The World of Storytelling

The World of Storytelling

by Anne Pellowski

R. R. BOWKER COMPANY
New York & London, 1977

Published by R. R. Bowker Company
1180 Avenue of the Americas, New York, N.Y. 10036
Copyright ©1977 by Xerox Corporation
All rights reserved
Printed and bound in the United States of America

Library of Congress Cataloging in Publication Data
Pellowski, Anne.
   The world of storytelling.

   Bibliography: p.
   Includes index.
   1. Story-telling. 2. Tales—History and criticism.
I. Title.
LB1042.P44   808.5'43   77-16492
ISBN 0-8352-1024-3

Contents

Illustrations

Preface

This work is intended for all who are interested in storytelling. It is not just for those who wish to become storytellers for children, but also for those who already are storytellers in libraries, schools, museums, parks, religious institutions, camps, homes, or other social or cultural institutions, and wish to know more about the historical traditions of this art and craft. It is meant, too, for students of children's literature as a source of information about the oral traditions out of which literature for children grew.

The book is not intended for folklorists, ethnologists, social scientists, psychologists and the like, although I shall be pleased if they find it of some interest. One may wonder about this seeming contradiction, especially since I have culled information for many parts of the book from the work of folklorists and ethnologists. To explain, I shall resort to personal experience.

When I first came to the New York Public Library and took the in-service storytelling seminar from Augusta Baker, I immediately sensed that I was embarking on something for which I had a natural interest. The greater my involvement became in storytelling, the greater my desire became to learn more about its history, and about the sources of stories. I began reading about folklore and about the peoples among whom it had been, and is still being, recorded.

To my dismay, I realized that folklorists, in general, have a very poor opinion of story compilers and storytellers for children. They criticize them for poor scholarship, for watering-down and changing original stories, and for the artificial manner in which they learn and tell stories. This is enough to put any children's storyteller on the defensive!

But, as I continued to read a great deal in the fields of folklore and ethnology, I learned some of the reasons behind the careful recording of informants, and began to realize that in many of the published story collections from which tellers were selecting their materials, the subtleties and nuances of the source cultures had certainly been changed, if not completely lost. Also, I had to admit that storytelling practiced in public institutions, in a number of instances, took on a decidedly formal, studied, and artificial air.

On the other hand, I also observed and took part in many fine storytelling sessions organized by various institutions or individuals. The best were characterized by telling of a very high order with great similarity, in the mood created between audience and teller, to that described by various observers of folk storytelling. To me it seemed distinctly narrow-minded on the part of folklorists and ethnologists to disdain such groups as unworthy of comparative study.

Subsequently, I myself was able to travel to several parts of the world where oral narration events are still a major form of entertainment and a cultural and social force of considerable significance. Once again, either as an audience participant or as an observer, I was struck by the similarity in mood to that of my best earlier storytelling experiences. This occurred in spite of the fact that the physical conditions, the stories, and the manner of telling were all quite different from any I had previously encountered.

My conclusion was that, as in so many professions or crafts, a good storyteller recognizes his or her own peer, and it matters very little whether the stories have been learned entirely from oral sources or from printed or mechanically recorded sources.

Storytellers for children usually refer to another's stories as folktales or fairy tales (or the equivalent in another language). This is in direct contradiction to the use of these same terms by most folklorists and ethnologists, who tend to follow rules such as that set by Sean O'Sullivan in *A Handbook of Irish Folklore* (Detroit: Singing Tree, 1970, p. 555): "Be sure to determine whether the storyteller has learned his/her stories only through oral sources, for if this is not the case, it is not folklore."

The World of Storytelling does not question the folklorists' definition of folktale, fairy tale, or any other oral type of literature. However, such terms are used in a much broader sense in this book, incorporating stories narrated by tellers of all kinds, whether they use oral, printed, or visual sources. Insofar as is possible, in each case the term used by a particular storyteller to describe story material is retained; and, when possible, it is pointed out where folklorists and ethnologists might disagree on the usage of these terms.

Last, but not least, this book is an attempt to rectify the relative obscurity of storytellers, especially the great ones. This is an area in which folklorists are likely to be in agreement, for of late there have been many criticisms of their past failure to record not only the name of the storyteller, but the specifics of style, manner of delivery, and the general ambiance of storytelling occasions, as Richard Dorson points out in *Folktales Told around the World* (Chicago: Univ. of Chicago Press, 1975, pp. xviii–xxii).

In the past, it was generally believed that folktales in and of themselves were such strong and meaningful stories that they were the product of a collective consciousness in a given culture, and all of them were automatically passed down from one generation to the next. More and more evidence suggests that this is not necessarily so. In all likelihood, many a story stays alive precisely because there was or is a gifted individual telling it frequently and well. Those stories no longer told with artistry and style die out for lack of interest on the part of listeners. There are many discussions of this point in both recent and past literature of folklorists and ethnologists. For a general review see the articles under "Folklore" and "Folktale" in the *Standard Dictionary of Folklore Mythology and Legend*, edited by Maria Leach (New York: Funk and Wagnalls, 1972), or *Albert Wesselski and Recent Folktale Theories*, by Emma Emily Kiefer (Bloomington: Indiana Univ. Press, 1947).

Folktales and fairy tales should be considered as much a literary property of the storyteller as written fictional stories are of the author. This poses many ethical questions for the publisher of folk and fairy tales, for the compiler and editor, and for the storyteller using printed material as a source. Among traditional storytellers there has generally been a very strong ethical feeling about using another teller's material. In *Folktales and Society* (Bloomington: Indiana Univ. Press, 1969, p. 89), Linda Dégh reports that among the Hungarian Szekler village storytellers there is great reservation about the use of another teller's stories. If stories belong to one individual, they are not told by another, unless they are passed on with permission or through inheritance. There are numerous other examples of such restraint, some of which are discussed by Robert Lowie in *Social Organization* (New York: Holt, Rinehart, 1948, pp. 131–134); Bronislaw Malinowski under "Myth in Primitive Psychology" in his *Magic, Science and Religion and Other Essays* (New York: Doubleday/Anchor Books, 1954, p. 102); and Paul Radin in *The Trickster* (New York: Greenwood Press, 1969, p. 122).

Sadly, this has not been the case among compilers and publishers, particularly in the case of collections destined for use by and with children. It is hoped that this book will encourage those who produce or purchase such collections to give more recognition to the specific storyteller from whom a tale was recorded, and to tell something about the background of the society and culture within which the stories were (or are) being told.

Acknowledgments

Thanks are due to the following persons who provided assistance or gave helpful advice:

Amy Kellman, Carnegie Library of Pittsburgh; Marilyn Berg Iarusso and the staffs of the Office of Children's Services, Central Children's Room, Picture Collection, Oriental and Slavonic Divisions, Rare Book Room, and Wertheim Room, all at The New York Public Library; Eva L. Kiewitt and Polly Grimshaw, Indiana University Library, Bloomington; Christa A. Sammons, Beinecke Library, Yale University; Virginia Haviland, Library of Congress; Verna Aardema Vugteveen; Lucia Binder, Vienna; Dr. Bernhard Bischoff, Munich; Rolf W. Brednich, Freiburg im Bresgau; Joan and Henry Ferguson, Thompson, Connecticut; Fritz Nötzoldt, Heidelberg; Koji Kata, Morio Kita, and Kiyoko Nozaki of Tokyo; Harold Scheub, University of Wisconsin, Madison.

Very special thanks are due to Victor Mair, Department of East Asian Languages and Civilizations, Harvard University, for guidance in the use of sources related to Chinese storytelling.

The author is grateful to the publishers of the following works for permission to quote selections at length:

"Translations of Buddhist Literature" and "Tun-huang Texts" from the *Dictionary of Oriental Literatures*, Vol. 1: *East Asia*, edited by Jaroslav Průšek and Zbigniew Słupski (London: Allen & Unwin, 1974; New York: Basic Books, 1974).

The Content and Style of an Oral Literature by Melville Jacobs (1959); *The Legends of the Hasidim* by Jerome Mintz (1968); *Folktales Told around the World*, edited by Richard Dorson (1975); all published by the University of Chicago Press.

Folktales and Society by Linda Dégh, translated by Emily M. Schossberger (Bloomington, Ind.: Indiana University Press, 1969).

The Book of the Gods and Rites and *The Ancient Calendar* by Fray

Diego Durán, translated by Fernando Horcasitas and Doris Heyden (Norman, Okla.: University of Oklahoma Press, 1971).

The Xhosa Ntsomi by Harold Scheub (1975); *Shinqiti Folk Literature and Song* by H. T. Norris (1968); *The Content and Form of Yoruba Ijala* by S. A. Babalola (1966); all published by Oxford University Press.

Growing Up in Dagbon by Christine Oppong (Accra, Ghana: Ghana Publishing Corporation, 1973).

Nireke No Hitobito by Morio Kita (Tokyo, Japan: Shincho-shi Publishers, 1964).

Thanks are also due to the American Council of Learned Societies for permission to reprint from *Russian Folklore* by Yuri M. Sokolov, translated by Catherine Ruth Smith (New York: Macmillan, 1950).

Although the material for this book has been gathered over many years and in many countries, the author is aware of the fact that there are a number of areas and periods that are only partially explored or not covered at all. She would be extremely grateful for any suggestions regarding corrections or additions, particularly with respect to early pictorial documentation of all forms of storytelling.

A Note on Abbreviations and Spelling

The reader of this book will find inconsistencies in spelling, in the transliteration of terms from non-Roman alphabets, and in the use of diacritic marks. This results from the fact that terms are generally used in the form in which they are found in the particular source being cited. For example, *ceilidhe* may appear in one source, while other sources use *ceilidh* or *celidh*. Exceptions to this are the three terms "folklore," "storyteller," and "storytelling." For ease of editing they are always used as single words without a hyphen, regardless of the form in which they are used by the authors quoted and cited in this work.

Abbreviations have been used as follows:

c.—circa
I.S.H.I.—Institute for the Study of Human Issues, Philadelphia
L.C.L.—Loeb Classical Library, Harvard University Press
p.—page
pp.—pages
Pr.—Press
S.B.E.—Sacred Books of the East
Univ.—University
v. or vol.—volume

I

Introduction

1

History and Definition of Storytelling

Most modern dictionaries define a storyteller, first, as one who tells or writes stories and, second, as one who tells fibs or falsehoods. This order is relatively recent. Until well into the nineteenth century, the more frequent use of the word was in the latter sense. The first definition generally was reserved for describing storytellers in the East, in the Levant, or in North Africa.

The earliest use of the English term "storyteller" that is cited in the *Oxford English Dictionary* is in 1709, by Steele in the *Tatler*, but it is likely that the word was used widely well before that date. The same dictionary, under the entry for "story," cites a line from William Dunbar's *Poems* (c. 1500–1520): "Sum singis, sum dancis, sum tellis store-is." Whether or not the term storyteller (or its equivalent in other languages) was in use, the telling of tales was commonly recognized as a form of entertainment from quite early on.

There are a number of early examples of stories or story fragments in texts from ancient Egyptian, Chinese, Sumerian, and Sanskrit. However, many of these contain no indication as to who told the stories, to whom they were told, and how or why. The first written description of an action that at least vaguely resembles storytelling appears to be in the Egyptian papyrus known as the Westcar Papyrus, recorded sometime between the twelfth and eighteenth dynasties (2000–1300 B.C.). It describes an encounter between Khufu (Cheops) and his sons:

> Know ye a man who can tell me tales of the deeds of magicians? Then the royal son Khafra stood forth and said, "I will tell thy Majesty a tale of the days of thy forefather Nebka. . . ."[1]

After Khafra has told his tale, another son, Baiufra, tells one from the time of Seneferu (father of Cheops) and the third son, Herutatef, concludes with a contemporary tale.

Another papyrus of approximately the same date, known as the Golenischeff Papyrus and now in the Hermitage in Leningrad, gives an account of the conversation between a nobleman and a sailor. The nobleman has returned from an unsuccessful mission and is reluctant to report to the ruling powers. The sailor, to convince the nobleman that he should not be afraid, then narrates his adventures as a kind of "proof" that such things can befall anyone! This has come to be known as the story of "The Shipwrecked Sailor."[2]

The Bible has, as Ranke puts it, "most of the forms of folktales in some shape or other, complete or incomplete."[3] But in the Old Testament there are few descriptions of actual storytelling occasions. The most striking one is in Judges 9:7, where Jotham tells a tale to convince the people of Shechem of the terrible deeds done by Abimelech, their ruler. The Chadwicks believe that this and other passages (Deut. 11:29, and Josh. 8:33, among others) reflect a custom followed by prophets or orators on public occasions. Their general conclusion is that "we cannot recall any reference to recitation for the sake of entertainment" in early Hebrew literature.[4]

Sanskrit scripture, on the other hand, does have a number of passages that indicate storytelling was practiced for religious and secular reasons. In the *Kaushitaki Brahmana Upanishad*, Part III (c. 500 B.C.), at the end of a story about Soma (a Hindu god), the narrator remarks that "it is thus told by those versed in legend (*âkhyânavidah*)."[5] Later, in several of the *Grihya-Sûtras*, or *Rules of Vedic Domestic Ceremonies* (c. 200 B.C.), appropriate times are mentioned for telling tales. Two examples are:

> They who have lost a Guru by death, or are afflicted by other misfortune, should perform on the new-moon day an expiatory ceremony. . . . Keeping that (fire) burning, they sit till the silence of the night, repeating the tales of the aged, and getting stories of auspicious contents, Itihâsas and Purânas, told to them.
> *Âsvalâyana-Grihya Sûtra*, IV Adhyâya 6 Kândikâ, 1, 6,
> Trans. by Hermann Oldenburg[6]

> [In preparation for a festival] therefore (husband and wife) should eat fast-day food which is pleasant to them. Let them sleep that night on the ground. They should spend that night so as to alternate their sleep with waking, entertaining themselves with tales or with other discourse.
> *Grihya-Sûtra of Gobhila*, I Prapâthaka 6 Kândikâ, 4, 5, 6,
> Trans. by Hermann Oldenburg[7]

Buddhist teaching also made use of stories. The *Tipitaka*, or sacred scriptures of Buddhism, contain many passages in which some story-telling device is used to make a point. The part known as the fifth Nikaya, which contains fifteen books, is full of dialogues, lives of sages and saints, fables, the birth stories (Jatakas), and numerous tales of all types. We know that the recitation of these stories was looked on with favor by the Buddhist authorities, and continued to be so regarded throughout the later centuries of Buddhist expansion and development. In a work that probably dates to around A.D. 300–400, *The Questions of King Milinda*, the sage Nâgasena reassures the king that the recitations are a good practice.[8]

Taoism and Confucianism did not have quite this richness of oral narrative, but they, too, used story to spread or reinforce belief. The *Tao-te-Ching* (c. 300 B.C.) contains little in the way of narrative, but the writings of Chuang-Tze (c. 100 B.C.) are full of parables, narratives, and short tales of all kinds. Chuang-Tze's work cannot be taken as reliable history, since it describes encounters and confrontations between Confucius, Lao-Tze, and a host of other sages, heroes, and characters that could not possibly have taken place. However, it is quite possible, and even likely, that Chuang-Tze did not invent these parables and tales, but recorded many from the oral tradition extant in his time. In describing how he believes Lao-Tze and Confucius told their parables and proverbs, Chuang-Tze was probably recording some of the ways he had heard tales told by members of the two philosophical systems.

Early Greek writing makes frequent reference to the art of telling stories, either through implication or by actually describing when and by whom it was done. Euripides, in the play *Heracles* (c. 423 B.C.), puts such a description in the mouth of Amphitryon. Advising his daughter-in-law Megara on how to spend the time waiting for her husband's return, Amphitryon says:

> Be calm;
> dry the living springs of tears that fill
> your children's eyes. Console them with stories,
> those sweet thieves of wretched make-believe.
> *Heracles*, lines 97–103, Trans. by Gilbert Murray[9]

Aristophanes also refers to storytelling in his plays. In *Lysistrata* (c. 411 B.C.) the chorus of old men says:

> I want to tell you a fable they used to relate to me when I was a little boy.
> *Lysistrata*, line 781, Trans. unknown[10]

The old men proceed to tell the story of Atalanta and how she fled from marriage to Melanion, except that they reverse the action of the characters to make their point with the women. In an amusing scene in *The Wasps* (c. 422 B.C.), Bdelycleon is trying to instruct Philocleon as to how to behave and talk in polite society. Philocleon then announces that he will tell the legend of Lamia, whereupon the following exchange takes place:

> Bdel.: Come, no fabulous tales, pray! talk of realities, of domestic facts, as is usually done.
> Phil.: Ah! I know something that is indeed most domestic. Once upon a time there was a rat and a cat. . . .
> > *The Wasps*, lines 1178–1180, Trans. unknown[11]

Earlier in the same play (line 566) is the statement: "Others tell us anecdotes or some comic story from Aesop [to get on their good side]."
    In *The Republic* (c. 400 B.C.) Plato writes:

> . . . we begin by telling children stories which though not wholly destitute of truth, are in the main fictitious; and these stories are told them when they are not of an age to learn gymnastics. . . . the beginning is the most important part of any work, especially in the case of a young and tender thing; for that is the time at which the character is being formed and the desired impression is more readily taken.
> > *The Republic*, Book 2, Trans. by Benjamin Jowett[12]

Aristotle, in his *Politics*, Book 7, Part 1336 (c. 322 B.C.), mentions that "educational directors, as they are called, should be careful what tales, fact or fiction, children hear." Two centuries later the Greek writer Dio Chrysostom imagines the following dialogue to have taken place between Alexander and Diogenes:

> Have you not heard the Libyan myth?
> And the king replied that he had not.
> Then Diogenes told it to him with zest and charm,
> because he wanted to put him in a good humour,
> just as nurses, after giving the children a whipping,
> tell them a story to comfort and please them.
> > *Discourse*, 4, 74 (c. 100 A.D.), Trans. by J. W. Cohoon[13]

Ovid depicts a scene of storytelling that would be seen later throughout Europe and the British Isles, namely that of women sewing or spinning and telling tales to make the work move more swiftly. He is here describing the daughters of Minyas, who do not wish to go out and celebrate the feast of Bacchus:

> Then one of them . . . says: While the other women are deserting their tasks and thronging this so-called festival, let us also, who keep to Pallas, a truer goddess, lighten with various talk the serviceable work of our hands, and to beguile the tedious hours, let us take turns in telling stories, while all the others listen.
>   The sisters agree and bid her be first to speak. She mused awhile which she should tell of many tales, for very many she knew.
> > *Metamorphoses*, Book 4, 36–44 (c. 7 A.D.), Trans. by Frank Justus Miller[14]

The historian Strabo does not depict one particular storytelling scene, but in several places implies that tale telling was a common human experience:

Man is eager to learn and his fondness for tales is a prelude to this quality. It is fondness for tales, then, that induces children to give their attention to narratives and more and more to take part in them. The reason for this is that myth is a new language to them—a language that tells them, not of things as they are, but of a different set of things. And what is new is pleasing, and so is what one did not know before, and it is just this that makes men eager to learn. But if you add to this the marvellous and the portentous, you thereby increase the pleasure, and pleasure acts as a charm to incite to learning. At the beginning we must needs make use of such bait for children. . . .

Geography, Book 1, Part 2, 8 (c. 7 B.C.–18 A.D.), Trans. by Horace Leonard Jones[15]

Even pre-Christian Latin literature includes a few brief mentions of storytelling occasions. In Cicero, we find one of the earliest denigrations of the fairy tale:

. . . as for your school's account of the matter, it is the merest fairy-story, hardly worthy of old wives at work by lamplight.

De natura Deorum, I, 34 (c. 45 B.C.), Trans. by H. Rackham[16]

Cicero does not say so directly, but he certainly implies that one of the things done by "old wives at work by lamplight" is storytelling, probably to make the task go faster.

Horace, in one of his satires (c. 30 B.C.), is much more specific in describing a storytelling scene:

O evenings, and suppers fit for the gods! with which I and my friends regale ourselves in the presence of my household gods. . . . Then conversation arises, not concerning other people's villas and houses, nor whether Lepos dances well or not; but we debate on what is more to our purpose, and what it is pernicious not to know. . . . Meanwhile, my neighbor Cervius prates away old stories relative to the subject.

Satires, Book II, 6, Trans. by Christopher Smart[17]

One of the stories that Cervius "prates away" at is "The Country Mouse and the City Mouse." This entire passage gives a vivid picture of one type of entertaining storytelling among well-to-do Romans.

These examples would suggest that folktales and legends were clearly perceived as entertainment (and sometimes education) to be enjoyed by adults and children. They were told by anyone who felt so inclined and in a variety of situations.

But what about the professional storytellers and reciters—the bards, minstrels and *rhapsodes*—also described in some detail in early Greek literature? The *Odyssey* has numerous references to bards, the occasions on which they perform, and the content of their stories. These examples are from Book 1:

Now when the wooers had put from them the desire of meat and drink, they minded them of other things, even of the song and dance, for these are the crown of the feast. And a henchman placed a beauteous lyre in the hands of Phemius, who was minstrel to the wooers despite his will. . . .

Phemius starts to sing of the return of the Achaeans. Penelope hears him, enters, and says to him:

> "Phemius, since thou knowest many other charms for mortals, deeds of men and gods, which bards rehearse, some of these do thou sing. . . ."

Later, Telemachus answers:

> ". . . men always prize that song the most, which rings newest in their ears."
>
> Trans. by S. H. Butcher and Andrew Lang[18]

Pindar, in one of his Nemean *Odes* (c. 485 B.C.), gives a picture of one of the ways in which the bard found material for his tales in song:

> Even as the sons of Homer, those singers of deftly woven lays, begin most often with Zeus for their prelude; even so hath our hero laid a first foundation for a tale of achievements in the sacred games by receiving a crown in the sacred grove of Nemean Zeus.
>
> *Odes*, II, 1–5, Trans. by Sir John Sandys[19]

Plato's *Ion* (c. 400 B.C.) gives an excellent picture of the *rhapsode* and his position in society:

> I often envy the profession of a *rhapsode*, Ion, for you have always to wear fine clothes, and to look as beautiful as you can is a part of your art. . . . you are obliged to be continually in the company of many good poets.
>
> Trans. by Benjamin Jowett[20]

A form of bardic storytelling is probably being referred to in this passage from the *Śatapatha-Brāhmana*, part of Sanskrit scriptures (c. 500 B.C.):

> And on the following day, he goes out to the house of the *sûta* (court minstrel and chronicler), and prepares a barley pap for Varuna; for the *Sûta* is a spiriter. . . . And he, the *Sûta*, assuredly is one of his jewels: it is for him that he is thereby consecrated; and him he makes his own faithful (follower).
>
> V Kanda 3 Adhyâya 1 Brâhmana 5, Trans. by Julius Eggeling[21]

There are even very early descriptions of the bard's position among the Gauls. Diodorus of Sicily, writing in Greek (c. 50 B.C.), comments:

> The Gauls are terrifying in their aspect and their voices are deep and altogether harsh; when they meet together they converge with few words and in riddles, hinting darkly at things for the most part and using one word when they mean another. . . . Among them are also to be found lyric poets whom they call Bards. These men sing to the accompaniment of instruments which are like lyres, and their song may be either of praise or of obloquy.
>
> *Library of History*, V, 31, Trans. by C. H. Oldfather[22]

The question has often been asked: Did these bards, minstrels, *rhapsodes*, and the like precede or follow the telling of tales by persons not looked on as professionals? Did this special career develop as a secularization of originally priestly or religious functions? Or were the first storytellers merely the best from among those who entertained their particular social group informally, then realized their special talents and power, and gradually sought to protect their status by devising systems regulating training, practice, and performance?

Going back to Strabo, we find that he has this to say:

> ... the fact that the ancients used the verb "sing" instead of the verb "tell" bears witness to this very thing, namely, that poetry was the source and origin of style.... For when poetry was recited, it employed the assistance of song.... Therefore since "tell" was first used in reference to poetic "style" and since among the ancients this poetic style was accompanied by song, the term "sing" was to them equivalent to the term "tell."
>
> Geography, Book 1, Part 2, 6, Trans. by Horace Leonard Jones[23]

The modern philosopher Johan Huizinga would agree with this. In *Homo Ludens: A Study of the Play Element in Culture*, he begins:

> Play is older than culture, for culture, however inadequately defined, always presupposes society, and animals have not waited for man to teach them their playing.[24]

Later he writes:

> Poetry everywhere precedes prose.... All poetry is born of play....
>
> Gradually the poet-seer splits up into the figures of the prophet, the priest, the soothsayer, the mystagogue and the poet as we know him; even the philosopher, the legislator, the orator, the demagogue, the sophist and the rhetor spring from that primordial composite type, the *vates*. The early Greek poets all show traces of their common progenitor. Their function is eminently a social one; they speak as the educators and monitors of the people. They are the nation's leaders....[25]

In light of these passages and others, Huizinga might well have answered the questions like this: Storytelling was first practiced by ordinary persons gifted in poetic speech, which had been discovered in play; gradually this playful aspect of poetic tale telling was grafted onto religious rituals, historical recitations, educational functions, and the like.

The Chadwicks, who divided oral literature into five types, were unwilling to state definitely that Type D (oral literature of celebration, including religious ritual) followed or preceded Type A (narrative poetry or saga designed for entertainment). They found too many instances in which the order apparently could have evolved in either direction. However, they imply that narration for entertainment preceded other types in quite a number of cultures. They do not speculate on whether the professional bard preceded the popular, nonprofessional poet-reciter.[26]

Arthur Ransome, in his chapter on the origins of storytelling, states unequivocally:

> At first there would be no professional storytellers. But it would not be long before . . . there would be found some one whose adventures were always the pleasantest to hear, whose deeds were the most marvellous, whose realistic details the most varied.[27]

A. B. Lord and his predecessor Milman Parry, both important scholars of oral epic narrative performance, also do not theorize about whether the bard preceded or followed folk storytelling, although they do firmly state their belief that written literature supplanted the oral but did not grow out of it.[28]

Other scholars in this century, from anthropologists to archeologists to linguists, have attempted to find evidence for one theory or another by studying peoples not yet touched by written, linear civilization or by examining still further the earliest examples of writing and artifacts from ancient civilizations. Each one propounds a different theory.

The best one can say about the earliest origins of storytelling is that there is evidence to support many theories:

1. That it grew out of the playful, self-entertainment needs of humans.
2. That it satisfied the need to explain the surrounding physical world.
3. That it came about because of an intrinsic religious need in humans to honor or propitiate the supernatural force(s) believed to be present in the world.
4. That it evolved from the human need to communicate experience to other humans.
5. That it fulfilled an aesthetic need for beauty, regularity, and form through expressive language and music.
6. That it stemmed from the desire to record the actions or qualities of one's ancestors, in the hope that this would give them a kind of immortality.

Documentation for the same kinds of storytelling, such as those cited above, continues up to the time of printing by movable type. It can be found in Sanskrit, Chinese, Greek, Latin, Anglo-Saxon, Old German, Icelandic, Old Slavonic, and probably in most of the other languages in use during that period. For example, depictions of bardic storytelling (see definition, page 19) are to be found in Lucan's *Pharsalia* (c. 60 A.D.), Athenaeus' *Deipnosophistae* (c. 200 A.D.), in *Beowulf* (c. 700 A.D.), in Bede's *Ecclesiastical History of the English People* (c. 700 A.D.), in Asser's *Life of King Alfred* (c. 970 A.D.), and in the old narrative poem *Deor* (c. 1000 A.D.), describing an Old Teutonic minstrel. These are, of course, different types of bards, and some suffered a decline in legal or social position before the arrival of mass printing. However, they all used material with a heroic/poetic content, and a formal style of presentation was common to all of them.

Descriptions of folk storytelling in the home or street or public place are encountered in numerous sources, as will be noted in Chapter 3.

The occasions remained essentially the same as those in classical times. Storytelling as a means of educating and socializing the child continued to be mentioned, just as it had been in the works of Plato and Aristotle. Quintillian (A.D. 35–100) wrote:

> Their pupils should learn to paraphrase Aesop's fables, the natural successors of the fairy-stories of the nursery, in simple and restrained language and subsequently to set down this paraphrase in writing with the same simplicity of style.
>
> *Institutio Oratoria.* Book 1, Chapter 9, Part 2, Trans. by
> H. E. Butler[29]

In the opening part of the *Panchatantra* (c. 400 A.D.), compiled for the education and enlightenment of the royal children of India, there is this "guarantee" of the efficacy of storytelling, with the use of tales from that collection:

> Whoever learns the work by heart,
> Or through the storyteller's art
> Becomes acquainted;
> His life by sad defeat—although
> The king of heaven be his foe—
> Is never tainted.
>
> Trans. by Arthur W. Ryder[30]

Only in what shall be called religious storytelling in this book (see definition, page 63) are there documented changes in the approach to storytelling style and content that can be called dramatic. In the Judaic, early Christian, and early Islamic tradition, storytelling for entertainment was frowned upon, in contrast to the Hindu and Buddhist traditions that encouraged this practice in both social and religious contexts. Particularly in the Judaic and Islamic traditions, stories could only be told if they remained true to the oral and written texts as passed down by orthodox religious authorities. Long before the advent of mass printing, however, there was a gradual secularization of both the style and content of religious stories among Jews, Christians, and Moslems.

Mass distribution of printed stories and tales began in Europe at the beginning of the sixteenth century, but did not so much usurp the place of the storyteller as use the devices of storytelling to advertise. Bardic performances did suffer a decline in those areas saturated by print where a sizable number of the populace learned to read. Their place was partly taken by street storytelling, usually promoting the sale of narrative ballads or news sheets or cheaply printed chapbooks. Sometimes these street performers tried to evoke the same kinds of heroic and high-minded feelings as had the bards, but they usually succeeded in appealing more to the curiosity of the folk. And they certainly never attained the respectability of profession that bards, and even wandering minstrels, had enjoyed in earlier centuries.

The market storytellers in the Arabic world continued to relate the elaborate tales-within-frameworks that had entered their oral repertoires via Persia, but they also added other elements that had evolved from Islamic tradition. In Hindu and Buddhist areas, the differences among Vedic, classical and folk myths, fables, and tales had always been difficult to perceive. With the spread of Buddhism under Asoka and, later, the increasing influence of the Moghul Empire, trade and travel (for war or pleasure) increased so much that peoples in all parts of Asia began to hear stories that once had been confined to a relatively fixed area. It became virtually impossible to sort out all of the origins of Hindu- and Buddhist-inspired tales. That these stories passed rapidly into China and East Asia, and then into Europe through Persia and through the Arabs living in North Africa and Spain, there is no doubt. Scholars all agree that certain elements now present in folktales throughout Europe entered during some period of trade with or conquest by Asian peoples. The method of entry may have been oral, but the stories were quickly converted into print. What is still widely debated, however, is whether there was a reverse flow, and to what extent European stories influenced those in Asia in the period prior to the nineteenth century.

Europe was also enriched by the firsthand, tale-bearing accounts of exploration and colonization coming from Africa and the Americas. Unfortunately, most of the records and manuscripts extant among the Aztecs, the Maya, the Incas, and the other Native American groups were destroyed by the colonizing powers. The only documentation one can find for storytelling is in those records that were re-created from memory decades or even hundreds of years after the destruction of the originals. Accounts of some of the more sympathetic explorers and missionaries also contain descriptions of myth, ritual, and legends, as well as information about how and when they were told. A good example of the latter is in Fray Diego Durán's *The Ancient Calendar* (1579), describing the ceremony after the birth of the Aztec child, subsequent to the use of prophetic pictures by the astrologer:

> The parents or kinsmen were told about these things, having first listened to assurances and then to long, flowery speeches. After this the soothsayers told two dozen lies and fables. . . .
> Trans. by Fernando Horcasitas and Doris Heyden[31]

The *Popol Vuh* of the Maya was also written down again shortly after the conquest, from the memories of those who had preserved it, probably through continued oral recitation. It is replete with myths, parables, and tales, but no actual storytelling occasions are depicted.

In Africa, storytelling obviously had been commonly practiced in many areas. There do not appear to be any written descriptions prior to the arrival of Arabic and European traders, but oral tradition speaks of the practice as being an ancient one. Ben-Amos finds at least tentative evidence of storytelling in the appearance of the *ak-pata* players in two of the Benin bronzes from the seventeenth century (see Plate 20). He theorizes that it is as likely as not that these performers accompanying the Oba (ruler) did praise singing and ritual-narrative singing. The *akpata* has lost most of its ceremonial meaning and use but is still employed by professional storytellers in present-day Benin (Nigeria).[32]

Whether or not this form of storytelling was practiced in seventeenth-century Benin, there is evidence from the work of Leo Africanus (c. 1600) and from a number of European travelers and traders that both heroic/poetic and folk stories were recited on occasion in different parts of Africa. Such accounts, together with those coming from the Americas and those that had already come from the East, enriched the possibilities of fantasy and imaginative speculation for the European storyteller. As Linda Dégh has pointed out, the storyteller is generally experienced and widely traveled, knowledgeable, and well versed in the ways of the world. The storyteller "attracts narrative material like a magnet."[33]

People tend to clarify their own identities in learning how others differ from them. It is no wonder then that, following their fascination with other parts of the world during the preceding centuries, the Europeans of the nineteenth century began to look more closely at their own traditions. The French critic of children's literature Isabelle Jan states that "there is a time in the evolution of every nation when it will seek to assert its specific identity by means of folklore."[34] For many of the European nations, this was the nineteenth century; for others, it was the first half of the twentieth century. For the United States, it is the present.

Among the educated and highly literate classes, oral narration as a form of entertainment for adults had died out by the eighteenth century. True, the same kinds of tales that delighted the listening audience among the folk were appreciated by the reading audience, but in polished form, as in Perrault or in the elegant versions of the *Arabian Nights*. For children, it was another matter. Folktales, legends, and myths were still considered appropriate in oral form, both for moral and entertainment purposes. Francis Bacon wrote:

> Men fear death, as children fear to go in the dark; and as that natural
> fear in children is increased with tales, so is the other.
> *Essays* 2, "Of Death"

Schiller, much impressed by the stories he heard, wrote in 1799:

> Deeper meaning
> Lies in the fairy tales of my childhood
> Than in the truths that life has taught.
> *Die Piccolomini*, III, 4

It was the appearance of the Grimm Brothers' *Kinder- und Hausmärchen* (1812–1815) that excited the educated and involved the literate adult population once again with oral tradition. After the erudite Jakob Grimm and the poetic Wilhelm Grimm had made folklore acceptable as a field of study, it became the rage of scholar and dilettante alike. It was probably fashionable to visit one's childhood nurse, listen to her tales, and report on them to one's intellectual and social peers at the next gathering. For the traveler, it became *de rigueur* to report on storytelling "among the natives." The only trouble was that all too often the stories and the manner of telling them were recorded and presented in such a refined and literary language that the flavor and style of the originals were sadly blunted. By 1891 Hartland was writing:

> To sum up it would appear that national differences in the manner of storytelling are for the most part superficial.
> *The Science of Fairy Tales*[35]

Modern scholars agree that most folktale or storytelling research of the nineteenth or early twentieth century is not valid in terms of present-day standards. The tales taken down by missionaries, travelers, anthropologists, psychologists, philologists, social scientists, and folklorists are all still studied and compared with later versions recorded under more stringent controls and conditions. But they are rarely accepted now as *the* authoritative versions, as was the case formerly.

Nevertheless, in spite of their disfavor among scholars, the Grimm tales must be considered as the single most important group of folk stories that affected storytelling for children. Their widespread appeal and their contemporaneous legitimacy helped European parents to believe it was important to continue telling stories to children, even though, in some cases, there was opposition from educational authorities. In the United States, with the public library just beginning to expand its work to children, the first children's librarians looked to such collections, and many later ones inspired by or modeled on Grimm, to justify the need for the story hour as a part of the regular work of every children's room. It is doubtful that this could have happened without the mantle of scholarship spread over the folktale collections of the Brothers Grimm, and later of Afanasiev, Asbjørnsen and Moe, and others.

It did not take long for this institutionalized type of storytelling to take hold. By 1927 it was an established part of most public library programs. Furthermore, it had also spread to municipal recreation departments. When these institutions inspired the establishment of similar ones in Canada, England, Scandinavia, Australia, and other countries, it was quite natural that the storytelling component would be carried along.

Storytellers in such cases were usually trained during in-service seminars and learned their stories from books more often than from oral sources. Not one of the more than fifty storytelling manuals published in the United States since the turn of the century suggests that the novice teller learn stories only (or principally) from oral sources. In fact, most of them have suggested books from which it is good to learn their first stories.

For whatever reasons—training, limitations of time and opportunity, or their own frame of reference—librarian-storytellers today tend to focus on already published stories as sources of material. They see storytelling, for the most part, as an introduction to books and a means of encouraging children to read.

As a matter of fact, a definition of storytelling widely used in library storytelling courses and workshops today is the following:

> Storytelling as an art means recreating literature—taking the printed words in a book and giving them life.[36]

This definition is unacceptable to most folklorists, since they are studying storytellers who have learned their stories orally. So the folklorists have developed their own definitions of storytelling. Axel Olrik, who coined the phrase "epic laws of folk literature," believed that the folk narrator was one who told tales by unconsciously obeying such epic laws as the "law of opening and closing," the "law of repetition," and others.[37] William Jansen, on the other hand, believes that the folk storytelling performance may be "at various times and for various reasons, an art, a craft, a common skill, or a universal and general capability."[38] Harold Scheub defines the type of storytelling he observed as "the creation of a dramatic narrative whose conflict and resolution are derived from ... remembered core clichés and shaped into a plot during performance."[39]

Dell Hymes[40] and Robert Georges[41] both describe at length the "communicative event," a culturally defined social event that is appropriate for certain forms of communication. Georges draws up a set of postulates that are contained in his definition of a "storytelling event," and one of these postulates is that the storyteller is an "encoder" who uses linguistic, paralinguistic, and kinesic codes to formulate, encode, and transmit the message of the story.[42] Linda Dégh believes that the narrator is the bearer of tradition (or the communal contribution of past bearers of tradition) to the storytelling community of which he/she is a part.[43]

Those who use storytelling for religious reasons today would probably formulate still another set of definitions. Mia Gerhardt, in her masterful study of *The Thousand and One Nights*, uses the term storyteller to encompass "those who created the stories, and those who repeated them, the narrators who worked them over, the redactors who wrote them down, the compilers who collected them, and the translators who made them accessible in other languages."[44]

Since all of these kinds of storytelling are still going on in different parts of the world, it was necessary to draft a new definition that would embrace both the librarian-storyteller's conception of storytelling and the folklorist's. For purposes of this book, then, the definition of storytelling is the art or craft of narration of stories in verse and/or prose, as performed or led by one person before a live audience; the stories narrated may be spoken, chanted, or sung, with or without musical, pictorial, and/or other accompaniment, and may be learned from oral, printed, or mechanically recorded sources; one of its purposes must be that of entertainment.

II

Types of Storytelling: Past and Present

2

Bardic Storytelling

In the previous chapter, a number of references to bardic story-telling were cited. The term "bard" is of Celtic origin, so, strictly speaking, bardic storytelling should refer only to a specific type practiced in Ireland, Wales, Scotland, and parts of Brittany. However, bard has come to be the commonly accepted English word for any poet/singer/performer. For purposes of this book, the term will mean a storyteller whose function is to create and/or perform poetic oral narrations that chronicle events or praise the illustrious forebears and present leaders of a tribal, cultural, or national group. In performance, the bard is usually, but not necessarily, accompanied by a musical instrument, either self-played or played by others.

If one accepts the above description, there were and still are bards in many parts of the world. A quick scanning of the dictionary in this book will find more than fifty different types. Some scholars would differ on whether or not to translate all of these as bard. Here they will all be treated as belonging to this general group, and the specific ways in which they can be defined and differentiated will be found either in a later part of this chapter or in the glossary.

In many instances it is extremely difficult to separate bardic story-telling from religious storytelling, because the performances honor heroes who have some religious significance or connection. This problem will be pointed out in the relevant passages, and will be discussed further in the section on religious storytelling.

The earliest recorded verbal depiction of a bard is probably among those to be found in Homer (see Chapter 1) or those found in the Sanskrit scriptures. One of the latter is cited on page 8. Another, taken from the same *Satapatha-Brahmāna*, is an even more explicit account of the probable role of the bard in early India:

> (In telling) this revolving (legend), he tells all royalties, all regions, all Vedas, all gods, all beings; and, verily, for whomsoever the Hotri knowing this, tells this revolving legend, or whosoever even knows this, attains to fellowship and communion with these royalties, gains the sovereign rule and lordship over all people, secures for himself all the Vedas, and by gratifying the gods, finally establishes himself on all beings.
>
> XIII Kânda, 4 Adhyâya, 3 Brâhmana, 15, Trans. by Julius Eggeling[1]

This passage refers to the elaborate preparations for the special ceremony conducted every ten days in a Horse-Sacrifice Year.

The bard or minstrel mentioned above and in Chapter 1, in the citations from Sanskrit scriptures, was usually referred to by the term *sûta*. There was, however, another early Indian bard called *māgadha*. This term actually meant a place and a people in ancient India. Magadha is mentioned very often in early Hindu and Buddhist scriptures, frequently as the source of the best wandering minstrels. Eventually, the place name came to refer to a minstrel in general. Magadha was later most famous as a great center of Buddhism, under Aśoka (c. 260–230 B.C.).[2]

Actually, although both these Greek and Sanskritic sources date to approximately 500 B.C., pictorial evidence and indirect verbal evidence can be found in earlier civilizations. The Sumerian myth of Enki and Eridu speaks of the gods feasting and banqueting until finally one pronounces his blessing, and in so doing, speaks of "this house directed by the seven lyre-songs, given over to incantations with pure songs...."[3] There are also several mosaics and sculptural reliefs with representations of harpists or lyre players who seem to be reciting. The beautiful lyre that was made in Ur more than 5,000 years ago has an inlay showing animals acting like men. Frankfort speculates that this type of illustration must surely have had something to do with the reciting or recording of myths or fables.[4]

Egyptian art from several early periods shows different scenes in which musicians and singers seem to be declaiming or reciting in front of a ruler or group of people. The beautifully clear relief from the tomb of Pa-Aton-em-heb that depicts a blind harpist reciting may well be one of the reasons behind the widespread belief that early bards were all blind.[5] This is romantic speculation, as Lord and the Chadwicks both convincingly show that there were numerous and gifted bards who were not blind. They also point out that, although a number of blind persons turned to this occupation because it was one that their handicap permitted, their blindness did not necessarily make them skilled singers and narrators.[6]

It is safe to speculate that the ancient peoples who preserved any records at all probably experienced their history, both past and present, as stories told orally by someone specializing in that art. For purposes of this book, these bardic performers will be divided into two types and referred to as chronicler-historians or praise singers. The chronicler-historian generally narrates what we shall call the oral epic or the historical ballad. The praise singer recounts and glorifies the names and deeds of one or more persons, living or dead, associated with the group from which the praise singer comes and for which he or she performs. Both the chronicler-historian and the praise singer can be subdivided into two types: one who recites or performs existing texts without changing them and another who composes anew each time a recital or performance takes place, using formulaic expressions and central themes, but combining them in different patterns. The two types of chronicler-historians are best exemplified by the Greek *aoidos* and the *rhapsode*. The former is the term used in Homer to distinguish the poet-singer who composes spontaneously. The latter term came into later use and denotes one who performs Homeric poems. The recitation of the *rhapsode* was studied, rather than spontaneous, and was judged by how well it corresponded to the written texts. Plato's *Ion* gives us a good picture of the life of the *rhapsode* (Plate 1).

The two types of praise poets are best observed in the different parts of Africa where they can be found even today. The Yoruba, Mande, Hausa, Sotho and Zulu are among those who have praise singers who compose and perform; once the narrative is well known and respected, however, it is supposed to be repeated without change. There are thus praise singers who can be known for their excellent performance of the praises composed by others.

Not all the performances of these various types of bards can be classified as storytelling events in terms of the definition in Chapter 1. But indications are that quite a number of them were.

Origin of the Term Bard

It was really the classic Greek and Roman writers who introduced the term bard into the English language, but in an indirect way, as will be indicated later. In Greek, Diodorus (see Chapter 1) and Strabo were the first to use the term to describe a person with a certain position among the Gauls:

> Among the Gallic peoples, generally speaking, there are three sets of men who are held in exceptional honour: the Bards, the Vates and the Druids. The Bards are singers and poets; the Vates, diviners and natural philosophers; while the Druids, in addition to natural philosophy, study also moral philosophy. . . .
> *Geography*, 4, 4, 3–4 (c. 7 B.C.–18 A.D.), Trans. by Horace Leonard Jones[7]

PLATE 1 A *rhapsode* with his *rhabdos*, from an Attic red-figure amphora, c. 400 B.C., British Museum No. E. 270. Photo courtesy of The British Library.

Later, the Roman writer Lucan had this to say:

> The Gallic bards, who compose elegies for heroes fallen in battle, and transmit these to posterity, were once more free to declaim their verses.
>
> *Pharsalia* 1, 447ff. (c. 60 A.D.), Trans. by Robert Graves[8]

Still later, the Greek writer Athenaeus, who lived in Rome, put these words in the mouth of a supposed visitor to the Celts in Gaul:

> And after he had set a limit to the feast, one of the native poets arrived too late; and meeting the chief, he sang his praises in a hymn extolling his greatness.... And the chief, delighted with this, called for a bag of gold and tossed it to the bard as he ran beside him.
>
> *Deipnosophistae*, IV, 152 (c. 200 A.D.), Trans. by Charles Burton Gulick[9]

Following this early mention of bards among the Celtic peoples, the term seemed to disappear about the fifth century in the written records concerning the Celtic and Teutonic peoples and did not come into widespread use again until the thirteenth century. By that time, the bards seem to have become so highly professional that there were many ranks of them, and the lowest one, called bard, was disdained by the higher ranks. In the *Leabhar na g-ceart* or *Book of Rights* (c. 1400) one of the passages translates:

> It is not known to every prattling bard;
> It is not the right of a bard, but the right of a poet (*fili*)
> To know each king and his right.[10]

On the other hand, the *ollam*, or highest ranking *fili*, was looked on as the poet laureate of his day. He was entitled to wear a *tugen* (also called *tuighean* or *taeidhean*) that apparently was made of feathers and must have looked most impressive:

> For it is of skins of birds white and many-colored that the poets' toga is made from their girdle downwards, and of their crests from the girdle upwards to their neck.[11]

The *ollam* had a retinue of twenty-four persons, a repertoire of seven times fifty stories, and sometimes sat in an official chair.[12]

Walker quotes an entry from the code of laws of an early Irish king, Mogha Nuadhad, that lists clothing due to the various bards (Plate 2):

> Three milch cows is the value of a free Poet's clothing, and of his wife's; it is the same from the chief Bard of a Petty Prince to the Ollamh; and the value of their wive's [*sic*] clothing is the same.[13]

Later, in a law called *Ilbreachta*, he found that whereas all other persons could wear clothing of one, two, three, or four colors, depending on their rank or social standing, the *ollam* could wear five colors, only one less than royalty, who wore six.[14]

IRISH BARD.

C. Maguire Sc.

PLATE 2 Irish bard. Reproduced from Joseph C. Walker, *A Historical Essay on the Dress of the Ancient and Modern Irish* (Dublin: J. Christie, 1818). Photo courtesy of the Metropolitan Museum of Art.

In Wales, the word bard is found at several points in the laws of Howel Dda, a Welsh king who died about 950. The earliest known manuscript containing these laws, however, is dated about 1200. Since these laws were constantly being changed and recodified, the later year must be accepted as more valid for the descriptions of the ranks of bard and *pencerdd*. The bard of the household or *bardd teulu* was one of the twenty-four officers in the court of the king. He received a steer out of every spoil that was captured while he was in service to the household. In return he had to sing the "Monarchy of Britain" before them on the day of battle. (This was probably a praise poem celebrating the lives and deeds of British rulers.) He received his harp and gold ring from the queen and sat second nearest to the chief of the household.[15]

On the other hand, the *pencerdd*, who was the chief of song, sat to the left of the chief of the household. He always sang first, followed by the *bardd teulu*. He became a *pencerdd* when he had "won his chair," states the law, but it does not stipulate how he went about doing this.[16]

In addition to the *bardd teulu* and the *pencerdd*, there was a bard in Wales lower in rank, called a *cerddor*. Not all scholars agree that this was one of the bardic group. He tended to be a wandering minstrel, rather than being attached to one household.[17] The *cerddor* gradually came to be associated with the telling of the popular tales, called *cyfarwyddyd*. Eventually, according to some authorities, they even came to be called *cyfarwyddiaid*.[18] They are probably the closest equivalent to the Irish *seanachaidhe* that the Welsh had.

Nash and Toland both place the *cler* among the bardic group, calling him a poet-minstrel whose "circuit was among the yeomen of the country."[19] Nash further mentions that the *cler* "maintained his ground against pressure from bards to come under their control," implying that the *clerwr* were not trained in the bardic schools and did not belong to the hereditary group.[20] Williams places the *clerwr* in Wales from the sixteenth through the eighteenth centuries and calls them the counterpart to the continental *clerici vagantes* or *goliardi*.[21] However, current scholarship tends toward the belief that none of these can be described as storytellers according to the definition used in this book because they were poets who composed in written rather than in oral form.

It can be seen that both Welsh and Irish bards had precise positions in their society, and at least some of the ranks seemed to coincide. The *fili* apparently did not have a Welsh equivalent. The Chadwicks speculate that the Irish *fili* had some connection with the Gaulish *vates*, mentioned in the quote from Strabo on page 21. They point out that there is an Irish word, *fáith* (prophet), that corresponds roughly to the *vates*. Perhaps at some point the function of the *fáith* was assumed by a bardic type, who then became known as a *fili*.[22]

In any case, from the thirteenth century onwards there are numerous mentions of bards in both Irish and Welsh manuscripts and documents. As the years passed, their positions and duties seemed to change somewhat, mainly in the fact that they began to inherit their posts. Bardic composition and recitation in Wales were formalized to such an extent that, starting in the late twelfth century, a gathering known as the Eisteddfod was established as an annual (or fairly regular) competition. It continues up to today.

The Minstrel Type of Bard

In the period between the time when Strabo, Lucan, and others wrote about the bards in Gaul, and the twelfth century when they again appear under that name in Irish and Welsh literature, there were other poet-singers who had positions similar to the bard. The Anglo-Saxons used the terms *scop* and *gleoman* to designate such a person. Most of our information about the *scop* comes from three sources: *Beowulf*, *Widsith* and *Deor*.

In *Beowulf*, Hrothgar is shown to have an official *scop* attached to his court:

> There was singing and music together in accompaniment in presence of Healfdane's war-like chieftain; the harp was played and many a lay rehearsed, when Hrothgar's bard (*scop*) was to provide entertainment in hall along the meadbench....
>
> *Beowulf*, 1063–1069, Trans. by John R. Clark Hall[23]

Deor speaks of having had a similar position:

> Of myself I will say this much, that once I was minstrel of the Heodeningas, my master's favorite. My name was Deor. For many years I had a goodly office and a generous lord, till now Heorrenda, a skilful [*sic*] bard, has received the estate which the protector of warriors gave to me in days gone by.
>
> *Deor*, A.D. 35–41, Trans. by Bruce Dickins[24]

Widsith depicts more the life of the wandering *gleoman*:

> Thus roving,
> with their devices wander
> the gleemen of men
> through many lands,
> their need express,
> words of thanks utter,
> ever south or north
> find one
> knowing in songs,
> liberal of gifts,
> who before his court desires
> his grandeur to exalt,
> valorous deeds achieve,
> until all departs
> light and life together.
>
> Trans. by Benjamin Thorpe[25]

The *scop* recited or sang not only sagas, but also poems on a variety of subjects. He was generally well traveled and could therefore comment on many things. Whereas many at the feasts were expected to pick up the harp and perform, it was the *scop* or *gleoman* who was looked upon to set the highest standards and be the most original. It is not known whether the *scop* accompanied leaders into battle, as did the Welsh and Irish bards.[26] From various passages in all three poems, we know that the *scop* did have a high position of honor and that his influence was considerable.

In *Beowulf*, another term used is *thyle*. This is usually translated as "spokesman" or "orator." In the early Norse of the Edda poems, it is *thulr* and seems to mean "poet." The Chadwicks also cite other meanings, depending on the context in which the word is used, and believe that the position of the *thyle* or *thulr* may have been a close approximation of the *fili*.[27] In any case, they obviously did recite poetry of a bardic nature occasionally.

The old Norse and Icelandic *skáld* was quite clearly the equivalent of the Anglo-Saxon *scop*. *Skáld* literally means poet. From quite early on, that is, well before the year 1000, it had become a regular practice for poets to recommend themselves to some noble patron in one or another of the areas now comprising the Scandinavian countries. More often than not, this poet was a traveling Icelander, because it was his language that was spoken and understood throughout the region. In the second half of the tenth century, the practice began to decline in Norway, but there were still a great number of *skálds* in Iceland during both the tenth and eleventh centuries. They did not begin to disappear until the late thirteenth century.[28] Snorri Sturluson, in his prologue to *Heimskringla* (c. 1225), wrote:

> There were *skálds* with Harald the Fairhaired and men still know their poems, and the poems about all the kings who have since ruled Iceland. And we take our statements most of all from what is said in those poems.[29]

The *skáld* is not to be confused with the prose *saga* teller, even though some of his poetic compositions were called sagas, and many were later taken up and incorporated into the prose family *sögur*. The *skáld* composed and recited a unique type of story in poetry of a strictly syllabic character different from the Eddas. The *skáld* was not a prose *saga* teller.[30]

Origin of the Term Minstrel

Starting about the fourteenth century, the terms "bard" and "minstrel" replaced *scop* and *gleoman* in the English language. Bard was apparently picked up by educated persons who read the Greek and Roman classics and found the term used there. Minstrel came from France. There is much disagreement among scholars as to how and why this took place, just as there is regarding the term bard. The most widely accepted view seems to be that some *jongleurs* who gave up wandering attached themselves to specific courts, began performing the works of *troubadours* and *trouvères* (depending upon whether they went south or north), and then set up guilds to train others and to protect their ranks. These were initially called *ménétriers* and then *ménéstrels*. They eventually spread all over Europe, and the accepted English term for them became minstrel. In German, it was *Spielmann*.

Before one can take up the question of the minstrels, one must consider first the development of the term *jongleur*, and the special position the *jongleurs* had in performing and spreading not only the poems of the *troubadours* and *trouvères*, but legends surrounding the lives of these two groups. The French scholar De La Rue believes the *jongleurs* were the continuation of the *bardi*, mentioned by classical writers as being prevalent among the early Gauls.[31] He believes that the Roman influence brought the Latin term *joculator* to the Gauls, applying it to the men who performed on instruments, perhaps accompanying the real *bardi*. Slowly, they came to add other entertainments to their repertoire, such as juggling, miming, magic tricks, tumbling, and more. The term *joculator* was gradually transformed into various medieval French terms, such as *jugler, jugleours, jongleors*, and finally *jongleur*. According to De La Rue, these changes began under the kings of the second dynasty (987–1328).[32]

Faral is of the opinion that there is no serious proof of this and that the connection cannot be taken into consideration. He also disagrees with those who consider the *jongleur* to be the direct descendant of the Anglo-Saxon *scop*. If the *jongleur* has an ancestor or predecessor at all, he feels it is more likely to have been the Roman mime (*mimus* or *histrio*). These were semitheatrical performers who were quite common in decadent Rome. Faral believes they may well have seen opportunities for support declining among the Romans, so they went north to other parts of the empire. He cites quite a number of documents from the ninth, tenth, and eleventh centuries that mention the *mimus* and the *jongleur* in the same place, as though they were similar in nature.[33]

Regardless of which group they might have descended from, the *jongleurs* were to be found throughout the Latin countries from the ninth century on, but especially in France. The Church tried to get rid of them and passed decrees forbidding lay persons, clerics, and monks to have anything to do with their amusements. During the eleventh and twelfth centuries, some of them were tolerated because they began performing the heroic *chansons de geste*, sometimes in churches at special feasts. On occasion, they also recited the lives of the saints in verse.[34]

But their "golden age" was the thirteenth century. There were literally thousands of them, and they were to be found throughout Europe. There were even female *jongleresses*. Not all of them recited epics or stories, so only a fraction of these can be considered storytellers.[35]

When the custom of composing lyric verse began at the turn of the twelfth century, the ultimate in performance at the elegant courts and wealthy homes was the singing or chanting of these lyrics. The composers, called *troubadours* or *trouvères*, were of a completely new tradition. This was not narrative poetry of the types previously extant. It was lyric verse. The work of the *troubadours* and *trouvères* attracted the more talented *jongleurs*, who were already performing in all the courts, and they either were hired by or attached themselves to the *troubadours* and *trouvères*. Sometimes they found they were themselves capable of composing this new form of poetry, and thus they raised their position within the court to that of *troubadour* or *trouvère*.[36]

According to the definition used in this book, the *troubadours* and *trouvères* were not storytellers, with the exception of a few who might be classified as praise singers. The characteristic that most distinguished their poetry from earlier types was precisely that it was lyric and only incidentally narrative, if at all. It did not concern itself with telling stories, as did heroic poetry. So the romantic view that *troubadours* were or are the antecedents of later storytellers is simply not the case. They are discussed here in detail merely because this confusion exists and because they were the inspiration for, and the subjects of, later stories used by *jongleurs* and minstrels. The notion that they belong in the ranks of early storytellers must be dispelled. Even illustrations of a number of types labeled as *troubadours* or *trouvères* must be looked at skeptically, for there are almost no contemporary depictions that show the difference between the bards, *scops*, minstrels, gleemen, and *jongleurs*, who often were storytellers, and the *troubadours* and *trouvères*, who were not (Plates 3, 4, and 5).

Once having settled permanently in a court, the *jongleurs* took on a new aspect, that of ministering to the whims of one master or mistress. It is from the root word *ministerialis* or *menestralis* that the words *ménétrier* or *ménéstral* probably were formed. They were first used in a general way and then came to mean a domestic *jongleur*, that is, one permanently attached to the household, with a salary and perquisites. It was this practice that spread throughout Europe, as mentioned previously. By the year 1300, most of the *troubadours* and *trouvères* had vanished. The *Minnesänger*, who were the German equivalent, survived only a little longer.[37]

The minstrel, by whatever name he or she was known, did continue to narrate stories in verse, chant, or song, as one of a number of entertainments. Other skills they displayed included juggling, tumbling and acrobatics, and short dramatic skits. They usually traveled in groups, and sometimes one in the group was more adept at tale tell-

PLATE 3 An early court minstrel or *scop* (often incorrectly labeled as a *troubadour*). Segment from Münchener Bilderbogen Series, No. 9, *Zur Geschichte der Costüme* (originally published in Munich by Braun and Schneider, mid-nineteenth century). Picture courtesy of The New York Public Library, Picture Collection.

PLATE 4 Theater of a *troubadour* or minstrel in Arles, France, 1622. Picture courtesy of The New York Public Library, Picture Collection.

PLATE 5 *Trouvère* accompanying himself on the violin; sculpture from the portico of the Abbey of St. Denis, twelfth century. Picture courtesy of The New York Public Library, Picture Collection.

ing, whereas another might be more talented at playing musical instruments, and still another was better at tumbling and juggling. The stories they told can be classified as bardic because of their subject matter, which was related to the noble families and frequently mentioned real personages who had lived in earlier times, although the accounts by then were highly fictionalized. It would probably be equally correct to classify them as folk storytellers, because their repertoires included tales that had come from the common folk, mostly because they had begun performing more and more in public places and less and less in the courts and homes of the wealthy.

Russian and South Slavic Bards

To a great degree, the same process took place in Russia with the *veselÿe lyudi*, the *skomorokhi*, and the *skaziteli*. However, although the performances passed from the homes of royalty and the wealthy into the homes of the peasantry, the subjects remained essentially the same. From the *byliny*, the oral poems chanted or sung by the Russian minstrels, we get bits of information about the performers themselves. But most of the contemporary descriptions of the early Russian minstrels are to be found in other historical sources. The Chadwicks in the second volume of *The Growth of Literature*[38] and Mrs. Chadwick in her *Russian Heroic Poetry*[39] record and discuss these historical references. They are the principal sources for the summary that follows.

Veselÿe lyudi means literally "joyous people," and this term, as well as the term *skomorokhi*, is the one most frequently encountered in the early histories to describe entertainers that appear remarkably like the minstrels of Western Europe. The *skomorokhi* are defined by the Chadwicks as "a confraternity of public entertainers, actors, wandering minstrels, dancers, singers, wrestlers, and buffoons."[40] They took a prominent part in all festivals. The two terms were used more or less interchangeably, except that the latter seem to be referred to as being more organized.

Just as in the *Odyssey*, *Beowulf*, the *Mabinogion*, and other oral epics there are descriptions of kings, nobles, and wealthy persons trying their hand and voice in the performing of heroic poetry and song as amateurs, we find similar indications in the *byliny* that this was done by the czars, the nobles, and the wealthy in Russia. But at the same time there are implications that the performances of the *veselÿe lyudi* and the *skomorokhi* included professional reciting of the *byliny* and other heroic verse much like that of the *aoidoi*, the *rhapsode*, the *scop*, and the *ollam* and *pencerdd*. Like them, the *skomorokhi* seemed to have honored positions in the courts and well-to-do homes, being regarded as equals.

They were not treated with as much respect by the church authorities, who found their unruly ways and their defiance of conventions a menace to ecclesiastical authority. In the sixteenth and seventeenth centuries there were a number of repressive decrees directed at curtailing their power. There was even a proverb that said "*skomorokh* and priest are no comrades." The czars and civil authorities did not seem to pay too much attention to the persecution until Alexis, father of Peter the Great, began to back up the religious authorities in the position they had taken; from then on the *skomorokhi* were oppressed in earnest. This occurred in the middle of the seventeenth century. By the end of the century, references to the *skomorokhi* grow rare and virtually disappear.[41] This persecution did not affect the *kalêki*, the religious counterpart of the *skomorokhi*.

In the next century there began to appear collections of *byliny* gathered from the peasant class. Many scholars thus speculate that the *skomorokhi* had gone "underground," that is, to the rural areas where people might be likely to protect them from the authorities, and had passed on their *byliny* to the peasants. This is not confirmed by any historical documents or written evidence, but neither is there any other speculation to the contrary.

The peasants who sing, chant, or recite these oral narratives, called *byliny* if they are metrical, and *pobyvalshchiny* if they are nonmetrical, are known as *skaziteli* (male) or *skazitelnitsy* (female). They come from the most humble origins and were and are to be found only in the very remote regions of Russia. They were usually of the artisan group of peasants, since it was easier to perform while working at such crafts as net making, cobbling, or tailoring than while farming or working in the fields. Most of those recorded in the last one hundred years were found in the region of Olonets, but they have been found in smaller numbers in almost all regions of Russia.

In Yugoslavia, the counterparts of the *skaziteli* are the *guslari* and the equivalents of the *byliny* are called *narodne pjesme* or *bugarštice*, depending on their meter.[42] The *guslari* or modern minstrel in Yugoslavia was, until very recently, the chief entertainer in small towns and villages, at least for the male population. In the really small villages, where there was no public gathering place, the singer was likely to perform in a private home. In such cases, it was likely that the women and children could also listen. In the bigger towns or villages, where there was a *kafana* (coffee or tea house), the performances were usually given in that public place. This was especially the case for Moslems during the month of Ramadan. In non-Moslem areas, or in areas where Moslems and non-Moslems both lived, there were performances in taverns and inns. No women or children were allowed. Another occasion where people might well have had the opportunity to listen to the singers was at weddings. However, there was often such confusion and merriment at these feasts that it was considered difficult to perform well without interruption.

Skendi reports that similar conditions prevailed in Albania. In that area the epic songs were called *këngë pleqérishte* or *këngë trimash*.[43]

Asian Bards

In Turkey, Iran, and the Asian parts of Russia there are also bards and minstrels who perform oral epics, but these epics tend to differ from those told in Russia and the Balkans. The *halk hikâyeleri* of Turkey are a mixture of prose and poetry, and the characters are heroic types rather than named, historical individuals. Eberhard[44] does not give the Turkish name for these minstrels, but it is surely similar to the Azerbaijani *ašyq* reported by Winner,[45] the Persian *aushek* referred to by Chodzko,[46] and the Armenian *ashough* mentioned by Hoogasian.[47]

The minstrels accompany themselves on an instrument. Since their works contain many Persian words, it is believed that they were influenced more by Asian sources than by European. However, they also have parallels in medieval Spain and France.

The epics were not the same as those performed for select groups, such as the nobles at court or for a ceremonial meeting. Such epics are known to have existed in the area in the past, and they were probably entirely in verse. These newer minstrel epics, on the contrary, are performed for ordinary men in tea or coffee houses, or at weddings, in small towns and villages. They are like the Russian and Serbo-Croatian songs in that they are performed on similar occasions, but their style and format are different. The Turkish minstrel can introduce improvisations to both the prose and poetry parts of the epic. Sometimes the epic is performed in its entirety; at other times only segments are recited.[48]

Kazakh bards are called either *aqyn* or *dšyršy*. The terms are virtually synonymous. They improvise songs and epics as well as performing those they have collected from already existing sources. They are also among the performers at the *ajtys*, a kind of singing competition that is part of every large Kazakh celebration, along with wrestling, horse races, and games. In such cases, however, they do not perform the epics or their own earlier compositions because the *ajtys* is totally spontaneous. It is a kind of singing "duel" in which the words, but not the tunes, have to be improvised on the spot, with one party starting one verse, and the other party alternating. Amateurs can also take part and, if they perform well, they can eventually become professional.[49]

The Kirghiz people obviously have or had a similar bard, for the Chadwicks cite four references to a minstrel called an *akin*.[50] Various travelers and visitors at the courts of Kirghizi sultans in the late nineteenth and early twentieth centuries commented on them. The Yakuts of eastern Siberia also had bards, but no name or current description could be located for them. Shklovsky gave only a very brief account of a woman bard he encountered, who performed at weddings.[51]

All of these forms of bardic storytelling were probably influenced by early Indian or Chinese forms, or both. In both cultures religious bardic storytelling generally was practiced in ancient and medieval times and then gradually developed into secular forms.

Modern bardism in India takes both a religious and a secular form. The *kalamkari* bards of Andhra Pradesh in southeastern India straddle both types. These wandering men carry their *kalamkari*, large cloths, with them from village to village. They spread out their picture cloths and then narrate the epic tales of India, using the pictures partly as an *aide-memoire*, partly as a stimulant to the audience (see Plate 26). The great majority of these tales deal with segments of the Ramayana and are narrated in Telugu.[52]

The *pabuji kaa pat* are scrolls telling purely secular tales of Rajasthan (see Plate 27). They are used by *bhopa*, local bards, who buy them and go from village to village, singing the story of the hero pictured in each one. The hero may have different names, but he always looks the same in the scrolls. A typical narrative will cover his birth, his adventures as a young man (usually involving killing a lion), his marriage, his fight with an enemy, and his eventual death.[53]

Chinese bards of the past included the *tze-ti*. They performed in wealthy homes during the Ch'ing dynasty (1644–1911) only for the honor of doing so and never for remuneration.[54] They sometimes were accepted into the storytellers' guilds or schools and came under their protection.[55] Although a considerable number of the storytellers in these guilds, in China and Japan, could possibly be termed bardic, they will be discussed together with other theatrical guild storytellers in Chapter 5.

An unusual form of bardism in Japan was practiced by the Ainu, a light-skinned people who lived in the northern part of the islands, and who were quite distinct racially from all other peoples of the region. Their language is unrelated to Japanese and Chinese. Their epics were recited sometimes by women, more often by men. The occasions could be connected with religious ceremonies, while waiting for a fish to bite, or around a fireside at home on winter nights. In other words, they practiced all-occasion bardism! How ancient this practice is one can only speculate, since the best-known epic was not written down until the 1920s, and Wakarpa, the bard who recited it, knew only that he had learned it from his predecessor. It is in the first person, which is the case for all other Ainu folktales as well.[56]

The Achehnese (or Achinese) of the island of Sumatra have epic poetry that concerns both ancient and more modern heroes. By 1900, the public recitation of these epics was rare. Yet new ones were still being composed at that time, so it was possible to document how such heroic poems came into being:

> Some one man, who . . . knows by heart the classic descriptions of certain events and situations as expressed in verse by the people of olden times, but whose knowledge . . . is somewhat greater than that of others; . . . who is endowed, besides, with a good memory and enthusiasm . . . puts his powers to the test by celebrating in verse the great events of more recent years. . . . The events of which he sings have not yet reached their final development, so he keeps on adding, as occasion rises, fresh episodes to the poem.[57]

Snouck Hurgronje shows a photo of Dōkarim, a bard whom he observed and studied at great length, in the process of composing and refining an epic poem having to do with the wars against the Dutch.[58]

Throughout Melanesia, Micronesia, and Polynesia there have been, and in some cases still are, performers of a bardic nature. The Polynesians have an especially rich history of such epic styles. As Katherine Luomala has stated, they "had a name for every narrative and poetic form, and each had its proper time and place."[59] The Maori of New Zealand were the most advanced of all. In a sense, every mother had to be a bard because she was expected to sing *oriori*, lullabies and songs full of historical allusions, while her children were still young, so they could learn about their ancestors.[60] The Samoans were famous for their "talking chiefs" who were skilled in composing and reciting traditions, genealogies, myths, and legends.[61] The *tohunga*, common to most parts of Polynesia, must be considered more a religious storyteller than a secular bard because of the sacred nature of his training and responsibilities.

Among the Melanesians, too, there were bards, apparently, who were similar to talking chiefs. Maranda reported that Timoti Bobongi, chief of a clan in the Solomon Islands, "is an acknowledged singer of tales and is often invited to sing myths in the memorial feasts. . . . He has also mastered genres other than myth and is a competent performer of songs."[62]

Mitchell states that, on the whole, "Micronesia lacks the complex mythologies found in Polynesia."[63] Nevertheless, there was the *sou fòs*, the person skilled in narrating *uruwo*, legend or history. *Uruwo* was often chanted in a special language, called *itang*, and had to be learned exactly.[64]

Native American Bards

Durán gives us a picture of Aztec bards that could apply to almost any of the preceding peoples mentioned in this chapter.

All these had their singers who composed chants about their own glorious deeds and those of their ancestors. . . . In their kingdoms songs had been composed describing their feats, victories, conquests, genealogies, and their extraordinary wealth. I have heard these lays sung many a time at public dances, and even though they were in honor of their native lords, I was elated to hear such high praise and notable feats.

Trans. by Fernando Horcasitas and Doris Heyden[65]

Durán lived and wrote in Mexico in the sixteenth century, less than one hundred years after the arrival of the first Spanish, so it is likely that the Aztec bards were still performing much as they had before the conquest.

The Incas of Peru did not seem to have the praise singer type of bard, but rather the chronicler-historian type. The *amauta* were oral specialists who decided what oral history was to be taught and which episodes of each Inca ruler's past were to be popularized and remembered. They were also involved in the selection and training of the *quipu-kamayoq*, the professional interpreters and reciters of the *quipu*,[66] a knotted cord that served as a memory device for historical traditions (Plate 6).

African Bards

It is in Africa that one encounters the richest variety of bards for the post-medieval period. There is disagreement among scholars as to whether many of the performers are truly bardic. Finnegan disputes the use of the term "epic" to describe most of the praise songs or chronicles of Africa, and finds little that is both narrative and epic.[67] Jordan does not express the belief that there are no bards, but simply states that the African performers have no exact parallels in classical or modern Western societies.[68]

Mafeje,[69] Biebuyck,[70] and others,[71] on the contrary, present fairly convincing arguments to show that there are African bards who are not very different from those in Celtic or classical history. Their functions, their social position, and the content of their performances are all similar to those of early European and Celtic bards.

Regarding the Nyanga people of the Congo, Biebuyck points out the differences between *muṣínjo*, their praise recitations for chiefs or headmen given on state occasions, and the *kárịsị*, their true epics. The former are recited without any musical accompaniment. The latter are first sung, then narrated, usually with rattles, bells, and percussion sticks as background sounds. The bards perform the *kárịsị* in episodes, rarely narrating the entire epic at one time, but sometimes it is done on consecutive evenings. The bard receives only very small amounts of money, but often accepts food and beer for himself and his

PLATE 6   *Quipu* or cord knotted in such a way that it could be used as a memory aid by
historical narrators of the Incas. Reproduced from Lord Kingsborough, *Antiquities of Mexico* . . . (London: Robert Havell, 1831), vol. 4.

assistants. For the bard, the act of reciting the epic has some religious significance, but the audience would generally consider the session a socially uplifting and entertaining experience rather than a religious one.[72]

The situation is essentially the same for the Lega, a neighboring people in the area. For them, the epic is called *lugano*. The bard is called *mugani wa lugano*.[73]

The *imbongi* of the Xhosa in South Africa is a self-appointed bard, but he could not remain so if he did not reflect in his poetry the feelings, aspirations, and interests of the group from which he comes and for whom he performs. His duties are to celebrate victories, chant the laws and customs of the nation, recite the genealogies of the royal families, and criticize the abuse of power or neglect of responsibility on the part of a chief. Mafeje recorded a modern bard of this type as he composed and performed his account of the history and politics of the Xhosa and the South African government.[74]

In Rwanda and Burundi, Vansina found as many different types of oral narratives and performers as Luomala found in Polynesia. Burundi mothers, just like Maori mothers, sing lullabies that border on the bardic, they are so full of references to family history.[75] Once a month, at the new moon, it was customary to publicly perform *ncyeem ingesh*, dynastic songs. Artistic, historical narratives called *ncok* are sung while persons who are about to take part in a masked dance are getting dressed and decorated.[76]

In Rwanda, there are both oral dynastic poems of a family nature and warriors' epic poems. It was the *abateekerezi* who had the tasks of composing, memorizing, and chanting the most important events of each reign, while the *abacurabwenge* added to and memorized the genealogies and other historical tales. The *abasizi* were similar to *rhapsodes*, reciting the praise poems of earlier poets from memory.[77]

The Swahili *utenzi*, a long epic-type poem, is now a literary genre, but was once composed and recorded through oral means for entertainment and inspiration.[78] It usually treated of the deeds of Moslem heroes, but more recently some *utenzi* were composed and recited on such occasions as the inauguration of the first presidents of the newly independent nations of East Africa. These *utenzi* naturally celebrated the lives of these new heroes.[79]

Because of the great amount of travel by explorers and missionaries into the region of the Baganda, their bards were described in detail quite early in English reports. Speke and Roscoe both gave verbal pictures that seem quite explicit:

> I found him [the chief] sitting on the ground with several elders; whilst Wasoga minstrels played on their lap-harps, and sang songs in praise of their king ... and the noble stranger who wore fine clothes ....[80]

> The old harp used at the court of the King and chiefs used to be accompanied by songs belauding the King's power and benevolence, praising him and belittling his enemies. The words were made to fit the tunes at a moment's notice, and were suited to passing events. ... The older and more popular songs were the traditions and legends of the nation, sung in a minor key.[81]

The Baganda lost their kingdom in the twentieth century, and bardic singing among them went into a decline. But there are bardic performers still in Uganda today. Morris describes the *omwevugi*, a praise poet who recites in the Runyankore language.[82]

In West Africa there are many epic bards and there are hunters' bards. The latter are performers whose original function was to prepare and accompany groups of hunters in order to bring them good luck in their search for game. The hunters' groups are now largely symbolic, but still quite active in social and cultural ways. The chief occasion on which their bards perform for them—for the Yoruba groups, particularly—is the annual celebration of the Ogun festival.[83] This falls sometime in the dry season between December and April. Each compound or village in which the hereditary members of the hunters' groups live decides on its own appropriate days for celebration. Other times when the bards are asked to perform are for the wake of a deceased member, for a housewarming, to celebrate a new farm purchase, or for a child-naming or marriage ceremony. The latter two occasions are now commonly used by the general public, that is, by those who are not members of the hunters' groups, as a time for inviting the bards to perform, simply for enjoyment and aesthetic satisfaction. The bards are themselves rarely members of the hunters' groups, and their office is not hereditary. In Yoruba, the bard is called *oníjǎlá*, and the narratives and songs that are chanted are called *ijála*.[84] In the Mande language, the bard is called a *donso-jeli*, partly after the six-stringed instrument with which he accompanies himself.[85] The training of these hunters' bards is fairly lengthy and is described in more detail in Chapter 13. Some aspects of their performance styles are discussed in Chapter 9.

The epic bards are known by a score or more of names throughout present-day West Africa, but the most commonly recognized term for them is *griot*. This is especially true since the appearance of the book *Roots* by Alex Haley, based in part on the recitations of a modern *griot* from Gambia. Other terms for the *griot* include *gêwel*, *gawlo*, *īggīw* (male) and *tīggiwīt* (female), *diaré* and *mbom mvet*. Charles Bird discusses the fine differences between the epic bard and the hunters' bard.[86] The chief difference is the fact that the epic bard is generally a hereditary type, while the hunters' bard is not. For some reason, Mafeje did not recognize or take note of this point, because he writes that one of the differences between Celtic bards and those of modern Africa was that the latter are never hereditary.[87] In South Africa these are not inherited positions, but in West Africa this entire type or group receives its training and social position solely through inherited means. Furthermore, they satisfy all the other conditions Mafeje cites as necessary in order to be called bards. Like the South African *imbongi*, the *īggīw*, *tīggiwīt* and *diaré* had a right to say what they liked with impunity.[88]

It is curious that one can find female epic bards among the Saharan and Sahelian peoples. In spite of the fact that most of these peoples are Islamic, the women bards always perform in public, to mixed audiences:

> He who loves to listen, goes to them in their homes, and they sing to him, both their male and their female, their youth and their elder, and not one of them has any feeling of embarrassment in front of the other.[89]

This custom probably was inherited from pre-Islamic times. In Mauritania, for example, the musicians' families are so ancient in lineage that they can usually be traced back to the time before the arrival of Islam. In fact, most of the hereditary bards of this region are a mixture of early Arab, Berber, and Sudanic cultures, and the Islamic tradition for them is relatively recent.

In Ethiopia, which has both Sudanic and Coptic cultural influences, there are a group of professional minstrels called *azmaris* who sing, dance, tell tales, and do improvisations, usually to the accompaniment of a one-stringed instrument called the *leqso*. They can be compared with the *skomorokhi* of Russia, or the medieval minstrels of Europe. The subjects of their songs are usually contemporary events or the personal history and background of someone prominent in their audience. These songs are usually complimentary, but sometimes they are outrageous or even offensive. *Azmaris* date back to at least the sixteenth century, when they were attached to courts much as were the early minstrels of Europe.[90]

There is a female type of bard similar to the *azmari*, called a *mungerash*.[91] A French musicologist recorded a vivid picture of one in the 1920s:

> There is one in Abyssinia named Tadigê, renowned in court and city. . . . she was much sought after. . . . she took part in official ceremonies on horseback, letting her long blue mantle flow behind her in the wind, while with an excited gesture she would accentuate the war songs or the praise songs in honor of Menilek and his illustrious guests.[92]

Both the *azmari* and the *mungerash* were known to have rather loose reputations, yet their social position was often stronger than it might have appeared outwardly because people feared their power to criticize.[93]

This brief survey of bardism throughout the world has probably omitted many types, for there was neither time nor space to trace each and every bardic group. Appropriately, the survey ends in a country neighboring Egypt, where, as mentioned, some of the earliest pictorial depictions of bards are to be found. Bardic storytelling seems to be the type that succumbs soonest to the modern media of print and recorded sound. It remains to be seen, then, whether these last surviving groups will, in time, survive or not.

3

Folk Storytelling

In the first chapter of this book a number of quotations from ancient sources were cited to indicate that there is written proof that storytelling took place in homes, during communal or group work, at social gatherings, and in streets or marketplaces. The persons who told the stories to adults and to children were not formally trained in that art, and they did not seem to be restricted to any particular educational level or social class. Folk storytelling, for purposes of this book, will be comprised of most of the qualities listed above.

Some early commentaries did seem to regard this kind of story with disdain, as though it were somehow less important than heroic literature or history. The Emperor Julian (A.D. 331–363), for example, wrote:

> But I am bound to say something in defense of those who originally invented myths; I think they wrote them for childish souls: and I liken them to nurses who hang leathern toys to the hands of children when they are irritated and teething. . . . So those mythologists wrote for the feeble soul whose wings are just beginning to sprout, and who, though still incapable of being taught the truth, is yearning for further knowledge. . . .
>
> *Orations* VII, 206 D, Trans. by Wilmer C. Wright[1]

This is an attitude that is carried over, to a certain extent, to modern times. As recently as 1935, the eminent anthropologist Ruth Benedict could find great interest in myths as socio-religious expressions of a culture when they were performed or transmitted in a serious manner or in what we would call bardic form; but as soon as the stories served as children's amusements they were, in her view, not worth studying.[2] Delargy also slighted the stories told for and by women and children. In his opinion they were obviously not as worthy of merit as those told by men at their gatherings.[3]

This disposition on the part of some folklorists and anthropologists appears strange in view of the fact that numerous testimonies to the power of the folktale stress that it was those heard during childhood that seemed to have the most profound and lasting effect. They might well appear in retrospect to have had little artistic or literary merit. And yet, writers, artists, inventors, scientists, statesmen, and a host of others have testified in memoirs and autobiographies that it was the stories they heard when they were very young that most profoundly affected them. T. S. Eliot was speaking of written literature for the young when he wrote:

> I incline to come to the alarming conclusion that it is just the literature that we read for "amusement," or "purely for pleasure" that may have the greatest and least suspected influence upon us.[4]

This will be one of the premises on which this chapter and the subsequent ones are based: that the stories told to children or overheard by them by accident or guile are indeed very important.

Storytelling in the Home

Linda Dégh is one folklorist who would agree to the importance of storytelling for children. In her opinion, it is the vital link that provides the means for transmission of the folktale tradition.

> It does not matter whether the children's stories are told well or badly or whether they are read. They constitute for the children the first real encounter with the folktale, and it quite often happens that it is decided then and there who will become, sometimes after many decades, a good storyteller.[5]

This is what must be kept in mind when reading the accounts of folk storytelling in many parts of the world. Some of the sessions might appear to have very little to do with children. Yet it is likely that even those meant strictly and exclusively for adult audiences had their secret child listeners who were deeply moved by the things they heard and remembered them all the better for having heard them illicitly.

Fortunately, children do not have to get all of their exposure to stories by secretive means. Storytelling in the home is one of the most universal of human experiences. Here we shall discuss only those accounts that specifically mention the importance of this activity for children.

Among many African peoples, there is still a high priority assigned to family storytelling. Béart quotes this maxim from the Ivory Coast: "The *gouros* gods only give children to those who can tell at least a hundred tales."[6] Children of the Ewe people of Ghana are sim-

PLATE 7 *Akpata* player and storyteller from Benin, Nigeria. Photo courtesy of Institute for the Study of Human Issues, Philadelphia; reprinted with permission.

ply not considered educated unless they have heard many times the *gliwo*, animal stories that are intended to teach basic lessons in obedience, kindness, courage, honesty, and other virtues through indirect example.[7]

According to Mbiti, children have to be present when a story is being told by the Akamba of Kenya. If one child has to go to another house to fetch something, the narrator will even wait until he or she returns.[8] The Shinqiti of Mauritania have a cycle of folktales especially for children that consist of episodes in the life of an imaginary woman, each one of which implies a moral or a virtue that is supposed to be absorbed by the young in entertaining fashion.[9]

Some groups in Africa have special names to describe the storytelling events within the family circle. For the Edo of Benin, Nigeria, such a gathering is called an *ibota*. It includes the children, youths, wives, and the head of household in one compound. It usually takes place in the largest room, and it can celebrate anything from the successful sale of a crop to the visit of a relative, or just being in a good mood. Anyone can tell stories or make riddles or sing songs at the *ibota*, except the head of the household who is the listener.[10] The *okpobhie*, in contrast, is a storytelling event also held in the family compound, but performed only by professional storytellers who play the *akpata* or *asologun* (Plate 7).

45

PLATE 8   Mrs. Nongenile Masithathu Zenani, gifted *ntsomi* teller from South Africa.
Photo courtesy of Harold Scheub.

For the Xhosa and Zulu children it is assumed that an accepted part of their social life will be not only listening to narratives, but also learning to perform them adequately, so that when they in turn are parents and grandparents, they will be able to tell them regularly to their offspring. The performance of the *ntsomi* among the Xhosa and the *nganekwane* among the Zulu is almost exclusively a family compound affair (Plate 8). This does not prevent it from being an art form that achieves a high degree of aesthetic harmony. The children in such situations are often just as demanding an audience as the adults, because they have had training in listening and narrating beginning at an early age. They are well aware of those performances that reach a peak of perfection and those that don't. Often they will join in the calls for bringing to a close a poor performance.[11]

Some families have storytelling activities only for short, fixed periods of the year. In rural Korea, this is during the month of October, or harvest time. At this time, the myths that usually are only performed during rituals will often be recited in the family.[12]

Cammann describes such a warm and intimate picture of the "*märchen* evening" in a West Prussian village home at the turn of the century that one can only envy the children and adults lucky enough to have been present.[13] The usual time for starting was on winter evenings at about four o'clock in the afternoon. A favorite request of the children, then as now, was for something scary or creepy.

One woman, Anna Spurgarth, remembered eight straight winters, from 1900 to 1908, of frequent storytelling in her home, at which most of her school friends from the village were also present. Some adults were always on hand as well, for Anna's father was well known as a good and entertaining storyteller. Whoever fell asleep had to put a fifty-penny piece in a saucer on the table. Smaller children might be sent to bed when there was a pause around ten o'clock for coffee, bread, and cakes. The older children could stay up as long as they managed to keep awake. Only occasionally were they asked to leave the room, when something of an adult nature, not considered appropriate for children, was being told. Most of the stories were told by Anna's father, Karl Restin, but other adults sometimes contributed a story. Birthdays, anniversaries, and other special days always called for a story evening.[14]

The Romansh tellers in Switzerland described by Uffer also told a great deal in the home.[15] One of them, Ursula Bisaz, reported a reaction common to children in many parts of the world, that is, their dislike of change once they find something they like. Bisaz, who was a gifted storyteller, would occasionally like to alter or change the words and even some of the events of the stories she told, but if she did, her grandchildren would invariably say with disappointment: "Granny, last time you didn't tell it that way."[16]

Because there has been a lessening of such family telling, grandmothers or older storytellers will frequently voice complaints that the younger generation is too lazy or too preoccupied to carry it out. Such was the case with an Indian informant, Anna Liberata de Souza, as recorded by Mary Frere in 1881:

> When I was young, old people used to be very fond of telling stories; but instead of that, it seems to me that now the old people are fond of nothing but making money.[17]

There is still a great deal of storytelling in the home, especially in Indian villages, so one suspects that Anna was exaggerating somewhat.

Some families not only had sessions for entertainment, but needed and wanted to perform regularly the tales that were considered as the sacred property of the family. This is commonly reported in the Pacific Islands and borders on religious storytelling. These were sometimes told in a special language and had to be told exactly, but their sacredness did not prevent them from being enjoyed as entertainment as well.[18]

The same situation is reported among the Australian aborigines. According to Allen, the telling of their myths was—and still is—"the most common form of aboriginal entertainment, one which included the women and children, so they, too, might learn some of the great stories."[19]

In some societies, wealthy homes had a man or woman among the servants whose special task was to tell stories for both the adults and children. Sometimes there was a different one for each group. This was frequently encountered in India and Russia in the nineteenth century and in the early years of the twentieth.[20]

Native Americans also perceive the narration of stories to children as being of the greatest significance. "If my children hear the stories, they will grow up to be good people; if they don't hear them, they will turn out to be bad," opined Yellowman, a Navajo informant.[21] This is substantiated by the fact that virtually all collections of Native American tales that mention the storytelling occasions at all include the fact that children were present and were expected to listen carefully and attentively.[22]

In the Bahamas, where stories are nominally directed toward children, it is usually they who begin the storytelling sessions.[23] Gorham does not say whether the children started the telling at the *serão* in Brazil in the past, but they were most likely included, for this was a family gathering during the evening when storytelling was practiced.[24]

In the Hungarian community of the Szeklers, folk storytelling took place both within the family and at other social occasions. The home-based telling was principally for the benefit of the children, but there does not seem to be any indication that the tales used were different ones, except that the average woman who did the home storytelling rarely used her creative talent consciously, as did the best storytellers (men and women) who told for the village at large. There were exceptions, like Zsuzsánna Palkó (see Plate 29), who put the same feeling into the versions of tales she told her grandchildren at home that she did when narrating at a more special, public occasion.[25]

On the other hand it must be mentioned that there are a few places where recreational storytelling was not considered appropriate for children. Ammar writes:

> There is hardly any adult ... who admits that he tells stories to his children. Stories ... are considered to be demonic, and of no particular value.[26]

Nevertheless, children in the village in Egypt where this was noted managed to tell eleven tales, so they must have heard them somewhere.

The only reference to storytelling practices in Africa south of the Sahara that could be interpreted as restrictive in any way insofar as children are concerned is the description Raum gives for the Chagga people of Tanzania. According to that account children are told a few very simple animal stories with a moral, for didactic purposes, but they are restricted in their permission to listen to the stories adults tell for entertainment.[27]

Gorer reported that the Lepchas of Sikkim also did not consider their tales, with the exception of one or two animal fables, as appropriate for children,[28] but it is likely that had he asked some of the younger ones to recount them, he would have heard at least the bare outlines of the stories told by the adults.

In an early study called *The Child in Primitive Society*, Miller implied that children heard stories only for purely didactic reasons,[29] but this flies in the face of much evidence to the contrary.

The reason for the lack of storytelling opportunities for children is much more likely to be a lack of interest on the part of the parents than it is a desire to protect or screen children from hearing stories. This trend can be noticed dramatically in immigrant groups or in those that are changing swiftly from rural to industrialized societies. Bianco reported, for example, that almost all informants among the Italian immigrants she interviewed had heard stories from their parents.[30] Those parents were in most cases born in Italy. But the younger age group, especially those under thirty, rarely told stories to their children or among themselves.

In some countries, storytelling took place in a home, but not in the home of the narrator. Such occasions often had special names also, and they cannot be treated as family storytelling because there were usually members from more than one family present. Typical of this kind of event is the Irish *céilidhe*. Delargy called a house where such an event took place a *toigh áirneáil*. The "season" usually opened near Halloween (October 31) and ended near St. Patrick's Day (March 17). The audience did not pay, but they were reponsible for bringing in turf for the fire, and plenty of water for the home owner.[31] Carmichael's depiction of a *ceilidh* in the Scottish Hebrides is a bit different, in that women and children seemed to be accepted members of the audience. He speaks of the women as knitting, sewing, spinning, carding, or embroidering in the background. The children squeeze in wherever they will fit, even in the rafters. "Occasionally a moment of excitement occurs when heat and sleep overpower a boy and he tumbles down among the people below, to be trounced out and sent home."[32]

There were other traditions of nonceremonial public gatherings for folk storytelling, but not in homes. Such an occasion is called *ma'rika* in Persian and is a custom dating back to at least the sixteenth century. Modern variations of it still take place occasionally in coffeehouses.[33] Both folk and bardic storytelling are practiced at such times.

Storytelling during Work

The tedium of work was often relieved by a background of tale telling. Sometimes the very rhythm of work became part of the rhythm of the story, or vice versa. Linda Dégh found that several members of the famous Hungarian storytelling family, the Zaiczes, told quite regularly in the fields of sugar beets. They were foremen and entertained the other workers while they hacked away. According to one worker: "Everybody was glad to work under a foreman who could tell good stories."[34] Other work during which storytelling had been done by this group of people included carting wood from the forest, fishing, and cobbling.[35]

Brinkmann mentions that a favorite time for storytelling in a rural German village was during weeding or during the harvesting of potatoes. He also observed it among a group of workers in a sand pit, and in a place where a building was going up.[36]

Gorer remarks that one of the occasions of storytelling for the Lepchas of Sikkim is while weeding. Often one skillful teller will be selected to tell short stories all day, while the others work. That person will even get special tidbits of food at the evening meal as a kind of extra pay.[37]

The work that seemed best suited for storytelling was that associated with cotton or wool. Sifting, carding, spinning, and weaving were so well suited to listening to stories that this is reported wherever such products were found. East mentions this as a favorite pastime of the spinners of cotton among the Tiv of Northern Nigeria.

> As soon as it was dark they lit a fire in the middle of the village, and the children, the older men and the women all gathered round it to spin cotton and tell hare-stories.[38]

Hoogasian found among her older Armenian informants in Detroit quite a number who had learned their stories while listening and sifting the seeds out of cotton, back in their Armenian childhood.[39]

50

Delargy mentions that at the Irish *airnéan*, a women's gathering to spin and card wool, storytelling was the expected accompaniment for at least part of the time.[40] Sometimes one of the women would tell, but at other times a shanachie would be invited in and even paid a bit to tell his tales. A gypsy teller in Romania mentioned to the folklorist Bela Gunda that he, too, had frequently been paid to come in and tell tales to women as they spun.[41]

The Szekler ethnic group from Hungary had a very strong tradition of telling tales in the spinning rooms of the village. This was true in the period when they lived in Bucovina, Romania, and also after they were repatriated to the area around Kakasd in southern Hungary. Spinning took place during part of the day, from Monday through Thursday, and on most winter evenings. For the day spinning, the women found tellers among themselves. In the evenings the men often gathered with their wives, and then some of the best tellers, usually men, would narrate, often until one or two in the morning.[42]

Some folklorists report that after long working days it is rare to find a storytelling occasion because people are too tired. But a community work project, in which all have shared the tasks equally, usually results in the shared good feelings necessary for a storytelling atmosphere. Such an occasion was called a *mingaco* in Chile.[43] It has apparently died out.

Other Occasions for Folk Storytelling

Personal celebrations and feasts on the occasion of a wedding or child naming are often the time to tell stories. Babalola reports that the *ijálá* chanters of the Yoruba, who used to recite only for members of hunters' groups, now are commonly asked by all to perform on those two occasions, regardless of whether they are members of the hunters' groups or not.[44] Cejpek also mentions that weddings and births were times for storytelling.[45] The Lepchas have a long story of from two to three hours that must be a part of every marriage ceremony.[46] The Suk, from the Sudan, also use the marriage feast as one of their favorite periods for a good long story session.[47]

Stories at wakes for the dead are common in Ireland and Europe and can also be found in some parts of Africa. For the Szeklers of Hungary, mentioned earlier, this kind of storytelling had tremendous social importance. The order of narration was an indispensable part of the ritual of the wakes, which lasted forty-eight hours. The wake served as the single most important social occasion for the married and elderly. A beautifully arranged wake would be discussed for years after the event, and all who had been present would remember the stories told. The storytelling alternated with singing and the saying of prayers. The stories told were usually short anecdotes and long, involved *märchen*.[48]

Although the above are recent examples, the custom of storytelling at wakes is very ancient. As cited in Chapter 1, it is mentioned in a number of the *Rules of Vedic Domestic Ceremonies*, compiled about 200 B.C. in India. The *sūtra* already cited referred to the death of a guru. There is another mention of storytelling at what might be called wakes for ordinary persons in a later *sūtra:*

> Now the water libations [which are performed for deceased persons]. . . .
> When they have come out [of the water] and have sat down on a pure spot that is covered with grass, those who are versed in ancient tales should entertain them [by telling tales].
> *Pâraskara-Grihya-Sūtra*, III Kanda, 10 Kandika, 1, 22, Trans. by Hermann Oldenburg[49]

In some Catholic countries, storytelling followed after special services during Lent. A Canadian informant remarks:

> At this time, young boys and girls in the region would set out from home after the daily family prayer and gather at his house to hear one or two folktales each evening.[50]

Delargy mentions that after the stations of the cross each week in Lent, it was customary to gather for a folktale session.[51]

Storytelling among soldiers has also been mentioned since ancient times. In Israel, a particular kind of storytelling session, called a *kumsitz*, developed among the Palmakhnik. This was a kind of paramilitary or underground group organized during the fight for independence and existence as a separate state. The men and women would usually get together for an evening of self-entertainment. The stories they told were known as *ha-chizbat*, derived from an Arabic word meaning "to lie." The stories could be fanciful, exaggerated, humorous, and even preposterous, but they had to be based on a kernel of truth. Sometimes the *kumsitz* was used as a device to recruit youths from the high schools.[52]

Some persons have such an urge to share their tales, they need no special occasion in order to be persuaded to tell them. Delia Poirier, a storyteller of French Canada, baldly confessed:

> One winter, I visited in turn every house in the entire village to tell my tales. I went out three nights a week. I would have gone more often, but I didn't want people to think I was a gadabout.[53]

She was reported to be well liked in the community, so her "gadding about" obviously was not a nuisance.

Street and Marketplace Storytellers

The most visible of folk storytellers have been the street and marketplace narrators of the past and the present. India may well be the source and inspiration for many of them. As will be discussed in greater detail in Chapter 4, the religious storytellers gradually absorbed a rather secular style and content. The "picture showmen," as the Indian scholar Coomaraswamy calls them, took to the streets and public places.[54] By the time this custom was spread by Buddhists to China,

Java, and other parts of eastern and southern Asia, it began to have more and more secular content and appeal. Traders probably carried the stories and the public manner of telling them in the other direction as well, through Persia toward the West.

Unfortunately, there is no history of storytelling in India as yet written down, at least none readily accessible to the Western reader. From the Sanskrit scriptures and other early works, it is evident that tales of an entertaining nature were told (see the citations in Chapter 1). How street storytelling could spring up from the traditions of family folk storytelling or from the courtly minstrel tradition in India is not clear, any more than it is in Europe. The only point on which scholars agree is that it is still impossible to entirely separate the folktales from the myths, the secular from the religious, the popular from the classical. They are inextricably intertwined. Since this is so, one can turn to the modern storytellers in an attempt to find out what they might have been like in the past. There is not likely to have been much change in their storytelling style and content over the last few centuries.

In present-day India, in rural villages, small towns, and even some of the bigger towns and cities, one can still encounter itinerant storytellers. Those that perform in a more elaborate style, using large picture cloths and scrolls, have been mentioned in Chapter 2 as being of the bardic type, mostly because the content of their stories is heroic. It must be admitted that this is rather arbitrary, since the *Ramayana* and other epics can be perceived by the average Indian as heroic, homey and folklike, or religious.

The less showy tellers, whom we shall call folk storytellers, use much the same tale material. Those that give it more religious emphasis are the *sadhus* and *fakirs*, the "wise men" of the Hindus and Moslems respectively. Those that tell the tales with more secular emphasis are called *kathakas, bhats, pauranikas*, or some other name, depending on what part of India one is in.

In her study of *The Thousand and One Nights* as a genre, Gerhardt states that such time-gaining frame stories are apparently of Indian origin, but they were adapted and taken over by Persians and Arabs fairly early. Virtually all these collections, she finds, have "highly ingenious devices to introduce, to justify, to authenticate the telling of a story, to set it off, to make it serve a purpose. Stories are fitted one into the other like Chinese boxes."[55]

These frame stories were probably performed orally at inns and in caravanserai in a manner similar to that described by a nineteenth-century traveler:

> ... they had lighted a fire in front of their tent, and were squatting around it.... One of the camel-drivers was engaged in telling stories to a rapt audience.... With a clear, unhesitating voice, which he raised or lowered as occasion required, he pursued his tale, pausing only when he had made a point and expected the applause of his hearers.[56]

PLATE 9   Kashgar market storyteller. Bettmann Archive.

After the Middle Ages, the time-gaining frame stories were written down in more and more versions. They could be found in manuscripts in Persian, Arabic, and many European languages.

However, public storytelling in the marketplace and in the tea and coffee houses survived in the Middle East and North Africa. English travelers of the nineteenth century describing such sessions were the first to use the term storyteller consistently in their written and printed accounts, as in the following example:

> In a Persian town they are to be met with in every street. In open sites, such as are often found near market-places, great sheds are erected, open on all sides and furnished with rows of steps capable of seating three to four hundred persons squatting on their heels. In front of the audience is a platform from whence a succession of storytellers repeat their stories to a succession of listeners from morning to night [Plate 9].[57]

One of the most colorful scenes still frequently encountered in present-day North African marketplaces is the animated storyteller, surrounded by a wide variety of listeners. The audience can be a mixture of young and old, in modern or traditional dress. An impressive aerial photographic view of one such crowd can be seen in the *National Geographic* for March 1932.[58]

When the tales of India moved in the other direction, to China and Southeast Asia, it was Buddhism that carried along this richness of narrative. After becoming secularized, the tales were added to and narrated by all types of tellers. The professional performers who told in teahouses and in special theaters are described in Chapter 5. There were also amateur storytellers who went from town to town and village to village, presenting their tales at marketplaces and on street corners. These street storytellers would try to attract attention by clapping together two small pieces of wood. Or they might play a two-stringed violin. Some of them were blind and deformed. Many of these latter were accompanied by other family members.[59]

Chinese marketplaces were often in temple courtyards. As recently as 1950–1954 the *T'ien-ch'iao*, Peking's Heavenly Bridge, was a place where one could encounter outdoor performers of all types. The storyteller sat at a small table, and the listeners were on benches in a semicircle around it. Fees and contributions were not fixed. They were collected in the middle of the story or just before the climax, as in Persia and Turkey. The narrator had to hope for the best and tried his utmost to perform well. Although the street storytellers were usually very poor and of the lowest social classes, they had a certain pride that lent them dignity.[60]

Japan had street and itinerant storytellers in the past (Plate 10), but it is much more difficult to locate precise information on how they performed and what their social position was. This does not refer to the *zenza*, the *kodan-shi*, the *rakugo-ka* or the *naniwabushi*, all of whom were special types of indoor performers who will be discussed in the chapter on theatrical storytelling (Chapter 5).

PLATE 10   Outdoor market storyteller in Yokohama, Japan, late nineteenth century. Picture courtesy of The New York Public Library, Picture Collection.

For the modern types of Japanese public storytellers, there is more documentation. Adams gives an excellent picture of a village folk storyteller who usually performed for groups of children in the tea and candy shop she ran. Tsune Watanabe told chiefly *mukashi-banashi*, the equivalent of *märchen*. It was interesting to note that although Watanabe perceived her role of storyteller as having been greatly diminished in recent years, she was still held in esteem by the young people of the village. She claimed that the children and young people no longer had an interest in her stories, and yet it was a young man who led Adams to her, pointing out that she was the best storyteller around.[61]

Another form of modern, popular storytelling in Japan was *kamishibai*. The term means "paper drama" or "theater of paper." It had its roots in earlier forms of storytelling, in *kabuki* theater, and in shadow-puppet plays. Satoshi Kako and Koji Kata have documented the gradual adaptation of earlier indoor theater forms into the outdoor form of storytelling with pictures known as *kamishibai*. Koji Kata was himself a *kamishibai* performer, and his recent autobiography has been a best-seller in Japan.[62]

In its modern, most popular form, *kamishibai* began around 1930. This was a time of economic depression, and *kamishibai* was used by many unemployed workers as a means of making a little money. The performers were exclusively men, and they were looked down on by middle-class parents because they were identified with the racketeers who had dominated earlier groups of outdoor performers. Also, the stories they told were considered to be vulgar and in bad taste, and the candies they sold were believed by many mothers to be unsanitary.[63]

It was the children who began to enjoy the *kamishibai*, especially the children of the urban poor and working classes. There were performers in most of the major cities. They usually went about on bicycles for greater mobility. Each had a repertoire of three or four stories which he carried with him in the wooden frame that also served as the means of presenting the picture cards during the telling of the tales. For a further description and illustration of the frame, see Chapter 11.

During the Second World War and immediately after, *kamishibai* was virtually the only entertainment available to children. There were about 25,000 players around 1950. Satoshi Kako estimates as many as 7.5 million children could have seen a performance on any given day when they were all performing, since the performers usually repeated their programs about ten times in different places during the day and had an average audience of thirty children each time.[64]

Educators tried to prohibit the *kamishibai*, but in vain. Later they attempted to adapt it to an educational format, with stories that were considered more "suitable" or proper. In this way, many of the favorite fairy tales were eventually printed in *kamishibai* format (Plate 11).

A contemporary writer, Morio Kita, has given a memorable picture (semiautobiographical) of one child's reaction to the *kamishibai*.

> The fact was this. Lately Shuji, all by himself, went out more frequently than before and was absorbed in *kamishibai*, which visited the neighborhood at twilight time. In comparison to other children, he could be described as unhappy. The reason for his unhappiness was that he had not a single *sen*. At the beating of clatters, a mass of children ran to the *kamishibai* player, each trying to be the first to give the tightly grasped one-*sen* piece to him. The player gave a candy, dyed red and white, in exchange for the one *sen*. Nibbling their candies, the children intently watched the illustrations painted on coarse papers, listening to the narrative given by the player in a husky voice. Shuji, however, had no capital to procure candies. Stationing himself, mostly by luck, in the front row, he was roughly thrust aside by the *kamishibai* player.
>
> "Those who don't buy candies go behind the others!"
>
> Shuji, stealing occasional, envious glances at the candies possessed by the other children, stretched himself from behind to catch glimpses of a monstrous figure of a man with the mask of a skull, long ominous fingernails and a flying red cape.
>
> "Here comes the man of justice! His name is no other than the Golden Bat!" At this point the player thundered a little drum.
>
> After several such experiences, even the little head of Shuji began to realize the importance and necessity of money.
>
> *Nireke no Hitobito (The Nine Families)*, Trans. by Kiyoko Nozaki[65]

PLATE 11   Modern, educational form of *kamishibai* being used in a kindergarten. Photo courtesy of editors of *Kamishibai*, Tokyo.

In Europe, the street storytellers usually did not relate long, complex tales of the *märchen* type. Their stories were more likely to be news events of the most sensational type, put into ballad form. Or they were short anecdotes strung together. Like the storytellers of India and China, some of them probably had their roots in the religious storytelling of wandering monks. Others were probably the remnants of the organized troupes of minstrels that had once been common at all public gatherings of any size. Wherever they came from, they quickly seized on the medium of print as an adjunct to their oral talents rather than viewing it as a totally competitive medium.

According to Coupe, the publisher-vendors first appeared in the sixteenth century. At that time, the engraver, publisher, and printer was generally the same person. They went to all the fairs and sold their wares to anyone who would buy.[66] Hans Fehr, who has also written on the mass printing media of the sixteenth century, states that the printers directed three types of printed matter toward three kinds of readers. The book was aimed at the learned and scholarly; the *flugschrift* (chapbook or pamphlet), at the educated, that is, those who could read; and the *flugblatt* (picture sheet or broadsheet), at the mostly illiterate folk.[67]

Booksellers, hawkers, peddlers, itinerant street singers, and others would buy the materials in quantity. The street singers were a motley crowd, looked down upon as the dregs of society. This contempt may well have been political or religious in origin because the authorities feared the growing awareness of the masses. And there was no question but that the masses listened to the street singer with all of his or her gory details. They then often bought the cheap broadsheets or chapbooks in hopes of finding still more detail that had been left out in the performance.[68]

The street singer was most often called a *bänkelsänger* in German because the performer stood on a bench in order to be seen better. The *bänkelsänger* usually had a long pointed stick, which was used to point to the pictures that showed all the lurid details of the most melodramatic events in the story (Plates 12 and 13; see also Plate 24). Most of the pictures were woodcut prints, painted in by illuminators. After the story had been sung, the singer (or members of the singer's family) passed through the crowd, either collecting coins outright for the performance, or selling individual broadsheets or pamphlets that contained the story ballads or news events. There is no concrete evidence for the prices at which broadsheets were sold, nor is it known in what numbers they were issued.

The broadsheets of the seventeenth century were the most artistic of all. The printers increasingly used copperplate engravings and woodcuts. During this period, the picture story played an important part in the imaginative life of all classes. This was true for much of Europe, for the peddlers and performers penetrated into all parts of the continent.[69]

PLATE 12 Etching, dated 1740, by C. W. E. Dietrich, showing a *bänkelsänger* surrounded by his audience. Author's private collection.

PLATE 13   Market scene showing a *bänkelsänger*. Reproduced from Münchener Bilderbogen Series, No. 120, *Der Jahrmarket* (originally published in Munich by
Braun and Schneider, mid-nineteenth century).

The quality of the picture sheets, the broadsheets, and the chap-books began to decline in the eighteenth and nineteenth centuries, and with the exception of a few publishing efforts, such as the *Münchener Bilderbogen*, they were designed for the poor and illiterate masses only. The middle classes thought it proper to purchase regular books and newspapers. There are few contemporary descriptions of that time to tell us how the singer might have changed performance techniques or how extensive the individual repertoires were. The best one can do is to speculate, based on statements made in the early twentieth century by some of the street performers. Dominik Rolsch was one who inherited from his father the profession of itinerant street singer. He remembered that his father had told him that short-ly after his marriage he owned a wagon in which to live, two dozen new *schilder*, and a music wagon with a built-in organ.[70]

In the twentieth century, a few performers survived, but for the most part they could not compete with films and radio.

4

Religious Storytelling

Religious storytelling is that storytelling used by official or semi-official functionaries and leaders of a religious group to explain or promulgate their religion through stories, rather than through laws. It employs at least a few elements that are dramatic and entertaining, so as to capture and hold the interest of the audience.

Hindu Storytelling

In the Hindu religion, the *Brahmanas* are prose commentaries explaining the relationship between the Vedas (sacred texts) and the ceremonies that had grown up around the early form of this religion. Although at first they were not considered as sacred revelation, in time they came to be regarded as such. In the *Brahmanas*, there are many myths and a large number of stories. Eggeling, one of the scholar-translators of the *Brahmanas*, believes that many of the stories were "invented by the authors of these treatises for the purpose of supplying some kind of traditional support for particular points of ceremonial. ... The style of narrative and the archaic mode of diction which they affect, readily lend themselves to syntactic turns of expression rarely indulged in by the authors in the purely explanatory or exegetic parts of their works."[1]

In other words, as in so many cases both ancient and modern, the story had the ability to engage the interest of the listener and to express symbolic meaning in a readily understandable way. It was seized on, therefore, as a logical device to use in the promulgation of religion. The stories attached to certain ceremonials in the Hindu religion (such as the marriage ceremony) remain in use up to the present day. Although they were written down approximately 500 B.C. for the first time, it is likely they are much, much older.

The Indian scholar Coomaraswamy gives perhaps the most complete listing of early Indian works that refer to picture storytelling, usually related to a religious theme (see Plate 25).[2] The short descriptions that he cites from ancient books could easily be used to describe as well the modern Indian storytellers who wander about, reciting and illustrating their narratives with cloths depicting scenes from the *Ramayana* or different aspects of the lives and qualities of various gods and goddesses. Typical of the latter are the Saurashtra temple cloths, used exclusively in worship to honor the Mother Goddess. Joan Erikson gives a full explanation of the long process by which these cloths are made. A typical one will contain images of the Mother Goddess surrounded by groups of worshipers, other gods, animals, warriors, hunters, and many symbols of one kind or another. These are meant to call to mind the myths and legends associated with the Mother Goddess.[3]

Mande describes the story cloths used by the *dakkalwars* in Maharashtra as depicting "the Basawa version of Purana myths."[4] The *kalamkari* cloths of the Andhra region usually show scenes from the *Ramayana*, or stories associated with such gods as Krishna and Ganesh (see Plate 26).[5] How they developed from the earlier scrolls, and indeed whether they are even the direct descendants of these scrolls, is still an unexplored area of research.

Lüders classifies the early "picture showmen" as actors and considers them as part of the history and tradition of the theater in India. He ties them in with the later custom of shadow-puppet plays, especially those of the *Ramayana*, that spread far and wide to Asia and had such a great and lasting influence on such places as Indonesia.[6] The effect of such versions is probably more theatrical and social than it is religious.

Buddhist Storytelling

Siddhartha Gautama, the founder of Buddhism, was born into a high caste, so it is likely that he was thoroughly familiar with Vedic ceremonials and the stories attached to them. Therefore, it is not surprising that the use of storytelling as a means of proselytizing would become a part of Buddhism as well. Furthermore, the very nature of certain beliefs in both Hinduism and Buddhism, such as their emphasis on rebirths and former lives, seems to encourage storytelling.

Tathâgata is another name for the Buddha, meaning "He who has come" in Sanskrit. In one of the sacred texts of Mahayana Buddhism, there is this passage:

> I am the Tathâgata, o ye gods and men! . . . and the Tathâgata who knows the difference as to the faculties and energy of those beings, produces various Dharmaparyâyas, tells many tales, amusing, agreeable, both instructive and pleasant, tales by means of which all beings not only become pleased with the law in this present life, but also after death will reach happy states . . . . Therefore, Kâsyapa, I will tell thee a parable, for men of good understanding will generally readily enough catch the meaning of what is taught under the shape of a parable.[7]

Several hundred years after the death of Buddha, when Theravada Buddhism was well established, a treatise composed for the purpose of explaining further some of its beliefs and practices questioned rhetorically:

> Why do the brethren concern themselves with recitation of, with asking questions about the discourses, and the pieces in mixed prose and verse, and the expositions, and the poems and the outbursts of emotion, and the passages beginning "Thus he said," and the birth-stories, and the tales of wonder, and the extended treatises?[8]

The answer was, simply, because "recitation was a good thing." In many parts of Asia, these Buddhist stories are so intertwined with their Hindu antecedents that it is impossible to say which is stronger or richer in its narrative tradition. It was Buddhism, though, that was the stronger medium of transmission.

In South and Southeast Asia, China, Korea, and Japan, Buddhism made a dramatic impact. Along with the manuscripts of the sacred texts and explanations, the traveling monks seem to have taken some of the pictorial scrolls mentioned earlier. There is some disagreement on this among scholars. Průšek, for example, translates a section of a Chinese work, dating from 1235, in this manner:

> . . . those narrating scriptures, which means the unfolding and narrating of Buddhist books; those speaking of visits and invitations, which means things like guests and [their] patrons, meditation and enlightenment.[9]

In 1279, in almost the exact same words, another Chinese work describes the storytellers who tell in the same manner, and then goes on to speak of "narrators of funny or humorous scriptures."[10] Průšek does not come to any firm conclusion but does speculate that there were probably storytellers of two types in the early centuries of Buddhist penetration in China: one type that recited or narrated existing Buddhist scriptures and another that created original works, religious in tendency, much influenced by secular tales.[11]

A student of Průšek, Věna Hrdličková, delved much further into this question. According to her, the gradual development of storytelling from sermons in the temple to stories in the marketplace occurred in the time from the later Han dynasty to the beginning of the T'ang (approximately A.D. 200–700). Sutras with an entirely religious content would be recited in a sermon, using the translated texts that provided only the core words. There was a strict form for

65

this. The monk-preacher took his place on a raised platform, paid respects to Buddha, and sang or chanted an introductory hymn. The recitation of the sutra followed, then another hymn, a closing obeisance to Buddha, and finally, with great dignity, the preacher descended from the platform.[12]

Gradually these performances were enriched with descriptions and illustrations from daily life, in which the preachers used their own words. These changes probably occurred as a response to questions from the audience. This was, after all, a new religious system to most of the hearers.

Průšek and Hrdličková confined most of their discussions to the texts used by these storytellers, and they did not comment much on the pictures that accompanied the texts on the back of the scrolls or appeared in temples. There was the possibility that some of the storytellers used some of these paintings, often found in long sequences on temple walls, to illustrate their telling. Arthur Waley was inclined to believe that the teller did not necessarily show the pictures to the audience during narration.[13] Victor Mair, a Harvard scholar presently working on a study of some of these early illustrated scrolls and storytelling texts, is more inclined to believe that the pictures were a natural adjunct to the storytelling.[14]

At any rate, the general consensus is that both the art and the literature of virtually all areas of Asia were influenced in some way by the spread of Buddhism. Buddhist propaganda was directed at the masses, and this helped to bring about the use of vernacular literatures. The scholar Demiéville summarizes:

> The earliest dated work of vernacular literature [in Chinese], in the middle of the 8th century, is a fictionalized amplification of a famous episode of the Buddhist legend, which lent itself to dramatic effects and also to figured representation.[15]

> Another specific feature of Indian literature which was to be adopted as a regular feature in the Chinese . . . was the mixture of prose and verse. The stories liberally included in their scriptures by the Indians, who are born storytellers, contributed to the development of literature in China.[16]

Demiéville is referring to the Chinese only, but the statements could fit equally well a number of other Asian countries influenced by Buddhism in much the same way.

Modern forms of Buddhism still use the story as a teaching and expository device, especially with children. The Jataka tales, relating to the adventures of the Buddha in his former existences, are used orally and in many printed versions. Since most modern sects of Buddhism do not have formal religious instruction schools for young children (of the Christian Sunday-school type or the Islamic Koranic-school type, for example), the informal use of stories is probably the method through which most Buddhist children first encounter the precepts and moral values of their religion.

Judaic Storytelling

As has been mentioned in the Preface to this book, the Old Testament contains fragments of stories and legends, but no real description of storytelling occasions. Gerhardsson points out that right from the start, the emphasis was on memorization of the Torah and other scriptures.[17] Talmudic literature makes many references to the fact that children were expected to learn to recite the scriptures by heart after reading or hearing them. When interpretive material was added, it was extremely conservative and traditional.[18] A parallel can be drawn with the Greek reciters, known as *rhapsodes*. They were conscientious in their attempts to render Greek epic narratives in the exact words, but they were not creative storytellers who allowed spontaneous changes. It is likely, then, that for orthodox Jewish purposes, storytelling did not serve too well. The nature of creative storytelling is that it changes with each teller, and this left too much chance of misinterpretation, in the view of many orthodox religious leaders.

Still, a certain amount of storytelling was acceptable, especially in the reciting of the haggadic portions of the Talmud. As Gerhardsson points out, this haggadic material had an advantage over the halakic precisely because it is easier to remember parables and narratives.[19] There is usually more leeway given to "free" transmission of such material, because word-for-word memorization is not required.

Thus, in the informal passing-on of Jewish tradition, storytelling has been and is used, usually in family or social situations rather than in formal Hebrew schools.

For Hasidic Jews, storytelling is very important. According to Mintz:

> Storytelling won an established place in the life of the earliest hasidim and it became part of the Shabbes ritual.... The Rebbes often wove their teachings into an extended metaphor or parable or told an illustrative tale.... The telling of tales can be a mystical expression on various levels. To tell tales of the tsaddikim is one means of glorifying the tsaddikim and of contacting their piety and power.... In this light, the hasidim believe that tales, like prayers, contain the potential to be active agents.[20]

The Hasidim consciously use storytelling as the best way of introducing their religion and its practices to the young.

In the United States, certain Jewish congregations have used storytelling with organized groups of children. There have even been manuals, like that of Shafter, outlining special methods and sources for the Jewish storyteller.[21]

Christian Storytelling

Just as the Buddhist religion could and did draw on its rich heritage of Hindu lore, so did the Christian draw on the legends of Judaism.

PLATE 14 Segment of an eleventh-century *exultet* roll. Reproduced from Add. ms. 30337 in the British Museum. Photo courtesy of The British Library.

Added to this were the oral versions of the Old Testament and of the gospels. Gerhardsson writes:

> We must take into account the fact that most of the gospel material is haggadic material and that haggadic material is often transmitted with a somewhat wider margin of variation in wording than halakic material.[22]

He was referring, of course, to the fact that so many of Christ's teachings were expressed in parable form, rather than in explicit laws or rules to be remembered.

Accumulating along with the Old and New Testament and other traditions were the orally transmitted stories and legends of early saints and the *exempla*. The *exemplum* is a classic fable or popular anecdote to which has been added a moral, in this case a Christian one. They were used as the basis of sermons, much as parables were used by Christ. The oldest known examples occur in the homilies of Saint Gregory the First (c. 600). They probably developed in much the same way that the stories of the Buddhist monks evolved, becoming secular enough in their use of illustrative material so that the masses could understand their meaning easily. In the thirteenth and fourteenth centuries, Dominican and Franciscan monks developed the *exempla* into a narrative art that was very successful. It could compete with the other performances to be found at marketplaces, on street corners and at fairs, where the monks collected their share of listeners.[23]

It is truly a remarkable coincidence that there also exists for the Christian religion a type of religious picture storytelling that parallels that of Buddhism in India and China. The format was not exactly like that of the Eastern scrolls, because it was shown vertically rather than horizontally. These Christian picture scrolls are known as *exultet* rolls, because all of the twenty-two rolls known to exist carry the same text. It is a part of the Easter vigil service that begins with the word *exultet*, meaning "rejoice."[24] The rolls were used in the liturgy at the moment of the blessing of the new candle. Plate 14, reproduced from an *exultet* roll, shows the deacon chanting the text while showing the pictures to the congregation.

Although all the rolls were produced in Italy during the eleventh and twelfth centuries, they were not identical. A few of the artists chose to illustrate different points, expanding the text by visual means. Old Testament vignettes are particularly emphasized. Although the text of the *exultet* portion of the liturgy is not a pure narrative, it becomes much more so by virtue of the narrative quality of the illustrations.

There seems to be no explanation as to why this particular segment of the liturgy was chosen for this purpose. Nor does there seem to have been any adaptation of the device into other uses related to religious instruction; that is, there is no *known* connection to later forms of teaching religion through pictures.

PLATE 15 Jacob Gole, *Sänger mit Triptychon* (c. 1600). Photo courtesy of Deutsches Volksliedarchiv, Freiburg im Bresgau.

A case might be made for the possible transformation of the *exultet* roll into the early form of triptychs or trunk altars that may or may not have been the forerunners of religious picture sheets used by early *bänkelsänger*. However, it is just as likely that the inspiration for the picture sheets came from altar paintings or church murals. At any rate, Leopold Schmidt was convinced that all readable picture stories of a sequential nature had their origins in religious art. It was religious promulgation of this type of art that made it popular with the masses and opened the way for the secular picture sheets, in which each scene occupies its own square.[25]

Brednich also believes that there was an early form of *bänkelsang* that was religious in character. The museum with which he is associated in Freiburg im Bresgau is attempting to assemble all the available pictorial evidence for the early history of *bänkelsang*. Brednich believes that the mezzotint by Jacob Gole, reproduced in Plate 15, is one of the examples of the precursors of the religious street and market singers.[26] The singer here is performing indoors, but there is no question that he is chanting or reciting some religious narrative, for the pictures can just be made out. Later examples of art from the eighteenth century show that there were outdoor market singers who told or sang religious stories. From their dress they do not appear to be members of religious orders, but there are not enough known examples to be conclusive.

The wandering type of Christian religious storytellers that survived the longest were the *kalêki* in Russia. They date to the early years of Christianity in that country. Originally, they were a mixture of well-to-do pilgrims, lower orders of clergy, beggars, handicapped or maimed persons, runaway serfs, and many others with no permanent home. Later, they were almost exclusively from the ranks of the poor, the crippled, and the blind. They wandered from monastery to monastery, always assured of a place to sleep and a bite to eat. They also got their religious training in the monasteries.

The *kalêki* reached their zenith in the reign of Alexis, father of Peter the Great. At that time, the secular performers of *byliny*, known as *skomorokhi*, were banned from performing publicly and the *kalêki* were not (see Chapter 2). While the *kalêki* usually performed oral narrative religious poems, known as *dukhovnie stikhi*, it was not uncommon for them to know some of the *byliny*. The Chadwicks speculate that the *kalêki* probably stepped into the gap left by the banished *skomorokhi* and learned to perform secular narratives too.[27]

The *kalêki* performed in churchyards, at church festivals, at funerals, and in the neighborhood of monasteries. There were both male and female groups, but they seemed to travel separately. The women had a distinctive form of dress that resembled that of the Carmelite nuns, except that they did not use a veil. The men wore rough peasant clothing. All carried a special type of knapsack that held their few possessions (Plate 16).[28]

PLATE 16 *Kalêki*, wandering religious storytellers of Russia. Reproduced from A. P. Bessonov, *Kalêki Perekhozhie* (Moscow, 1861–1864). Photo courtesy of the Library of Congress.

Modern forms of Christian storytelling are those associated with the Sunday-school movement and with parochial schools. The Protestant Reformation had discouraged the telling of legends of the saints; even the use of *exempla* was frowned upon. Stories from the Old and New Testaments were considered quite appropriate, however. These did not have to be told word for word, but were not supposed to deviate from the basic text.

By the late nineteenth century, virtually every village and town in the United States had a Sunday school, most of which had small libraries of storybooks with Biblical themes.[29] In the early years of this century, several manuals for Christian storytellers were published. The most influential was that of Edward Porter St. John. He advocated the use of selected folk and fairy tales, for he believed that they offered as good a sense of morality as did many Bible stories. He reported that in New York City there was even a special Sunday School Storyteller's League.[30] After his work came out, it became quite acceptable and common for Sunday schools to use storytelling of a much broader type, not exclusively based on biblical themes.

The Baptists were particularly strong in their promotion of storytelling. In the years from 1930 to 1940, they set formal guidelines for storytelling procedures[31] and even began a quarterly magazine to help their Sunday-school teachers.[32]

Curiously, although there were many more stories and legends of saints current among Catholic groups, there does not appear to have been a conscious effort made by any authorities to guide teachers in a Catholic method of storytelling. The parochial schools did not seem to have organized storytelling of the kind found in Protestant Sunday schools. Religious instruction in parochial schools was usually catechism learned by rote and selected Bible stories read aloud or silently, or even used as the basis of reading lessons. Only in recent years has there been a tendency to absorb some of the Protestant Sunday-school storytelling techniques in Catholic religious education.[33]

Islamic Storytelling

Stories were not told in the time of the Prophet, according to Islamic belief. Only later did storytelling of an approved kind grow up, within the strict boundaries of prescribed, orthodox tradition. Of course, just as in other religious movements, there were a number of persons who attempted to create new stories by embellishing accepted tradition. In a manuscript dating to approximately 1200, an Islamic scholar lauds the commendable character of storytelling:

> Storytelling is an innovation, but how wonderful is that innovation! How many a prayer is answered, request granted, companion won, and how great is the knowledge received, through it! . . . a jurist or reader of the Quran is not capable of bringing to God a hundredth of the people the [preacher] is capable of bringing . . . .[34]

At the same time he strictly admonished the believers to listen only to those who were trained in "special branches of learning and knowledge" and those who were commissioned by the *imam* to tell stories. True stories were those that followed orthodox thinking regarding the life of the Prophet.[35]

The Arabic word for tale, *hadith*, came to mean, in an Islamic context, sayings or parables associated with Mohammed. In the third century after his death, there was already a saying: "Woe to him who spreads false *hadiths* to entertain the people, woe to him, woe." Goldziher mentions passages from many Arabic sources in which the secular storyteller is made fun of and taunted. He used the term *qāṣṣ* or *qāṣṣaṣ* to denote the religious narrator:

> Only the holy subject of their tales differentiated them from the profane tellers of anecdotes who gathered audiences at street corners in order to recite piquant stories and yarns . . . .[36]

The term *qāṣṣ* gradually came to have a negative connotation in orthodox Islamic circles. But Goldziher points out that the Prophet himself used the alternate term, *qāṣṣaṣ*, to describe his message.

In orthodox Islamic families, boys were sent to Koranic school when they reached the age of four years, four months, and four days. This is usually interpreted loosely now, but children are still started on their Koranic memorizations when they are very young. In some cases, girls are also sent to such schools. Most of the time is spent in having the children listen to simple verses and then repeat them after the teacher. However, there are some schools, particularly the more modern ones in parts of North Africa, where there are other activities similar to those in a kindergarten, including the telling of stories with social and religious morals.[37]

Other Religious Storytelling

It is far more difficult to discuss religious storytelling for those peoples whose moral code is based partly on animism and partly on a strict system of social ethics. Native American groups, for example, considered most of their storytelling as having at least some religious value. For the outsider, it is often impossible to perceive just what elements in the stories make them religious. Nevertheless, in case after case it is recorded that stories were looked on as "holy" or "sacred."

The Mandan-Hidatsa group had special words to distinguish stories that had to do with creation and the origin of things, called *māshī* or *hoge*; but in addition there were *māshī aruhopa* or *hohohopini'i*, stories explaining origins of ceremonies and of powers considered holy. The latter stories were extremely sacred.[38]

Interestingly, for the Winnebago, *waikan*, a sacred story with spirits or deities as heroes, ended happily; ordinary stories about human beings often ended tragically. The *waikan* had a high monetary value.

They could be passed on through bequest, or they could be sold from one teller to another.[39]

Opler told of the Apache custom of painting the face with red ochre after a night of storytelling. The paint was supposed to stay on all day as an indication that the wearer had been influenced by the holiness of the stories.[40]

Peoples of the Pacific, such as the Polynesians, used storytelling for religious purposes in the past. The telling of these stories was usually accompanied by dance. The early forms of the hula were semireligious in nature.[41]

The Maori used storytelling in their *whare wananga*, or house of knowledge, where young people were trained in the sacred traditions of their clan. The stories were, for the most part, secret and unknown to all except the *tohunga*, the graduates of the houses of knowledge. Best concludes:

> A people like ourselves . . . who hold our sacred teachings so cheaply as to make our Bible as common as the daily newspaper, simply cannot conceive the feeling the old-time Maori had for knowledge of the above kind.[42]

Other Polynesian groups had the equivalent of the houses of knowledge. Because of such restrictions, it is impossible to describe just how storytelling was carried out and the true impact it had, both for the special groups like the *tohunga* and for the common people.

African religions also seem to use song and dance to express religious feeling. There are quite a number of citations referring to religious chants, but none that indicate that the prose narrative story was used for religious teaching.

Biebuyck and Mateene report a situation in which the act of storytelling was looked on as a religious experience for the teller but did not necessarily have such a meaning for the listeners:

> For the bard himself, the act of narrating the story has religious significance. He believes that *Kárìsì*, deified, wanted him to learn the epic; to perform the drama adequately makes the narrator "strong," protects him against disease and death.[43]

On the whole, though, most storytelling in modern Africa is intended to entertain or to teach social values rather than to promulgate religious beliefs.

5

Theatrical Storytelling

There are some parts of the world in which storytelling developed as a form of theatrical entertainment. Many of the forms of storytelling described in earlier chapters are as dramatic as the type of storytelling being considered in this chapter. What distinguishes this kind is the fact that it was or is performed in actual theater-like buildings, and the audience that goes to see and hear it pays entrance fees in much the same fashion as it would for entering a legitimate theater. In other words, this kind of storytelling is barely distinguishable from legitimate theater.

The most elaborate and studied type of theatrical storytelling was common in China, Mongolia, and Japan for at least seven centuries and still is practiced in the latter two countries. There is very little documentation for this kind of activity in present-day China. Hrdličková's research, conducted mostly in Peking, Tientsin, and the small towns of northern China dates to the early 1950s. But according to her it was in Shanghai that the *shu-ch'ang*, or storytelling halls, were most popular, especially in the latter half of the nineteenth century and the early part of the twentieth.[1] Eberhard found a few storytellers of this type still practicing in the late 1960s in Taiwan, but no longer in special theaters. They generally told in a temple or in a teahouse.[2] The audience consisted only of old men, indicating that the tradition was a dying one.

Chinese Storytelling

The origins of Chinese theater storytelling are religious, as indicated in some detail in Chapter 4. In the later years of the Sung dynasty (960–1279) and all during the Yüan dynasty (1279–1368) these storytellers increased in number and became almost completely secularized. They were organized in guilds throughout China.[3] So important was their work to the development of the written literature of China that it is impossible to separate their oral performances from the written versions of their tales. Scholars disagree about certain aspects of the works of these storytellers. The most frequent point of contention relates to whether these texts served as memory aids to the storytellers, or whether they were printed, literary versions of the oral stories, designed for reading.[4] The common term for them is *hua-pen*. Some of them may or may not have been intended to accompany the picture scrolls described in Chapter 4, dealing with religious storytelling, and in Chapter 11.

Průšek, a sinologist who has written extensively on the subject, believed the *hua-pen* was used as a kind of secret prompt book by the storyteller. In his view, printers later managed to acquire some of them, had scholars polish and flesh them out, and then published them. After the scholars heard and saw the stories recited again and again, they would perfect the printed editions.[5]

Hrdličková, on the other hand, believed that the *hua-pen* were not to be confused with the *tz'e-tze*, also called *ti-pen* or *chiao-pen*, handbooks of secrets handed by the master to each student upon completion of the apprenticeship. In her opinion, the *hua-pen* were definitely meant to be read, either in public recitation or privately.[6]

In any event, there were many guilds, each specializing in teaching and performing certain genres or types of stories. It was the guild that negotiated the contracts for each of its members to perform, first in teahouses and then in the storytelling theaters.[7] They told their stories in an idiom approximating the vernacular, with lively coloring and long and inventive descriptions. The proof of their liveliness lies in the fact that virtually none of the works written in the literary language from the Sung and Yüan dynasties is considered above average, while quite a number of the works recorded from the oral storytellers of the period, in the vernacular, are still considered outstanding. The majority of the famous long novels of the Ming period (1368–1644) were developed from the works of these storytellers.[8]

Kara's researches in Mongolia date to 1959–1960, but it is not entirely clear if the public storytelling halls, the *üliger kelekü tangkim*, that he encountered there are of the same tradition as the Chinese *shu-ch'ang*.[9] The epics that the Mongolian bard performs start with a rhythmic prose recitative. The body of the epic is in verse and is generally accompanied by a four-stringed instrument. Another performer in the halls is the *üligerčin*, the folk storyteller.[10] This would

PLATE 17   Entrance to a *yose* in Tokyo. Reproduced from Jules Adam, *Japanese Story-tellers* (Tokyo: T. Hasegawa, 1912). Photo courtesy of The New York Public Library.

seem to indicate that the same varieties of storytelling styles are to be found in these Mongolian halls as were found in the Chinese, and are still found in the Japanese *yose*. There is an admission charged upon entry, and one is expected to take tea, just as in the *yose*.

Japanese Storytelling

With regard to these Japanese *yose*, there is a considerable body of descriptive documentation in English and German. In 1897, Brinkley recorded that there were 180 *yose* in Tokyo and many more in other parts of Japan. The storytellers were divided into schools, usually under the direction of a master, of whom there were ten at the time. Brinkley called the tellers *koshaku-shi*.[11]

Adam,[12] a French visitor to the *yose* in 1912, and Meissner,[13] a German folklorist studying them in 1913, give even more details. Adam cites the number of *yose* as 243, but it is not clear if he is referring to all of Japan or only Tokyo. Each *yose* could seat 500 to 1,000, he claimed. He called the apprentices *zenza*, the storytellers *hanashi-ka*, and the master, *shin-uchi*. The most interesting aspect of his book is the illustrations. They include an exterior of a *yose* (Plate 17), an entryway, an interior, a stage setting, a typical audience, and numerous other fine details.[14]

Meissner's count of the *yose* in Tokyo in 1913 came to 151, including all types, but he stated that each *yose* seated only 250 to 300 persons rather than the 500 to 1,000 suggested by Adam. The entrance fee was about ten *sen*, and another 15 *sen* usually had to be spent in ordering tea and for gratuities. Thus, this was an entertainment in reach of the middle and working classes.[15]

Meissner lists the ranks from apprentice, the *zenza*, up to *shin-uchi*, the master. He also describes in some detail the various types of storytellers who performed in the *yose* at that time.[16] Both Adam and Meissner reported the oddity of a European performer who had become a master in one of the *yose*.[17]

A later study by another German folklorist, Barth, expands the picture considerably.[18] Barth concentrates on the tales and the tellers. There were the *kodan-shi*, who performed narratives of warriors, more or less historically based, and the *rakugo-ka*, who presented witty, humorous narratives of much shorter length. The *naniwabushi* told almost exactly the same historical warrior tales as the *kodan-shi*, but they accompanied themselves on the *samisen* and, from time to time, would break their narrative with a song.

Barth mentions that all of these performers were turning to radio because people were not going to the *yose* as frequently as they had previously. Some of the performers were employed in a new profession, that of providing the running commentary and dialogue for the silent films! It was Barth's impression that the *yose* was an institution that was peculiarly Japanese, without any foreign influence.[19] However, Průšek and Hrdličková have shown in their research that the origin was almost certainly Chinese, with certain aspects possibly traceable back to India. Barth does mention the *biwa-hoshi*, monks or persons in monks' clothing who went around playing lutes and singing epic songs of wars and folk heroes. And most of the early *kodan-shi* were poor *samurai*, warriors, or former monks.[20]

In 1815 a number of decrees were promulgated against the *rakugo-ka*, but there was such a public outcry that the authorities had to desist. They did, however, insist that the *rakugo-ka* begin performing stories that were more "truthful" and filled with good example. After that the stories changed somewhat, but not entirely.[21]

The modern updating of this picture can be found in the articles of Hrdličková.[22] By the time she began her research in the 1960s, there were only two schools or guilds of the *rakugo-ka* remaining. There was a total membership of 227. They performed in seven *yose* that still remained in Tokyo.[23] There was only one hall left where the *kodan-shi* were performing. The twenty-two *kodan-shi* had only a few pupils. The *kodan-shi* still performed with a little table in front of them, where formerly they used to place the handbook of texts that was used as a memory aid.[24] This would seem to indicate strongly that the origin of this kind of storytelling was influenced by the Chinese medieval tellers, whose use of the prompt books was apparently quite common. For ordinary appearances, the tellers have a kimono embroidered with the family crest, but on festive occasions they wear much more ceremonial dress.

The storytelling performances are sometimes interspersed with other acts, such as jugglers, magicians, and singers, but the good tellers are always placed toward the end of the program, and they have no interruptions. The majority of the audience is now composed of older men, but family groups are still seen on occasion. Some of the performers also appear on television and radio, and this has enhanced their reputation. Although definitely waning in numbers, the tradition of the *yose* seems to cling tenaciously to its position in the cultural and social life of Japan.

The Far East seems to be the only part of the world where this particular type of storytelling flourished. There are no exact parallels in other cultures, especially not in terms of the strict training, the manner of payment, and the presentation in a formal theater type of building. The only storytelling that remotely resembles it are the occasional theatrical narrators who performed in Europe and the United States. But in no case were they the product of a strict apprenticeship and of completely oral training. In most cases, they learned the art through dramatic training and got their stories from books. Germany and the United States seemed to have more of them than did other countries.

German Storytelling

Grimm's *märchen* were very popular as the selections in these dramatic recitals. Rougemont recounts how thrilling it was to hear them told in a concert hall by Vilma Mönckeberg-Kollmar, back in the 1930s.[25] In fact, the performance so impressed her that she vowed to become a storyteller and later did just that.

Others based the drama of their presentations partly on the ability to describe a "picturesque" or "exotic" people that they might have visited, and from whom they purportedly gathered their tales. Such was the case with Elsa Sophia von Kamphoevener, who had spent many years living with a group of Turkish nomads.[26] She returned to Germany and began presenting evenings of oral narration of their tales in theaters throughout the country. The author Hans Baumann recalls finding one of these performances most impressive.[27]

American Storytelling

In the United States, the best known of such performers is probably Eva Le Gallienne, who has made a specialty of reciting the tales of Hans Christian Andersen. Such entertainments often have started out as "readings" but soon developed into dramatic narrations with the book serving more as a stage prop than as a necessity.[28]

Gudrun Thorne-Thomsen, Ruth Sawyer, and Marie Shedlock had all done this kind of storytelling, as well as the institutional type. All three used largely folk material or stories by writers such as Andersen, who wrote in folktale patterns. It was Miss Shedlock's manner and style of telling that most influenced the development of the storytelling programs of the New York Public Library.[29]

Russian Storytelling

There are some examples of Russian folk storytellers who attempted to transfer their art to the formal setting of the theater. Sokolov reported that a woman who had been honored by the state for her unusual storytelling gifts went to Voronezh and Moscow in the winter of 1935–1936. There she performed in public halls and theaters the same stories she told in her village.[30]

Indonesian Storytelling

If it is extremely difficult to draw the line between storytelling and theater in the Chinese *shu-ch'ang* and the Japanese *yose*, it is doubly so in the case of the *dalang*, the narrator who is both storyteller and puppeteer in the *wayang kulit*, the shadow-puppet play of Indonesia. Most accounts and studies seem to treat the *wayang kulit* as theater, which it certainly is in its totality. Yet the *dalang* performs alone, except for the members of the orchestra who accompany him. He could and would be considered by some to be a storyteller.[31]

> Even today, he never fails to burn incense and to pronounce the *kochap ing pagedongan* (invocation to the audience) at the opening of the stage. Then he stations himself behind the screen which he will not leave during the whole performance, beginning after evening prayer and continuing until dawn.

Thus, he must have, above all, physical endurance against all strains for he cannot allow the high tension of the play to fall for a single instant lest he could lose the attention of the spectators during the performance. In addition, he must possess a prodigious memory in order to recite correctly the whole repertoire in verse; he must have a certain sense of humour, great deftness and range in his vocal chords (for he must make the puppets speak in different tones according to their sex), and a refined musical sense.[32]

Coomaraswamy found parallels between the *dalang* and the early picture showmen in India and those of Persia and China.[33]

Of course, an element of storytelling is inherent in much of theater, as it is in the ordinary conversation of some creative individuals. But this does not fall within the definition of storytelling as formulated at the beginning of this book.

6

Library and Institutional Storytelling

It is not quite clear just which public library in the United States first began to have regular story hours for children. Nor is it possible to state definitively which children's librarian first propounded the idea. Caroline Hewins, a pioneer in public library work, is known to have read aloud on Saturday mornings in the Hartford Public Library from approximately 1880 on.[1] But this was definitely reading aloud, and no mention of oral narration was made in her reports.

The Carnegie Library in Pittsburgh, which began regular story-hour programs in 1899, is usually credited as being among the first, if not the first, to have offered this activity as an accepted part of children's work.[2] This might well be true, but there is some evidence that other libraries began a regular story hour much earlier than 1899. For example, Mary Ella Dousman, writing in 1896 and describing the notices that were put up in Buffalo prior to the opening of the public library there, cites the text of the placards:

BOYS AND GIRLS—Books for You to Read
Pictures for You to Look At
Maps for You to Put Together
Magazines for Everybody
Someone to Tell You Stories[3]

The new librarian is quoted as saying: "We shall have a regular hour for storytelling."[4]

There surely must have been further discussion among the pioneer children's librarians on this subject. Yet no other references to a regular story hour in public libraries could be located for the years prior to 1899.

Carnegie Library and Pratt Institute

The programs of the Carnegie Library in Pittsburgh and the Pratt Institute Free Library in Brooklyn seem to have sprung up spontaneously at about the same time. Their impact was great because they were the two most important centers at the turn of the century for the training of children's librarians. The graduates took positions in Brooklyn and Pittsburgh and also spread out all over the country. They took with them the experience of actually having seen story hours; perhaps they had even directed or participated in one as part of their training.

Some of the early story hours, at least at Pratt Institute, seem to have been delightfully free of any pretensions. They probably were close to folk storytelling experiences, because as Anne Carroll Moore wrote, "the people who have told stories for us are volunteer visitors."[5] Here is how she described one of them:

> A most delightful improvised story was told about two children who were lost in a forest. . . . The sixty children in attendance ranged from three to twelve years and formed an ideal group.[6]

She mentions also that for a Christmas story hour, a librarian of German origin told simply and expressively of her childhood experiences during the Christmas season.

In Pittsburgh, the programs seemed a bit more formal and literary from the very beginning. The series that opened the formal storytelling programs in 1899 was of stories based on the plays of Shakespeare.[7] For the second year an outline of sixteen stories from the *Iliad* and the *Odyssey* was prepared; these programs were held simultaneously in the Central Library and in all of the branches.[8] The story hour in Pittsburgh was not meant to be a formidable experience or to approximate a literature class in school, however. On the contrary, as F. J. Olcutt pointed out:

> We have found that even our weekly storytelling lectures are seized on by the teachers as material for compositions and tests of memory, which, if not prevented, would defeat our main object in telling the stories. We aim to produce an unforced, natural love for the best in literature.[9]

The very fact that a flexible length was suggested, rather than a fixed one-hour session, implied that the storyteller was not expected to overdo it. The storyteller was supposed to watch out for "audience fatigue" and bring the story to a stop as soon as attention lagged.[10]

The cycles of stories told in Pittsburgh included the three already mentioned and the following: the Volsunga Saga, Robin Hood, *Beowulf*, Cuchulain, King Arthur and His Knights, and the *Chanson de Roland*. These were told in story hours for children aged ten and up.[11] In 1902 a story hour was organized for children nine years old and younger. For them the selections were fairy tales, fables, nature myths, and Bible stories.[12]

Richard Alvey, in his dissertation "The Historical Development of Organized Storytelling to Children in the United States," analyzes in great detail the early philosophical differences between Anne Carroll Moore and Frances Jenkins Olcutt. Moore, he felt, emphasized the story hour as a "sociocultural event" whereas Olcutt never deviated from her insistence on tying in the story hour to books, literature, and the specific goals of the library in promoting them.[13]

By 1900, at least five libraries were reporting regular story hours of the types recommended by Pittsburgh or Pratt advocates.[14] They were usually held weekly during the months from November through April. This activity was soon to mushroom, not only because of the spreading out of Carnegie (Pittsburgh) and Pratt graduates, but also because of the first storytelling and lecture tour of Marie Shedlock.

Marie Shedlock

Marie Shedlock, a teacher in a successful girls' school in London, abandoned teaching to become a public lecturer.[15] When, in 1900, she was brought by Charlotte Osgood Mason to lecture at Sherry's in New York in an ongoing afternoon lecture and concert series, she had one lecture in her repertoire. This was titled "The Fun and Philosophy of Hans Christian Andersen." In the course of her talk, she told seven Andersen tales. One of the persons who heard her was Mary Wright Plummer, then head of the Pratt Institute Library School. Plummer invited Shedlock to lecture at Pratt in 1902 and to tell stories in the Children's Room the following year.

Mary Wright Plummer and Anne Carroll Moore must have talked at length to their colleagues around the country about this excellent teller of Andersen tales. In the subsequent years of her first U.S. tour, from 1902 to 1907, Marie Shedlock performed in many public libraries,[16] whereas in her first two years of the tour she had lectured mostly in tearooms, small concert halls, kindergarten training schools, and the like.

Shedlock's style was polished and skillful, yet very simple and with little gesture. It emphasized delight in the story. It was the antithesis of the style propounded by elocutionists of the day. She often wore gowns that suggested the costume of Mother Goose or a fairy godmother.[17] Over the years, she increased her repertoire greatly, telling legends and folktales of many types. But she was always to remain closely identified with the interpretation of stories from Hans Christian Andersen.

Gudrun Thorne-Thomsen

Another person who had a strong influence on organized storytelling in the United States was Gudrun Thorne-Thomsen. An immigrant from Norway while still in her teens, she became a teacher at the University of Chicago, lecturing in the school of education. Like Marie Shedlock, she was soon also giving lectures and demonstrations in other places, particularly in library training schools. Her influence was greatest in the Midwest and the West, but the fact that she made several disc recordings that were distributed by the American Library Association also helped to spread her quietly inspiring style to all parts of the country.

May Hill Arbuthnot, author of *Children and Books*, found in Gudrun Thorne-Thomsen "the greatest expression of the folk art of storytelling that this generation has known." She describes her as "the quietest of all the storytellers and the least humorous. Sometimes in telling a saga she is almost austere, and her stories are apt to fall continuously into a minor key. Her art is the essence of dramatic simplicity—no embellishments, no exaggeration, but a complete integrity of words and spirit, and all so quiet, so still that you can hear the heart speaking."[18]

Many of the reports of storytelling in libraries over the next few decades revealed the influence of either the "Carnegie Library" or the "Marie Shedlock" style. If a library's printed program showed a series of story hours based on heroic epics or Shakespeare, there was almost sure to be a librarian on the staff who had attended the Pittsburgh school or had gone there for a summer of observation and study. If the programs included more Andersen stories, short legends, and unusual and poetic folktales, chances are the person who planned them had studied at the library schools of either the Pratt Institute or the New York Public Library.

Storytelling in Schools

There had been earlier attempts by educators to stress the importance of storytelling. In fact, the Kindergarten Teachers' Group of the National Education Association had been very active in the promotion of storytelling, as had the kindergarten training schools. Kindergarten teachers were among the first to write extensively about storytelling to class groups of children, at least in the United States. They wrote so much that Alvey concluded:

> One could nearly summarize kindergartners' claims for the benefits of storytelling ... by stating that they suggested that almost every conceivable benefit or desirable non-physical need of the child could be realized through properly employed storytelling.[19]

But in spite of the enthusiastic support for storytelling among such prominent educators as Friedrich Froebel, Maria Montessori, John

Dewey, Johann Friedrich Herbart, and others, teachers did not take to storytelling as enthusiastically as did librarians. Of the four professional groups in the United States analyzed by Alvey—teachers, librarians, religious educators, and recreational directors—it was the educators who were the least involved in the actual practice of storytelling.[20]

The only educational group in the United States (above the kindergarten level) that accepted storytelling and even insisted on it as a necessary part of the school curriculum was the Ethical Culture Society. This group was founded in 1876 by Felix Adler, who expounded his beliefs on education and on the importance of storytelling in his book *Moral Instruction of Children*. Most of the schools operated by the society still include storytelling as a part of the regular curriculum.

The formal school systems had not achieved anything comparable to what the public libraries had succeeded in doing within a very short time, namely, to establish as part of their operative policy and philosophy the importance of scheduled story-hour programs. These programs were administered in a number of cases by special staff, whose responsibilities included training storytellers, planning programs for the entire season, and arranging to have them printed in special bulletins or in regular library programs.

Library Supervisors of Storytelling

Carnegie Library in Pittsburgh and the New York Public Library were the first to have full-time supervisors of storytelling. Edna Whiteman of Cleveland was appointed the first supervisor at Carnegie in Pittsburgh, in May 1912. One report discreetly reports that "at first there was some opposition from librarians to this special supervision."[21] But this seemed to disappear as newer members of the staff were added. Apparently, some of the more established staff members with years of experience felt it was an intrusion to have someone observe their storytelling.

The New York Public Library position was created earlier, in 1908. The first person to fill the post was Anna Cogswell Tyler, who as a student at Pratt had heard Marie Shedlock tell Andersen's "The Nightingale." She had decided then to become a children's librarian so that she could tell stories regularly.[22]

Another library that added a full-time supervisor of storytelling was the Enoch Pratt Free Library in Baltimore, c. 1925.

Opposition to Storytelling

Not all public library administrators were completely in favor of storytelling. John Cotton Dana, a well-known librarian and lecturer in library schools, believed that the function of storytelling belonged in the public schools. "It is probable that the schoolmen know better when and how to include storytelling in their work with a given group of children than do the librarians," he wrote in 1908. He conceded that there were more librarians than teachers who were skilled in telling stories, or who *wanted* to do storytelling, which was also important. To satisfy these creative urges on the part of some children's librarians, he recommended the following:

> If, now, the library by chance has on its staff a few altruistic, emotional, dramatic, and irrepressible child-lovers who do not find library work gives sufficient opportunities for altruistic indulgence, and if the library can spare them from other work, let it set them at teaching the teachers the art of storytelling.[23]

Dana did not reckon with the wide appeal that storytelling had among public librarians. Nor did he take fully into account the fact that administrators generally like visible signs of library use. The lines of children waiting to get into the story hours were obviously impressive. Also, the number of books checked out on a day during which there was a program was invariably higher than on non-program days.

The most persuasive answer of all to the Dana arguments was the fact that large numbers of children were not in school. The children that did go to urban public schools were of immigrant families, more often than not, and English was usually their second language. Many of these immigrant children were in crowded classrooms where the likelihood of storytelling was remote. The teacher was probably hard put to cover all the basic skills that were supposed to be included in the curriculum.

The public library took seriously its responsibility to serve these children, especially with a view to helping them to improve their English. They believed this could be done more easily through informal reading aloud, story hours, and the use of simple books with many pictures. A 1909 article on storytelling in the Cleveland Public Library mentioned that 76 percent of the children in the public schools of that city were of foreign parentage, and that many more were out of school. The article cites as one of the main goals of storytelling, "the presentation of stories which children have found difficult to read."[24] This referred not to reading difficulties per se, but rather to those encountered by non-English-reading children.

By 1927, there were regular storytelling programs in 79 percent of the public libraries of the United States.[25] Furthermore, in many urban areas, children's librarians were also providing storytelling services for park and recreation departments, for schools, for hospitals and other institutions.[26] With the Great Depression, however, came a decline in the number of staff. The amount of time that could be given to storytelling was reduced. For the decade from 1930 to 1940, there are fewer articles on the subject in periodicals than for any other decade between 1900 and the present. The story-hour programs were not by any means discontinued. In the libraries themselves, they very much held their own, but librarians did cut back on the number of story hours in outside institutions. Radio and films were also beginning to make inroads on the attendance figures. Some libraries switched from the Saturday morning story hour to one held after school on a weekday afternoon.

Preschool and Picture-Book Hours

The first preschool and picture-book story hours were begun in the decade from 1930 to 1940. Gross cites the Detroit Public Library as having the first preschool picture-book story hour, for three-to-five-year-olds.[27] Other early story hours for preschool children were in Maumee, Ohio (1939–1940),[28] and Milwaukee (c. 1940).[29] Many of these still used mostly orally told stories, followed by a session in which children looked at the pictures in the books. This was in line with the recommendations of Marie Shedlock, the most widely followed model insofar as librarians were concerned.

The public libraries were just beginning to come out from under the pall of the depression when World War II broke out. Once again there was a shortage of staff, and many children's librarians had to do more administrative work and also work with the public. Some librarians, however, used the war as a special impetus to expand the storytelling program, contending that the children needed stories at such times more than in a time of peace.

Picture-book storytelling had become more and more popular. In 1944, the Library Extension Division of New York State's Department of Education found it expedient to issue guidelines and instructions for carrying out picture-book programs.[30] After the war, and in the decade of the 1950s, there was a spate of articles dealing with the picture-book story hour, both for preschool children and for slightly older children. The impact of this on picture-book publishing is discussed in Chapter 11.

The traditional story hour received additional momentum in the 1940s, 1950s, and 1960s, partly through the inspiring articles and teaching of librarian-storytellers such as Elizabeth Nesbitt and Frances Clarke Sayers. Nesbitt, formerly supervisor of storytelling at the Carnegie Library in Pittsburgh, was later a lecturer in the library school there. Sayers had been coordinator of work with children at the New York Public Library before going on to teach at the University of California, Los Angeles. There were also numerous attempts to revitalize the training of library storytellers by having symposia, seminars, and festivals at which the less-experienced tellers could hear and observe those with many years of telling behind them. Gudrun Thorne-Thomsen (until her death in 1956), Ruth Sawyer, author of a popular manual on storytelling, and Augusta Baker, storytelling specialist and later coordinator of children's work at the New York Public Library, were frequently asked to lecture informally about storytelling and

PLATE 18   Augusta Baker conducting a storytelling hour at the Chatham Square
branch of The New York Public Library. Photo courtesy of The New York
Public Library, Public Relations Dept.

then to demonstrate their skill in telling stories (Plate 18). In England, librarian Eileen Colwell took on this task. In Japan, Momoko
Ishii did the same, passing on what she had learned during her stay at
the Toronto Public Library.

Nevertheless, by the mid-1960s, the traditional story hour had de-
clined in public libraries, and its place was being taken by the pre-
school hour, or the picture-book hour, or the combination film and
story-hour program. Whether this was caused by the expanding influence of films, radio, and television, or by the lack of time and staff
needed to prepare good story hours that would consistently attract
children, has not yet been sufficiently explored. Alice Kane of the Toronto Public Library was inclined to believe that it was a lack of enthusiasm on the part of librarians and an unwillingness to expend the
extra effort needed to sustain a good story-hour program.[31]

In the early 1970s, while doing field work for his dissertation, Alvey
observed storytelling in school and public libraries of all sizes as well
as in other institutions and organizations. It was his general con-

clusion that the professional librarians in the small libraries and in school libraries rarely had the time or the incentive to prepare and present a traditional story-hour program. Only in the larger libraries were such programs being sustained. However, there were still a large number of enthusiastic storytellers individually carrying out programs by dint of special, personal effort.[32] These observations are confirmed by the author's own experiences during appearances at numerous storytelling seminars or workshops.

It must be emphasized that the above refers to the story hour that involves only orally told stories, unaccompanied by films, pictures, and other recording devices. Almost all libraries of all types and sizes were managing to carry out picture-book story hours for young children of preschool age or under eight.

The most recent country-wide survey of storytelling in libraries was that undertaken by Ethna Sheehan and Martha Bentley for the Queensboro Public Library in 1961.[33] Of the thirty-six library systems queried then, over 77 percent said they still had the traditional story-hour program. Since only systems serving populations over 100,000 were included in the survey, this would seem to indicate that there had not been much change in the decade between the early 1960s and the early 1970s. It also adds weight to Alvey's conclusion that the traditional, organized story hour for children in the United States grew and matured to steadiness *only* in the libraries. The storytelling programs in school classrooms, in parks and playgrounds, and in religious education programs have been all but lost to other forms of education through entertainment and can be found only sporadically.

It is interesting to speculate why this is so. Alvey believes it was because the personal presence of outstanding storytellers, such as Shedlock, Thorne-Thomsen, and Sawyer, had such a positive effect on library staffs. The librarians, he believed, more than the other groups, saw to it that there were continual personal contacts and multiple personal storytelling performances for the beginner as well as for the experienced practitioner to observe. He concluded:

> This exposure, coupled with an adequate printed model for referral and continual training and practice emulating the expert, no doubt largely accounted for the success of librarian storytellers. On the other hand, lack of these—or most of them—or possibly the absence of the peculiar effect of the *combination* of all of them, perhaps largely accounted for the ineffectiveness of teacher storytellers.[34]

This would seem at first to be a good explanation. But the fact remains that certain groups of teachers had an equal amount of exposure to outstanding storytellers, had adequate printed models, and had access to further training. Yet they did not produce a cadre of exceptional storytellers.

It would seem just as logical to search for the answer in the conditions under which librarians and teachers have been telling stories. The greatest difference lies in the fact that, in most cases, when librarians tell stories to children in groups, those children know that there is nothing in particular that "has to be" or "should be" learned. Whether in their home institution or outside, storytelling is usually simply a case of entertainment offered by the librarian, without the element of a lesson to be remembered or some vague thought that in the future the child might be called upon to recount what happened in the story. The very nature of pedagogy seems to demand this of the teacher's use of storytelling. Thus, a subtle change in the storyteller/audience relationship occurs.

It is likely that the conditions and expectations of the school classroom, as well as a lack of models to follow, were some of the reasons that prevented the teacher-storytellers from realizing their full potential. Pedagogy generally exerts pressures for explanation, interpretation, rationalization, and justification. This is the antithesis of storytelling as practiced by the well-known tellers that librarians emulate.

Another reason for the paucity of storytelling in the classroom may well be the extensive course requirements demanded by various public authorities. Teachers in training must take many courses that cover subject areas as well as teaching methods and do not always have time for specialized courses such as storytelling. Nor are these courses always available in teachers' colleges. However, there have been and are some schools of education that include courses in storytelling for teachers as an elective. A good example of such a school is the Bank Street College of Education, where there has been a storytelling course for many years. The courses in library schools are usually open to education students in the same university and can often be included in education credits. It is not unreasonable to assume that at least a small percentage of those teachers who have taken such courses manage to include the story hour on a regular basis in their classrooms, in spite of heavy demands created by required subjects and activities.

7

Camp, Park, and Playground Storytelling

There have been four types of organized storytelling to children in groups in the United States and Canada according to the folklorist-librarian Richard Alvey. These types he calls educational, religious, library, and recreational.[1] Only the last-named type had as its chief and only goal, right from the start, the pure fun of storytelling. For park and recreation leaders, for camp counselors, and for club or playground supervisors, the one aim has been to amuse the children, and comparatively little time has been spent in trying to justify the amusement with edifying reasons concerning the liberating social value of communal entertainment.

Recreational storytelling of the organized type had its beginnings in neighborhood and settlement houses of heavily populated urban areas, in municipal parks and playgrounds, in camps run by scouting groups or philanthropic agencies, and in boys' clubs. According to Harriet Long, in her history of library service to children, it was in the years between 1869 and 1875 that the first directed playground was established, the first settlement house was opened, and the first boys' club was founded.[2] In these early years, however, there is not much mention of storytelling.

Jacob Riis, social reformer and journalist who did much to further the cause of free parks and playgrounds, obviously favored storytelling, for in his autobiography he writes:

> I hear of people nowadays who think it is not proper to tell children fairy stories. I am sorry for those children. I wonder what they will give them instead. Algebra perhaps. Nice lot of counting machines we shall have running the century that is to come![3]

But in the early articles and books he and other social reformers wrote, urging the establishment of municipal parks, playgrounds, and recreation centers, there is mostly an emphasis on the need for physical play space.

Neighborhood and settlement houses stressed the study of both practical matters and the sharing of intellectual, culturally uplifting ideas, all in an atmosphere of social conviviality. The value of storytelling became apparent in these places a bit sooner than in the playgrounds. Jane Addams, in her autobiographical book recalling the early years of work in Hull House in Chicago, mentions the use of storytelling almost from the start. One of the first residents was a "charming old lady" who read aloud tales from Hawthorne and interspersed them with her own tales of recollections about Hawthorne, whom she had known.[4]

Hull House was also the scene of some of the early boys' clubs meetings. Jane Addams reminisced:

> Another memory ... is that of the young girl who organized our first really successful club of boys, holding their fascinated interest by the old chivalric tales, set forth so dramatically and vividly that checkers and jackstraws were abandoned by all the other clubs on Boys' Day, that their members might form a listening fringe to "The Young Heroes."[5]

Notice that no mention is made of the fact that one activity is "better" than the others. The implication is simply that when there is a talent and it is shared with pleasure, the group will take up the offer with alacrity. In these early efforts, there is a remarkable freedom from "do-goodism" at least in the theories of so exceptional a person as Jane Addams. Few of the other social workers documented their early work as vividly and frankly as she did, so there are not many other accounts of the uses of storytelling in social agencies prior to 1900.

The decade after the turn of the century brought the greatest impetus to recreational storytelling. The Boy Scout movement began in England in 1907 and in the United States in 1910. Camp Fire Girls, Girl Scouts, and Girl Guides followed closely after. The custom of sending city children away to summer camps in the country for at least a week or two began to be more prevalent.

Playground Storytelling

The Playground Association was established in 1906. The members of this professional group worked in the newly established parks and recreation centers maintained by municipalities. In some cities their jobs lasted only over the summer months. In others they were year-round, full-time occupations. These workers began to be trained in the special techniques of directing or supervising group play of all types.

All of this activity brought about an expanded interest in anything that proved to be fun for children. Storytelling was a natural outlet, especially for those workers with a talent and bent for it. During the second annual congress of the Playground Association, a storytelling committee was established. The chairman was Maud Summers. In an early article she had written:

> In the municipal playgrounds which have been built in so many cities, large and small, there is always a house known as the Recreation Center. If the playground is in a noisy section of the city near railroads, elevated trains, or factories, the children should be taken into one of the rooms of this neighborhood house for the story hour.[6]

Summers died before her committee could present its report, and Anne Carroll Moore was named the chairman.

Summers believed that the parks and playgrounds should use outside professionals for such specialized programs. In her view, the training and talent needed was too exacting to be expected of the average playground worker.[7]

The committee presented its report in 1910.[8] Not too much came of it, except that for many cities the trend was established: The storytellers for the parks and playgrounds were provided either by the public library (Plate 19) or by some other group, such as the local chapter of the National Storytellers' League.

Gudrun Thorne-Thomsen, on the other hand, advocated the training of regular staff to carry on such programs in recreation departments. In her view, the best assurance for long-term follow-through on such programs was best assured by having them done by regular staff members. Thorne-Thomsen made all of her recommendations after a summer of experimentation in the parks and playgrounds of Chicago.[9] It is ironic, but her report probably did much more to develop reading rooms for children in the Chicago Public Library than it did for the development of continued storytelling programs to be maintained by the Parks and Recreation Department of Chicago.[10]

Some cities probably did pay attention to Thorne-Thomsen's suggestions. For example, a report mentions that "storytelling in the playgrounds of New York City is considered an important feature of the work of the playground assistant whenever the conditions are favorable to carrying it on."[11] This was in addition to the storytelling assistance provided by staff of the New York Public Library. The pattern remains the same in New York up to the present time, with staff from both agencies undertaking storytelling in the public parks each summer.

Another city that had a professional recreational storyteller very early was St. Louis. That person was responsible only for the story-hour programs and occasionally assisted in directing games. The assistants also did some storytelling, as did a number of volunteers.[12] San Francisco is reported to have had a professional storyteller for its

PLATE 19   Playground story hour, August 1910, in Hazelwood Playground (now Tecumseh), Pittsburgh. Unknown storyteller was from staff of Carnegie Library. Photo courtesy of Carnegie Library of Pittsburgh.

parks and playgrounds during the 1930s.[13] On the whole, though, the majority of recreational storytellers were itinerants.

In some cities the playground storytellers were encouraged to use costumes. A favorite choice was that of a "gypsy." These were often more romantic than authentic, as evidenced by surviving descriptions and photographs.[14] A steady sprinkling of articles in the pages of the official journal of the professional recreation association indicate that some attention was paid to storytelling throughout the decades of this century. There is no question, however, that this activity, as well as all other organized park and playground activities, began to dwindle with the arrival of a much wider choice of free-time entertainment for urban children.

Campfire Storytelling

Another reason for the decrease in summer activities was the rise in summer camping outside the city for children of all social classes. The scouting groups established many camping programs in the decades from 1910 to 1930, and social agencies followed after, arranging for children from even the poorest families to spend two weeks or more in a camp. In most of these camps it was traditional to end the day with stories told around the campfire. For the commercially or philanthropically run camps, such storytelling was likely to be an informal, spontaneous event rather than a consciously adopted program.

Among scouting groups it was more firmly established as policy, right from the first appearance of the *Handbook for Scoutmasters*. That book insisted that scouting was recreational and that the method to be used in all cases of teaching should be the story method, and not academic instruction.[15] The campfire was looked upon as a logical place for recreational storytelling. Once Franklin K. Mathiews became chief librarian for the Boy Scouts, the organization's literature made even more reference to the fact that storytelling around the campfire was a "must." Mathiews insisted that the stories be entertaining.[16]

Such campfire storytelling is the least organized and the most informal of all the types of organized storytelling to groups of children in the United States and Canada. In spite of a wide array of more modern and sophisticated forms of entertainment available to many camps, it remains persistently a recognized camping activity. This could provide the researcher with some interesting questions to investigate. Is there something intrinsic in the campfire that demands an almost instinctive response of narration on the part of those sitting around it? Does the child—even the urban, sophisticated child—suspend the usual expectations of entertainment while in a camping situation? Is the absence of television from most camps a factor?

A careful exploration of such questions might well lead to more conclusive evidence about the relative strength and appeal of oral, visual, and print media among children.

III

The Format and Style of Storytelling

8

Opening of the Story Session

Most theaters use the curtain to inform the audience that something is beginning or ending, and as a psychological device to suggest to viewer/listeners that they must suspend belief or time. So, too, do most storytellers use special opening and closing actions or phrases to prepare their listeners and themselves.

Delargy describes how in Ireland the scene was set for storytelling by the man of the house, who passed a fresh pipe with tobacco, first to the most honored guest, then back to himself, and continuing to the rest of the company.[1] This was not unlike the preparations of a number of Native American groups prior to their storytelling. According to Beckwith, among the Mandan-Hidatsa Indians it was the custom to begin by opening the tobacco pouch, filling a pipe with tobacco, and offering a smoke to all. The smoking continued during the entire storytelling session. Indeed, the very word for ending a story, *Kiruskidits*, is the same word used to describe the act of pulling the drawstrings on a tobacco pouch to close it.[2]

In folk storytelling in the village, sessions didn't have a fixed beginning or end. In one of the tale cycles cited by Brinkmann, there are ten pages of conversation before one gets to the first complete telling of a folktale. This conversation is full of short anecdotes and hints from the audience, such as "How was that again with the —" or "How did that go again—?" Sometimes these hints are picked up by the storyteller, and he or she launches into the full tale. At other times the narrator passes them by, obviously not in the mood to tell that particular tale at the moment.[3]

West African Method of Story Selection

A most unusual form of preparation for a storytelling session was recorded by Mary Kingsley in West Africa during the last years of the nineteenth century. In a number of places she had come upon traveling narrators, each carrying a net. Her description of these tellers carrying their unusual objects bubbles over with enthusiasm and admiration:

> I have seen one in Accra, one in Sierra Leone, two on board steamers, and one in Buana town, Cameroon. Briefly, these are minstrels who frequent market towns and for a fee sing stories. Each minstrel has a song-net—a strongly made net of fishing net sort. On to this net are tied all manner and sorts of things, pythons' backbones, tobacco pipes, bits of china, feathers, bits of hide, birds' heads, reptiles' heads, bones, etc., etc., and to every one of these objects hangs a tale. You see your minstrel's net, you select an object and say: how much that song. He names an exorbitant price; you haggle; no good. He won't be reasonable, say, over the python bone, so you price the tobacco pipe—more haggle; finally you settle on some object and its price and sit down on your heels and listen with rapt attention to the song, or, rather chant. You usually have another.... These song-nets, I may remark, are not of a regulation size. I have never seen on the West Coast anything like so superb a collection of stories as Mr. Swanzy has tied on that song-net of his.... The most impressive song-net that I saw was the one at Buana. Its owner I called Homer on the spot, because his works were a terrific two. Tied on to his small net were a human hand and a human jaw bone. They were his only songs. But they were fascinating things and the human hand one had a passage in it which caused the singer to crawl on his hands and knees, round and round, stealthily looking this side and that, giving the peculiar leopard-questing cough, and making the leopard mark on the earth with his doubled-up fist. Ah! that was something like a song![4]

The only other person to have recorded a custom similar to this was Rattray, writing in 1923:

> That evening I strolled down to see the chief to ask him about the next day's ceremony. I found him sitting in the court-yard of his "palace" listening to a storyteller. Somewhat like the late Miss Kingsley's "Homer" he was, for he derived his inspirations from his hat, round the entire rim of which were suspended articles that represented or reminded him of some proverb, story or riddle. You chose your little fancy, and he "was off."[5]

A modern folklorist, Verna Aardema, used this intriguing image of the "story hat" as the title for one of her collections of African tales for young readers.[6]

Another African variation in opening a storytelling session is reported by Junod. This was the custom of "riddling," that is, of making up riddles and guessing the answers to them. According to his report, those not good at this back-and-forth word game had to pay a forfeit by being the first to tell stories.[7]

Other Methods of Story Selection

In preparing to perform the *penglipur lara* in Malaysia, the tellers frequently prepare a dish of offerings, burn incense, and murmur invocations.[8] In the special Japanese halls or theaters called *yose*, apprentice storytellers prepare the stage for the master by bringing tea, arranging the cushions in the prescribed manner, and setting out any special items that are called for.[9] These formal, ritualistic preparations are echoed a bit in the ceremony of candlelighting that initiates the story hour in a number of public library systems in the United States and Canada.

By far the most common preparation for folk storytelling is the spontaneous gathering, often around a fire, of a group of persons whose past experience has led them to believe they can expect stories under such conditions, especially when there is a certain mood or atmosphere created by the cumulative events of the day or the seasonal weather. One Taos Indian informant related how, during his childhood, an elder of the village would assemble up to twenty children for an evening's session:

> Each boy would bring with him two sticks of firewood. All would sit around the walls, and each in turn would tell a story.[10]

A Nez Percé informant mentioned two special winter lodges that were made: one for boys and one for girls. The best tellers were then invited in for long nights of storytelling.[11]

Among most North American Indian tribes, there was no storytelling allowed during the summer, spring, and early fall. Also, many believed that it was better to tell stories at night rather than during the day. Adamson mentions the fact that among the Coast Salish Indians it was the custom for people to prepare for stories by lying flat on their backs around a fire, so as not to get humps.[12]

In Africa there was a commonly reported proscription against telling stories during the day, especially during the planting or hoeing season. Vague, superstitious reasons were suggested for this. Some informants said that horns would grow on the storyteller if stories were told during the day or that the teller would grow bald.[13] Others predicted only that dire things would happen. Scheub is doubtful of these reasons, based on his observations among the Xhosa. In his opinion, the proscription was on economic grounds. If the work of the children lagged behind, especially during the hoeing season when everything grows by leaps and bounds in the tropics, it would be difficult to harvest a good crop later. So the threatening reasons for not being able to tell stories during the day were invented by the elders as a means of keeping all at their tasks.[14]

Although no other folklorist or anthropologist seems to have put forth this explanation, it appears to be sound in view of the fact that few informants, whether African or Native American, were able to cite specific religious, historical, or cultural reasons for prohibiting stories during the planting, growing, and harvesting seasons. His reasoning also seems logical since the forbidden times for storytelling are always during the productive hours of the day or year.

Bardic storytelling did not differ greatly from folk storytelling in its preparations and openings. In ancient Greece, it consisted of a few strains on the cithara as a prelude, followed by a short address to Zeus or to another god or goddess, as the occasion demanded.[15] *Byliny* singers in Russia occasionally start with something striking and original, but the majority begin with familiar or formulaic phrases to make the audience feel at home. A stock device is to open with a feast at which a wager is made.[16] Yugoslav openings of this type are even shorter and more direct.[17]

Opening Words and Phrases

To actually begin the story, storytellers most frequently call out or say slowly an opening word, phrase, or rhyme and then move right into the story. In English, we are all familiar with "Once upon a time—" or "There was once—." For those who wish to compare them in the original, here is a list of these well-known opening phrases in some of the languages of Western and Eastern Europe:

Albanian	*ishte njëherë*
Czech	*kdysi za onoho času*
Danish, Norwegian, Swedish	*det var en gång* (Swedish, *gang*)
Dutch	*er was er eens*
Finnish	*olipa kerran*
French	*il y avait une fois*
German	*es war einmal*
Greek	*mià forà k' ëva kairó*
Italian	*c'era una volta*
Polish	*byl sobie raz* or *pewnego razu*
Portuguese	*era uma vez*
Romanian	*era odată*
Russian	*zhil byl*
Serbo-Croatian	*nekada*
Spanish	*érase una vez*

Occasionally, the opening has a more stately variation that seems to warn the listener the story will be long and complex, and will probably have royalty as central characters:

> There was once, in old times and in old times it was, a king in Ireland....
> Yeats, *Fairy and Folktales in Ireland*[18]

> In a certain kingdom, in a certain land, in a little village, there lived....
> Afanas'ev, *Russian Fairy Tales*[19]

Peoples in other parts of the world who utilize the same or similar type of openings include:

Toucouleurs: *Woneko wonodo* (There once was here)[20]
(Mali)
Sinhalese: *Eka mathaka rata* (In a country one recalls to mind)[21]
(Sri Lanka)
Japanese: *Mukashi, mukashi* (Long, long ago)
Aro tokoro ni (In a certain place)[22]

The *tekerlemeler* of Turkey are rhymed introductions that usually have a nonsensical twist to them, but in essence, they, too, put the setting of the story in the past:

Once there was and once there was not, a long time ago, when God had many people but it was a sin to say so, when the camel was a town crier and the cock was a barber, when the sieve was in the straw and I was rocking my mother's cradle, tingir, mingir . . .[23]

Native American opening phrases were also generally set in the past. Some of them were very terse, as, for example, the typical Clackamas introduction:

He lived there. *or* She lived there.[24]

Others were closer to the European type of opening phrases, or at any rate, this is how they have been translated:

White Mountain Apache: Long, long ago, they say . . .[25]
Navajo: In the beginning, when the world was new . . .
or
At the time when men and animals were all the same and spoke the same language . . .[26]

Not all peoples begin their storytelling by putting the tale into the vague and distant past. Among the Xhosa of South Africa, as Harold Scheub reports, the folktale usually begins with: "Now for a *ntsomi*," or "A *ntsomi* goes like this." It is the action and singing during the story that help to build up atmosphere, not the preparation and setting of scene.[27]

Other short introductory phrases are: "I can tell lies too!"—a playful challenge by the Tiv of northern Nigeria[28]; "*a gbae se*," an untranslatable phrase, the closest equivalent of which is "Let's throw stories," from among the Bandi people of northwest Liberia.[29]

"And now listen how the *dombra* tells about it," is a frequent device found among Kazakh storytellers. They use it to enter into the real story, after they have given a short synopsis or introduction.[30] This is similar to the "prelude" device used by some Russian storytellers, who follow it up with words to this effect:

That's the flourish, just for fun;
The real tale has not begun.[31]

Call-and-Response Openings

In some parts of the world, the storyteller calls out a word or phrase, the audience replies, and the teller continues. This is most common in Africa, although it occurs in other parts of the world as well. In Cameroon, the exchange might go like this:

> Narrator: Listen to a tale! Listen to a tale!
> Audience: A tale for fun, for fun.
> Your throat is a gong, your body a locust;
> bring it here for me to roast!
> Narrator: Children, listen to a tale,
> a tale for fun, for fun.[32]

Among the Hausa of Northern Nigeria, the exchange that is heard most frequently is:

> Narrator: *Ga ta, ga ta nan.* (See it, see it here.)
> Audience: *Ta je ta komo.* (Let it go, let it come back.)
> *or*
> *Ta zo, muji.* (Let it come, for us to hear.)[33]

Ben-Amos reports that in southwestern Nigeria, among the Edo-speaking peoples of the Benin area, "the storyteller opens his recitation with a string of proverbial phrases which include praise for the host, greetings to the audience, and wishes of blessing to everyone present." These are interspersed with responses from the audience or the storyteller's helper. Only after these have been completed does he actually begin the story, with a phrase such as:

> *Umaranmwen sion sion sion.* (This is a nice story.)[34]

Simpler and shorter call-and-response openings are the following:

Hungary and Central Europe[35]
Narrator: { Bones, people } *or* { Bones } *or* { Bones }
Audience: { Soup } { Meat } { Bricks }

West Indies[36]
Narrator: *Cric*
Audience: *Crac*

Massignon does not say whether the *Cric-crac* opening found in France is a call-and-response type. Common variants and their translations are:

> *Cric crac; cuiller à pot; marche aujourd'hui, marche demain; à force de marcher, on fait beaucoup de chemin . . .*

> Cric crac; clog, kitchen spoon; walk today, walk tomorrow; by walking and walking we cover a lot of ground . . .[37]

In the Bahamas and other West Indian islands, one or another of the following rhymes is used to start off a tale, often after the *Cric-*

crac exchange between teller and listeners, or after the teller calls out "Bunday":

> Once upon a time, a very good time
> Monkey chew tobacco and spit white lime . . .
> > *or*
> Once upon a time, a very good time
> Not my time, nor your time, old people's time . . .[38]

Similar rhymed verse beginnings are found in Chile:

> To know and to tell
> A lie does quite well.
> I walked by a creek
> Thrashing my stick.
> I went through the corner
> Stumbling along . . .[39]

Another place where they are encountered is Romania:

> Once upon a time when
> Bears had tails as big as their head
> And Willows bore a fruit, juicy and red . . .

> Once upon a time, a long, long time ago,
> When mice ran after cats
> And lions were chased by rats . . .[40]

These are probably related in source to the *tekerlemeler* of Turkey, mentioned above. However, they could also be representative of a spontaneous and playful period when, according to Huizinga, most speech of a special character was in poetic form, including laws. This would explain why the practice is common to so many parts of the world.

Finally, it must be noted that there are places where there is virtually no "setting the stage" or creating of atmosphere by actions, words, phrases, or rhymes. For example, Mbiti reports that the Akamba in East Africa begin storytelling spontaneously by saying "The story of. . . ."[41] Among Amapa storytellers in Mexico, it was recently noted that there was no particular preparation or opening and closing phrases.[42]

9

Style, Gesture, and Voice Change

According to John Ball, the storyteller's style includes "intonation, voice rhythm, continuity, speaking rate, pitch, voice intensity, pauses, facial expressions, gestures, pantomime or reenactment by the speaker, voice imitation (even of the opposite sex or of animals), and methods of reacting to audience response."[1] Such a specific listing of components should make for relatively easy definitions of the different types of storytellers, classified according to style. Nothing could be further from the truth.

While there are accounts of groups within which all storytellers seem to have the same or similar styles, there are many more reports and studies indicating the presence of diversity in the performance of any given group of tellers. This provides the reader or listener with the delightful opportunity of discovering still another way of achieving effect, but it makes it more difficult for the scholar to report.

For the teacher of storytelling, the task of describing and cultivating style is even more formidable. Most students wish to know whether it is suitable or not to use voice change, to expend few or many gestures, to pantomime action, to use subtle or exaggerated facial expressions, or none at all. It does not help at all to be told that a worldwide survey would indicate that all of these elements can be present in good storytelling style. Most newcomers to the field are encouraged to observe and imitate the manner in which master storytellers approach each story, but there comes a moment when the new story-teller must decide whether to continue imitating or to begin innovating.

Putting the component parts of an oral style into written words presents difficulties that are often insurmountable. As Robert Georges and others have so clearly stated, every storytelling event is unique. One cannot even capture it on film.[2]

This section can only suggest the barest outlines of that which comprises personal style in telling, as recorded by many observers and listeners. Some of these observers were probably more "in tune" with the storyteller than others. Their reports and comments are mentioned here only as clues and guides to that which is visible in storytelling style. This might suggest to the present-day student of storytelling some of the things to look for when analyzing style at a live storytelling event.

The groups that are most extensively described, insofar as styles are concerned, are Native Americans, Africans, Central Europeans, and the Gaelic peoples. This does not mean that a composite style can be drawn up for each one, or that the descriptions are all accurate. Far from it. But the variety and extent of the reports on these groups does allow for better comparative study than is possible for other regions or peoples of the world.

Native American Styles

Melville Jacobs has written one of the few book-length attempts to analyze the oral style of a Native American group.[3] He examines the style and the qualities oral literature has not only as literature, but also as a visible performance and as an expression of inner belief in a particular world view. His study concerns the Clackamas Chinook tribes, but frequently refers to other related groups.

According to Jacobs, these Northwest raconteurs used a style that was "terse, staccato, or rapidly moving." Yet the terse delineation of characters and situations, he feels, was not conscious on the part of the storyteller.

> He was succinct because he had learned no other way of expressing himself. The few choices of things which could be expressed were items that had to be articulated with utmost brevity. Such a blanket characteristic of literary style must have been maintained during long eras because of several factors, including the exhaustive familiarity with actors, plots, and stylizations which adult villagers shared. Therefore story content was not repeated *ad nauseam* during formal recitals. Each person's acquaintanceship with literature because of formal recitals was heavily reinforced by year-round chitchat about and discussions of stories.
> These conversations were stimulated not only by psychological needs rooted in the cultural and social heritage but by challengingly different versions and treatments of plots given by in-laws, visitors, and alien peoples. The very manner of performance and the limited time available during an evening encouraged compactness.[4]

Quite a few other folklorists, ethnologists, or anthropologists who recorded tales from Native American groups mention this same succinctness and lack of descriptive matter. It was mistakenly believed by a number of those recording the tale telling that the absence of emotion in the words of the story extended to the gestures and voice that the teller was allowed to use. This was probably because the recording sessions were not before a live audience, or because they were taken down in the summer season when the informants were often uneasy about telling stories. But as Jacobs points out, even though the Clackamas storyteller never used words to convey the feelings of a character in the story, "voice, gesture and other devices for dramatic expression permitted a raconteur to act out the emotions of the characters."[5]

Reichard also mentions one teller among the Coeur d'Alenes who was so dramatic in his movements that he once "got up from his chair, went out the door, lay down on his stomach on the porch and worked his way in, crawling sneakingly as one would up to a tent in the dark." All during the pantomime, he had been telling the tale, and when that particular scene was finished, "he returned to his chair and quietly continued."[6]

A Kiowa woman storyteller observed by Parsons was found to be an excellent pantomimist, very dramatic in her presentations.[7]

Toelken's Navajo informant, Yellowman, also perceived the narration of tales as dramatic events. Without an audience they were very dull, he explained.[8] Although Yellowman used a "pretty" or "older" language for telling stories than was used for everyday conversation, there does not appear to be among Native American groups the general use of special languages for different types of stories.

The listening style of the audience is often equally as important as the teller's style. Among most Native American groups, children were expected to be very attentive and not to interrupt the storyteller. The exceptions to this were among tribes such as the Assiniboines, Crow, and Nez Percé, where the listeners were expected to exclaim "*E*!" (yes) after every few sentences. When this response was no longer forthcoming, the narrator brought the session to a close.[9]

Opler mentions that among the Jicarilla Apache, the older narrator would often stop if the children were misbehaving. It was probably partly to keep the children satisfied and interested that there evolved the custom of giving them kernels of corn to chew during the storytelling. The deeper meaning has to do with the sacredness of corn as a symbol of life and the holiness of the stories. It was believed that the children would be helped by the eating to remember the content of the stories and their importance.[10]

Others who noted that children and adults were expected to be quiet and almost unmoving during the storytelling were Beckwith,[11] who recorded myths and ceremonies of the Mandan-Hidatsa, and Adamson,[12] who wrote about the Coast Salish of western Washington.

The patterns of Eskimo storytelling style appear to be similar, except that the audience could respond more freely. Hall reports that vocal and visual mannerisms are heavily used. "A very long pause accompanied by an almost imperceptible change of facial expression may turn the audience to bursts of laughter or expressions of pity, as the case may be." There is much mimicry, and the tellers often "try to talk like people from where the story took place."[13]

African Folk Style

Just as there seems to be general agreement that the usual, most common style of Native American storytelling was terse and staccato, but sometimes accompanied by dramatic gestures or body movement expanding upon the words, so also there seems to be a general consensus that the prevailing style of African folk storytelling is ebullient, with much more social interaction between teller and audience. This is not as explicit in the writings of observers from the past century as it is in the commentaries of modern folklorists.

In the nineteenth century a number of travelers to Africa recorded their impressions of the storytelling sessions they had witnessed. The most widely read were those of Stanley. Scholars of today do not regard as very accurate the texts of the stories related in *My Dark Companions and Their Strange Stories*, because they were obviously only loosely translated at the time of performance and the language was romanticized and anglicized in Stanley's recasting. The descriptions of each of the tellers, and how they told, ring truer. A typical example is:

> Sabadu was unequalled in the art of storytelling; he was fluent and humorous, while his mimicry of the characters he described kept everybody's interest on the alert. To the Rabbit, of course, he gave a wee voice, to the Elephant he gave a deep bass, to the Buffalo a hollow mooing. When he attempted the Lion, the veins of his temple and neck were dreadfully distended as he made the effort; but when he mimicked the dog, one almost expected a little terrier-like dog to trot up to the fire, so perfect was his yaup-yaup. Everyone agreed as Sabadu began his story that his manner, even his style of sitting and smoothing his face, the pose of his head, betrayed a man of practice.[14]

This description and a number of others coincide with later and even present-day descriptions of storytellers in action in the same region.

Other nineteenth-century writers who commented on the style of African narrators, rather than merely recording their tales, were Heli Chatelain,[15] A. B. Ellis,[16] and Edward W. Lane.[17] Chatelain named and described in detail the various types of tales told in Angola. He placed "poetry and music" as separate types and stated that "not even a child finds difficulty, at any time, if excited, in producing extemporaneous song." He may well have been referring to poetic recitations, but he apparently did not understand that the poems and songs were often connective parts of the tales, and he could well have been referring to the singing interludes that make up a large part of Angolan folktales even today. This was probably because, as many of his notes indicate, he had his informants write down or dictate their stories directly to him; he seems to have had little opportunity to observe them told in groups, under natural circumstances.[18]

Ellis, in writing about the Yoruba professional storyteller, mentioned the use of a drum to fill up the pauses in the narrative and also implied that there was much audience participation.[19]

Lane described the coffeehouse storytellers in Egypt who were, of course, following the Arabic style.

> The reciter generally seats himself upon a small stool on the *mastab'ah*, or raised seat, which is built against the front of the coffee-shop: some of his auditors occupy the rest of that seat, others arrange themselves upon the *mastab'ahs* of the houses on the opposite side of the narrow street, and the rest sit upon stools or benches made of palm sticks—most of them with the pipe in hand, some sipping their coffee, and all highly amused, not only with the story but also with the lively and dramatic manner of the narrator.[20]

After the turn of the century, language study had become sufficiently advanced so that more accurate transcriptions of folktale texts appeared. Also, folklorists began to take more and more interest in the individual informants and in the circumstances of narration, and their notes began to reflect this. Torrend noted, for example, that the narrators in Northern Rhodesia (now Zambia) were free to borrow words and phrases from any language and were supposed to be able to understand and interpret the language of the birds and animals, in order to imitate their sounds better. He compared a storytelling session there with the Latin rites of the Catholic church, in which the servers and congregation knew exactly when to break into chant, or what phrase to intone, often without being able to read or understand the Latin.[21]

Fortunately, bardic and folk storytelling are still practiced in Africa today, and a few scholars have recorded in writing, on tape, and on film some of the styles of present-day tellers. Among the most graphic short descriptions is that of a storyteller observed by A. C. Jordan in South Africa:

> There began the most spontaneous cooperation I have ever seen in storytelling. No less than six of the audience went with the principal narrator. They began "fattening" the narrative with dialogue, mimicry, bird calls, graphic descriptions of the grass-warbler's stunts when left alone in the sky, etc. etc. What was most revealing was the attitude of the original narrator to all this. Far from feeling he was being interrupted, this man was the most delighted of all. He was obviously getting fresh ideas for future occasions of storytelling.[22]

It becomes clear, from this and other observations made by Jordan, that there is no distinct demarcation between tellers and listeners in this style of African storytelling. All are drawn into the tale and become involved in creating it as well as enjoying it.

It was the inspiration and guidance of Jordan that led one of his students, Harold Scheub, to undertake an intensive study of the style of Xhosa storytellers, referred to earlier in Chapter 3.[23] This work is invaluable for the person studying storytelling style, for it shows the great diversity that can occur within a relatively small geographical area and within the constraints of using one type of narrative.

The general style of the *ntsomi* tellers, if one can use that term to represent an amalgam of the styles of a large number of individuals, is a lively mixture of verbal and body language, often dramatic and exaggerated, using core-clichés, and interspersed with song and a great deal of audience participation. But as Scheub points out, the finest performer he encountered, Mrs. Nongenile Masithathu Zenani (see Plate 8), seemed to perform in a manner contrary to the general style.

> She uses gestures sparingly, her face rarely betrays occurrences and emotions involved in the *ntsomi* she is creating, and her approach to her audience seems condescending.[24]

This apparent outer calm and indifference prove to be deceptive.

> A careful analysis of her style reveals that all of the usual technical and stylistic devices are utilized, but in highly subtle ways. Furthermore, so incisive and exacting are her words, and the actions they describe, that the experience is especially vivid and moving, one in which the audience, her petulant attitude towards its members notwithstanding, is eager to participate.[25]

Other performers that Scheub singles out as exceptional are:

Mrs. Macutsha Sidima

[She] often drops to her hands and knees to give character and vividness to one of her creations. Her techniques are broad, her style approaching hilarious slapstick ... episodes and details erupt with staccato rapidity from a deep and bellowing voice. Character development ... is achieved through frenzied (but always controlled) action and constant use of mime. Narration is uninterrupted, gestures are bold, and the world that she creates ... is stormed by a humour that is direct and bombastic.

Mrs. Martha Makhoba

[She] performs with quiet skill, lacking the arrogance of Mrs. Zenani and the animated antics of Mrs. Sidima. Hers is instead a calm, assured competence often concealing by its very smoothness the complex strands that combine to create the illusion of a single textured production.

Mrs. Mahlombe Nxesi

Hers is a declamatory production.... When her *ntsomi* deals, for example, with diviners, it is in that part ... that Mrs. Nxesi makes maximum use of her skills and demonstrates her total control over the audience. With exquisite timing and growing suspense, she addresses the questions of the diviner to an audience which she knows so intimately that it has little difficulty becoming a part of her production. . . . Mrs. Nxesi artfully interrupts the rapid and rhythmic flow of her narrative with the audience-sequences; then, as the final response of the audience is still being uttered, she has again caught smoothly . . . the momentarily lapsed strand of the *ntsomi* plot, building to the next segment of the participation, so that there is a constant and pleasing overlapping of narrative and response. . . . It is a breath-taking exchange to witness. At the conclusion of such a performance she is quite exhausted.[26]

These are only a few from among the more than 2,000 performers observed and recorded by Scheub, with much more detail than can be quoted here. Reading about them, one can only comment that, had the opportunity allowed, one would have liked to follow Scheub in his miles of walking from village to village, as did the local children, so as to hear (and see) one *ntsomi* performance after another.

Scheub is not alone in expressing wonder at the variety and individuality of African folk storytelling. Evans-Pritchard, who as an anthropologist recorded tales in the Sudan many years ago in conjunction with other material he was more interested in, was later asked to edit and publish the tales. He found that even after the lapse of forty years he could still tell by the stylistic traits alone the name of the informant from whom he had taken down any particular story.[27]

Perhaps it was storytelling sessions similar to those described by Scheub and Evans-Pritchard that Béart refers to when he states that the atmosphere of storytelling in the French West African countries was almost like a game.[28] Unfortunately, he gave no details, so we cannot compare further.

Mbiti's introduction to the Akamba stories of Kenya depicts conditions of telling quite similar to those for the *ntsomi*, but he makes the pointed observation that grown-ups must refrain from interruptions. He does not make clear whether this means they cannot break in with the responses, or whether it only means that once the teller has begun, the adults must let him or her finish.[29]

Ben-Amos does present a vivid picture of another style of storytelling in present-day Africa, one that is not comparable to the *ntsomi*-telling sessions.[30] The term *ibota* describes an event roughly equivalent in social makeup to the storytelling sessions observed by Scheub. But Ben-Amos chose to describe in detail the *okpobhię*, an event at which professional tellers perform. He does not provide much information about the individual styles of the persons who perform at the *ibota*, except to say that it is usually the women of the household who are the most active participants. Just as in the *ntsomi*, the narratives are interspersed with songs, and there is much audience interaction.

The professional tellers at an *okpobhię* are called either *okp'akpata* or *okp'asologun*, depending on which of the two musical instruments they use (see Plate 7). The instruments are very different and will be discussed in greater detail in the following chapter. The styles used by both types of tellers, however, do not seem to differ measurably. In contrast to the *ibota*, at the *okpobhię* there is no audience participation. The narrator usually brings with him a small choir of supporters, and it is they who give the proper responses whenever he signals them. According to Ben-Amos, they are usually persons whom the narrator knows well. "Once started, the telling can last all night long; till daybreak; often it will involve a single story."[31]

These stories usually treat of chiefs, magicians, and heroes outside of the court and are full of precise details. Each character, however minor, is fully delineated, and the narrator makes certain that the exact relationships of all the characters, one to another, are clearly mentioned. This is in contrast to the folk narratives told at the *ibota*, and indeed to folktales in many parts of the world.[32]

In many ways these professional Benin storytellers resemble bardic tellers, but due to their "outsider" position in their society, they cannot be considered bards.[33]

African Bardic Style

Bardic style in Africa does take many forms. Here we shall group them together into two main types, which for want of better names we have been referring to as chronicler-historian and praise singer. As mentioned before, the distinctions are not at all fine, and few scholars would agree as to just which types are to be considered as equivalents in the various languages.

The style of all of them is, more often than not, formal and precise. Some of the earlier descriptions of chronicler-historians are to be found in Ellis[34] and Johnson.[35] They both referred to someone called the *ologbo* or *arokin* in the Yoruba king's court. Ellis referred to the *ologbo* as the chief of the *arokin* and stated that they "narrated traditions."[36] Johnson wrote that they "repeat daily in song the genealogy of the kings, events in their lives," and other narratives.[37]

Alagoa writes that there are bards among the Ijo in the Niger delta, equivalent to the Yoruba *oriki*, who recite *kule* in a singsong fashion.[38] This would seem to match the earlier descriptions of Ellis and Johnson, so that *oriki* may be the same word as *arokin*, or may come from the same stem. Babalola, in his book on Yoruba chanting, mentions the *oriki* only very briefly:

> As the children do obeisance before their parents, first thing in the morning, the parents burst forth into *oriki* recitation in commemoration of their ancestors whose achievements their young descendants are to be inspired to emulate.[39]

The *kwadwumfu* in the Ashanti court were described by Rattray as minstrels who "drone like a hive of bees in the chief's ear."[40] Still another chronicler type is the bard found among the Nyanga and the Lega in Zaire, called *shékárìsì* and *mugani wa lugano*, respectively. While singing and narrating, these bards take the role of the hero and often dance or mime the action. They also shake a calabash rattle and anklet bells at various times, for emphasis. Accompaniment is by percussion sticks played by apprentices. Members of the audience shout encouragement or clap their hands. The interesting point is that the entire epic would never be recited in one sequence.[41]

In contrast to this, the *hwenoho* tales in Dahomey, which include myths and clan chronicles, are narrated with little attempt at dramatization. Ordinary speech is used, and there is little or no audience participation.[42]

The praise-singer type of bard in Africa seems to use more or less the same style of performance, at least in terms of voice. It is high-pitched, singsong, with a rapid, sometimes staccato, delivery. Occasionally, as with the *shékárìsì* of the Nyanga in Zaire,[43] the *ebyevugo* of the Bahima in Uganda,[44] and the *imbongi* of the Xhosa,[45] there are short pauses to allow the audience a chance to participate by hums, murmurs, or shouts of agreement. The Bahima *ebyevugo* also snaps his finger and thumb at the end of each verse.[46]

Sometimes these bards are accompanied by drums, as in the case of the *oníjàlá* among the Yoruba[47]; or by rhythm and string instruments, as in the case of the Mande hunters' bards, called *donso-jeli*.[48] The *imbongi* of the Zulu usually walks up and down very fast while reciting, more or less to match the rhythm and tempo of the words. Occasionally, the *imbongi* will even leap about and gesticulate.[49]

Taken as a whole, all storytelling in Africa, whether folk, religious, or bardic, whether in prose or poetry, seems to be strongly influenced by music and rhythm. It is rare to find stories that do not have some rhythmical or musical interlude or accompaniment, using either the voice, body parts, or special instruments. Raum implies that the use of music in conjunction with the story has a didactic or psychological purpose:

> The child quickly grasps that songs are a means of controlling the emotions. ... The Chaga, like the American Indian, sings a song when in need of self-control.[50]

But the comments of other scholars would imply that its function is much more for aesthetic or entertainment reasons.

European Bardic Style

Of the bardic manner of performing in pre-Christian and medieval Europe, we know practically nothing. There is not even much documentation about the performing style of those at the periphery of bardism, such as the *troubadours*, *trouvères*, and *minnesänger*. All that is known for sure is that the style was musical, similar to that of the ancient Greek *aoidoi* and *rhapsodes*. As to the use of gesture, voice change, pauses, and many other points, we are in the dark.

The exceptions are the singers of heroic epic songs in the South Slavic areas (Yugoslavia and Albania) and in Russia. Enough examples have been collected during the past two hundred years to conclude that their style has not changed much. The style of these *byliny* singers, as they are called in Russia, was fairly constant. Sokolov mentions that they "performed leisurely, smoothly, with few changes of tempo. The long-drawn monotony of the melody not only does *not* draw the attention away from the content ... it soothes the listeners, harmonizes exceedingly well with the tranquil measured account of events of distant times."[51] The creativeness of the narrators lay in how the formulaic phrases were used and in the way some details of language and content were changed to suit the occasion. They did not rely on dramatics and voice change or gestures.

European Folk Styles

The storytellers of modern Europe, on the other hand, rarely used or use song and musical accompaniment as part of their presentation, even though such precedents are there from the past. The folk storytellers of Germany, Scandinavia, Hungary, and Russia, whose styles have been recorded in as much detail as possible, indicate that there is a wide variety in the use of gestures, voice changes, and body movements, but it is not nearly as extreme as that found in African storytellers. Azadovsky was one of the first to record such storytelling style in detail. The Russian narrators he described fell into three main types:[52]

1. One who used a disordered, episodic style; often lost track of the story in all the detail and then had to find it again; long-winded.
2. The exact repeater; desired to pass on the tradition just as it was received, with each detail intact; narrated slowly and calmly.
3. Sparing of detail; uniform; used all the traditional formulae, but in poetic and inventive patterns; showed personality and character in telling; attempted to get across the psychology of the story and the characters.

Sokolov, on the other hand, felt there were many more types than just these three:

> ... we find tranquil, measured epic poets ... also fantastic dreamers ... moralists, searching after truth ... realists specializing in the romantic tale dealing with everyday life ... jokers, jesters, humorists without malice ... bitter, sarcastic, satirical storytellers with exceedingly malicious and pointed social satire ... storytellers who relate chiefly "shameful," that is, indecent, or even downright cynical erotic tales ... storyteller-dramaturgists, for whom the center of interest and artistic invention lies in the manner of narration, in the skill and animation of the handling of the dialogue ... bookish storytellers who had read plenty of cheap popular works or other novels of excitement and adventure, who were exceedingly avid for the "educated" bookish speech, and at times overly zealous in transmitting it ... women who told stories for children....[53]

Among the northern types, Tillhagen gives us a good picture of the animation of the Swedish gypsy storyteller Johan Dimitri Taikon, who had wandered all over Europe. Taikon reminisces about how dramatic it was, narrating among a group of people in Russia, called the *Kölderascha*:

> Sometimes there were four, five persons who were telling stories. One was the wolf, one the prince, another the giant, caliph or whatever was wanted. That was real theater you understand. In the middle of work it would start. But only in the beginning. All the workers kept on working until after a while it got more and more tense, they didn't give a hang and listened, waiting to take their turn as a character. Because the more the tale progressed, the more persons appeared. One, for example, was the judge and he sat down. He twirled his moustache, looked very serious, and then would start judging and giving wild opinions. And there stood the accused, and bowing and full of fear. There was the guard, and the folk and God knows what all. Ah, what a trial; that was funny, so funny![54]

Liestøl quoted the Norwegian folklore collector Jørgen Moe as he gave a vignette of an entertaining narrator:

> One cannot say he related his folktales, he *played* them: his whole person, from the top of his head to the withy thongs of his shoes was eloquent; and when he came to the place in the story where Askeladd had won the princess and all was joy and wedding bells, he danced the "snip! snap! snout! my tale is out" to an old rustic measure.[55]

Haiding made a special study of the gesture language of several Austrian storytellers, recording them in photos and words. A night watchman, Ernst Nemeth, "grabbed me on the shoulders, shook me strongly, then showed me how the ugly gypsy woman lighted her pipe and thereby turned her eyes upwards."[56] This was while Nemeth was telling the tale of "The White and Black Bride." There are very few studies such as this that give the specific gestures at specific moments in specific tales.

The German tellers in the village observed by Brinkmann used very different styles. Some underlined the meaning of various words and phrases by different forms of emphasis; others did not. Still others would use gestures, body movement, or a modulation of the voice to mysterious tones.[57] Flori Aloisi Zarn, a masterful Swiss storyteller recorded by Uffer, told in a very even style, smooth and flowing. "You have to tell such stories really well, with lots of beautiful words and with words the old people used," he is quoted as saying.[58]

The manner of delivery of two of the narrators that Linda Dégh observed was outwardly quite different.

> Mrs. Palkó's strength is not in a dramatic performance of the tales. ... Her talent is, in the main, epic; and the narration is the important thing for her. She used few gestures or movements of her body. Her delivery could be called dramatic only insofar as she lived with the story as it

went along, making reflex gestures in her identification with the hero. It was only in her anecdotes that her gestures became more vivacious. . . .[59]

Andrásfalvi was a better performer than Mrs. Palkó. While he was telling a story he would rise and underline what he said by gestures and mimicry. . . . When he told a story, the listeners did not crowd in closely about him but left a space open, because they were accustomed to his rising and moving around while telling a story.[60]

Yet in spite of Andrásfalvi's more animated performances, it was Mrs. Palkó who ranked as the finest storyteller because the internal style of her *märchen* was so special (see Plate 29). It had great richness of expression and was completely flexible, being lyrical and poetic, or hard and concise, or satirical and full of humor when the occasion demanded it. Her language was oftentimes "rhythmical, full of compact, expressive turns and idioms, of beautiful poetic images and alliterations."[61]

In addition to the narrators she observed and recorded, Dégh cites numerous other comments on Hungarian storytellers made by other folklorists. In general, she finds that the Hungarian narrators prefer "epic width to dramatic conciseness."[62]

Gaelic Styles

The Irish storytellers would hardly be accused of being concise. We do not know how the *scélaige*, the medieval folk narrator, performed. But the style of his modern counterpart, the *seanchai*, more commonly known as the *shanachie*, has been sketched by Delargy, Carmichael, and many others.

Obviously much affected by his narrative, he uses a great deal of gesticulation, and by the movement of his body, hands and head, tries to convey hate and anger, fear and humour, like an actor in a play. He raises his voice at certain passages, at other times it becomes almost a whisper. He speaks fairly fast, but his enunciation is at all times clear.[63]

The storytellers of the Highlands are as varied in their subjects as are literary men and women elsewhere. One is a historian narrating events simply and concisely; another is a historian with a bias, colouring his narrative according to his leanings. One is an inventor, building fiction upon fact, mingling his materials, and investing the whole with the charm of novelty and the halo of romance. Another is a reciter of heroic poems and ballads, bringing the different characters before the mind as clearly as the sculptor brings the figure before the eye.[64]

Jackson implies that the Gaelic storyteller usually sat in a chair, as would be appropriate in a cottage by a peat fire. But he also remembers one teller who would jump up and stride about the room, swinging his arms and declaiming when he reached an exciting passage.[65]

There are not a sufficient number of studies covering the style of storytellers in other parts of the world to be able to make valid comparisons or draw conclusions that would apply to entire regions or peoples. There seem to be no in-depth studies that discuss the style of

Italian, French, Spanish, and other Latin folk storytellers. None could be located for either the nineteenth or twentieth centuries. Massignon briefly portrays a few of the narrators she observed in France and Corsica in the middle of this century. From some of her comments, it might be safe to speculate that the delivery was probably full of emotion and gesture. About a Corsican storyteller, she writes: "She used to take my hand and place it over my heart in order to link me with the parts of her tale which she thought most moving."[66]

Asian Styles

The storytellers in the *yose* or *kodanseki*, public halls in Japan, use a style that is outwardly very simple. Only a few gestures are used, but they count for a great deal. Since the storytellers are seated, there is not much movement, but the little that is used is of great subtlety. There is extensive use of voice change, but not in overly exaggerated tones.[67] An amusing story in *Newsweek* in 1973 related how a young woman who began performing rather erotic stories in one of the *yose* in Tokyo used many more gestures and postures than the ones traditionally allowed. It was the posturing, more than the content of the stories, that caused a split in the *Kodan Kyokai*, the professional association of storytellers. The basis of the break was the disagreement between members who felt that such a style was permissible, and those who did not.[68]

Other Asian groups whose style has been commented on at some length include the various categories of Turkish storytellers. Eberhard gives a general idea of the style of some twenty minstrels who performed the *halk hikâyeleri* (minstrel epics) during the early 1950s. They varied from good performers to poor or mediocre ones who could only tell fragments of epics, because the custom was beginning to die out. In all cases, a good voice was considered necessary, and the animated performers were more appreciated by the audiences than the passive ones.[69]

A more recent picture of Turkish tellers can be found in Barbara Walker's article in the *Horn Book*. They ranged from janitors to maids to prison inmates. One of them, Behçet Mahir, a janitor at Atatürk University, believed that he had to stand in order to perform well, so that all "two-hundred-and-fifty veins could be vibrating."[70]

It is a curious coincidence that the frequent and regular interruption of the storyteller by the audience is common to all parts of the Indian subcontinent, just as it is among those misnamed Indians, the Native Americans. As previously mentioned, the latter were supposed to say *"E"* or make some other sound signifying assent at the end of every few sentences of the narration. In India, the sound was usually "Hum" or "Mmm," or something similar.[71] Not much is known about the manner of narration in family storytelling other than this. Bardic style, especially that using picture cloths, uses a kind of singsong chant, probably similar to some African bardic styles.

The Rawang of Burma have a very conservative style of narration. If the teller varies too much from what is considered to be the proper way of telling the story, the audience is sure to ask "Where did you hear it that way?" Myths especially must be remembered in word-perfect order. Any deviation is corrected.[72]

Myths among the Ifugaos in the Philippines were recited in barked-out, terse phrases or sentences. The conciseness of language reminds one of the patterns common among many Native Americans.[73]

Folk storytelling in the Pacific, to be successful, was supposed to put people to sleep, so the style probably is not particularly animated. Mitchell's study covers fairly recent observations of a Polynesian group, and, according to his account, a good storyteller chants or recites in such a manner that at the end the entire audience is asleep.[74] In Tonga, the very word for the most common type of folktale, *fananga*, means "stories that put to sleep."[75]

Maranda indicates that in Melanesia, when epics are recited for entertainment or didactic purposes, they are told; but when they are used for sacred purposes, they are sung. He gives no further indications as to use of gesture and voice change.[76]

Gorer mentions that although the Lepchas of Sikkim narrate their stories very vividly, there is almost no attempt at dramatization. Voice change and mimicry were observed only in a very few humorous stories. But all tales employed minute and specific details in the language.[77]

North American Ethnic Styles

Among the ethnic groups that came to the United States and Canada, storytelling style has not been recorded in great detail, but the general consensus of folklorists probably would be that the characteristic styles were carried with the tales from the country of origin. The Armenians of Detroit appear remarkably similar in their storytelling style to the Armenians of Turkey and the Armenian Soviet Socialist Republic.[78] Bianco[79] and Sklute,[80] however, noticed a marked deterioration in style among an Italian-American and a Swedish-American community, respectively.

The best overall view of a group of native and immigrant tellers in North America can be found in Dorson's "Oral Styles of American Folk Narrators."[81] The Polish-American teller Joe Woods used fresh, colloquial, and idiomatic language in English even though it was his second language. He could handle dialogue with great ease. The Swedish-American Swan Olson had a gentle demeanor, but he told extremely violent stories. His neat, episodic shockers were based on personal experience and were all the more effective for the understated manner in which he told them. Burt Mayotte, a French Canadian, told with phrases that fell into a rhythmic beat.

Botkin is another folklorist who has included brief descriptions of American storytelling style in his various compilations. In the foreword to one of them, D. S. Freeman remarks:

> What may be said of the style of story-telling in the South?...There were artists in narration but art no more was universal in this than in any other form of human endeavor. Herein is disappointment because in the rural South there was time enough for perfecting any embellishment the narrator devised . . . but the regrettable fact stands: story-telling was not as artful as it should have been. It was too long-winded, and it had too much of the echo of the political platform. Spontaneity was lost in the polishing of paragraphs.[82]

Marie Campbell[83] and J. Frank Dobie[84] have also given word pictures of the styles of a number of regional United States storytellers.

Religious storytelling style seems to be characterized by earnestness and a moral seriousness that is only occasionally lightened by slight exaggerations or humor. This latter exception appears in some of the tales of the Jewish hasidim, which on occasion permit religious law to be parodied and the Rebbe to be turned into a comic figure.[85] There are, to be sure, parodies in regard to other religious groups, but they tend to be unacceptable to the authorities, or else they are simple anecdotes that only poke fun gently.

Library Styles

Library storytelling style generally tended to imitate that of bardic and folk storytellers. In the early days of library story hours, from approximately 1900 to 1920, there was a concentration on telling hero tales, long myths and legends, and prose versions of some of the epics. In such cases it was usually recommended that the children's librarian use a formal, rather serious style. The early reports of the Carnegie Library in Pittsburgh indicate that the purpose of storytelling then was less for entertainment and more for the purpose of introducing the classics to children who might otherwise not get to know them. Librarians in all of the branches generally had to follow a fixed series of programs: for example, in 1901, stories from Norse mythology and the *Nibelungenlied*; in 1902, legends of King Arthur; in 1903, legends of Charlemagne; in 1904, tales of Robin Hood, and so forth. The storyteller-librarians were "given a series of seven lectures on Homer for the purpose of arousing literary interest in the epics and serving as an inspiration."[86]

Such story hours were for children ten years and older. For the younger children, fairy tales, fables, and folktales were used. Most of the storytelling manuals and the courses in library schools recommended a natural style, one in which the teller felt at ease with the material. On the whole, dramatic gestures, excessive voice change, and histrionics were frowned upon. Stories that were from literary sources, such as Andersen, Kipling, and Farjeon, were to be memorized almost word for word and were considered far too complicated for the beginning storyteller.

In recent years there has been a "loosening up" of these strict rules. Many libraries have used folk storytellers from the community in regular programs. Strict standards of performance are no longer being demanded of the children's librarians, chiefly because they require far too much staff preparation time for the library to absorb. Some administrators believe this is the cause of declining attendance at story hours in their systems. And yet, the interest and range of styles that one can encounter in present-day children's libraries is very broad.

This is, in fact, true of all types of storytelling being practiced in the world today. It is alive and well, and has many different styles. The mass media have not entirely overwhelmed this ancient form of entertainment.

10

Musical Accompaniment

Many of the previous chapters have mentioned various kinds of storytelling that were accompanied by some form of musical instrument, or that used the voice or a part of the body as an instrument. This chapter will concentrate on the instruments themselves. Insofar as possible, any instrument known to accompany storytelling will be described in such a manner that the reader should be able to recognize each one when encountering it in a museum, in its place of origin, or in any other place. The instruments will be treated here in the commonly accepted groups of chordophones, idiophones, membranophones, and aerophones.

Chordophones

Chordophones include all stringed instruments that are plucked, struck, or bowed. Those that were used earliest for storytelling appear to be the plucked types, including the musical bow, the lyre, the harp, and the lute.

The musical bow is one of the oldest known examples of stringed instruments. It can be seen in prehistoric cave and rock paintings in North Africa that date back many thousands of years. The musical bow consists of a curved stick of wood, with a cord of string, leather, gut, fibre, or the like. One end rests on the ground during playing. Often a hollow gourd or calabash is attached and used as a resonator.

The musical bow is used in parts of Africa to accompany certain types of narrative poetry. Norris mentions that in Mauritania it is popular with children for practicing narrative singing as well as for performing.[1] A more complex type of African musical bow survives in Brazil, where it is called a *berimbao* or *berimbau*. It is used mostly to accompany a specific type of acrobatic, narrative dance, but there is also a historical, narrative quality to many of the songs that are performed with it.[2]

The bow-lute, also called the *pluriarc*, is actually a multiple musical bow, since it consists of a series of curved bows, each with its own string. They are attached to one sound box. The *akpata* used by professional narrators of Benin is a seven-stringed bow-lute. The *akpata* is quite old, for it appears in at least three Benin bronzes from the seventeenth century (for one example, Plate 20). It has rattlers or bells made from split palm seeds, discarded caps of bottles, or other bits of metal at the top of each bow (Plate 21). From these depictions, it would appear that the *akpata* had a ceremonial use, but that is not the case in modern times. In fact, the use of the *akpata* has rather somber symbolic overtones. There is a superstition that an *akpata* player who appears before the king to tell stories will die unless he breaks his instrument. The origin myths associated with the *akpata* are also rather doleful.[3]

Two ancient stringed instruments that are plucked are the harp and the lyre. The harp is generally distinguished from the lyre by the position of the strings. In a harp the strings are on a plane perpendicular to the sound box, attached to it and also to a curved or straight neck. In a lyre the strings are stretched from the sound box, and parallel to it, to a straight crosspiece held in place by two "arms" extending upward on either side of the lyre. Both kinds of instruments appear to have been used to accompany narrative singing and reciting from very ancient times on.

Lyres

A Sumerian lyre of Ur, dating back about 5,000 years, shows animals playing the lyre, eating, dancing, making merry, and behaving, in general, like humans. There are other similar scenes found in the art and artifacts of Ur. Frankfort theorizes that these scenes could have a bearing on some of the Sumerian and Greek fables and myths.[4] It is tantalizing to speculate whether this same lyre, now located in the University Museum, Pennsylvania (Philadelphia), was once used to accompany a singer who recounted animal tales similar to those in Aesop's fables.

The *kitharis* or *phorminx* mentioned so frequently in Homer is an early form of lyre. It is not definitely known if either or both of these were of the *lyra* type (bowl lyre) or the *kithara* type (box lyre, similar to those found in Ur). In Homer, the *kitharis* and *phorminx* are both associated with the *aoidos*, the poet-narrator. He used the instrument

PLATE 20 A Benin bronze from the seventeenth century showed an *akpata* player
(small figure, lower right). Photo courtesy of The British Library.

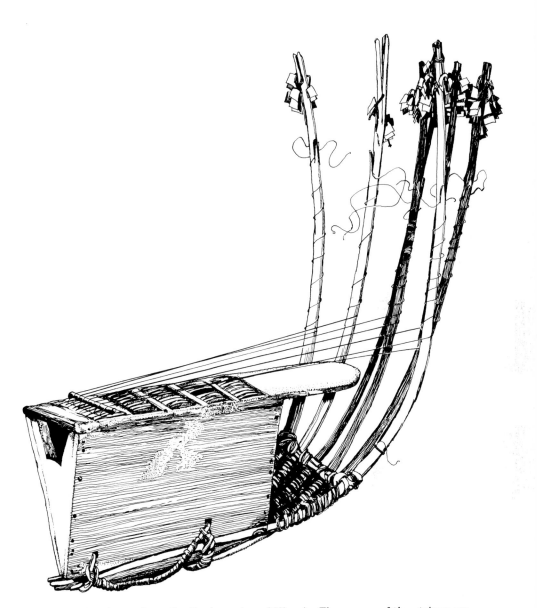

PLATE 21   An *akpata* from the Benin region of Nigeria. The names of the strings are
(from left to right): *ẹkhue*, "beginning" (uncertain), *ayere*, "memory,"
akugbe, "unity," *iye ema*, "mother drum," *ẹkhue*, "beginning," *ozi*, "strong
wind," *uke*, "small drum that men use." There are variations on this naming
system. Reproduced with permission from Dan Ben-Amos, *Sweet Words*
(Philadelphia: Institute for the Study of Human Issues, 1975).

to accompany his sung or chanted narrations that were recomposed spontaneously at each performance. Kirk expresses the belief that the natural accents in each Homeric hexameter line were further accented by a plucked note or chord on the *kitharis*. This was used to cover up any hesitation on the part of the composer-performer. Kirk concludes that it was precisely because the *rhapsode* did not change any of the text, but merely recited it, that the need for the musical accompaniment was lost. Therefore, the *rhapsode* used a staff for emphasis (see Plate 1) instead of a *kitharis* or other musical instrument.[5]

Thus, the musical instrument is very functional in the case of the poet-performer. It helps to fill gaps and cover hesitations, and allows the performer time to think of the next phrase. For the declaimer or reciter of already existing oral epic poems with fixed texts, such accompaniment would have been a hindrance; it would have slowed down the performance and taken away the use of the hands so that no dramatic gestures would be possible. Other scholars have suggested that the reason the musical accompaniment was dropped by the reciter-storytellers (*rhapsodes*) in Greece was because it could not be heard by large audiences.[6]

The only place where the lyre seems to have survived up to modern times as an accompaniment to storytelling is among the *kalêki* in Russia. They were wandering groups of performers of religious narrative poems (see Chapter 4). In the south and west of Russia, one member of each group generally carried a lyre to accompany its performances.[7]

Harps

The harp is one of the instruments most closely associated in the popular mind with storytelling. There are probably many cases where the term "harp" was used incorrectly, to describe lyres or lutes; just as there is reason to believe that terms for "lyres" were used when a harp was clearly the instrument in question. There is enough pictorial evidence to indicate that the harp was a favorite of narrators from ancient Egyptian times to the nineteenth century. These instruments seemed to be equally at home in the drawing room or the inn, the castle or the more humble hearth.

Teutonic, Anglo-Saxon, Norse, and Icelandic poets were known to have used musical instruments to accompany their narrative poetry. In *Beowulf*, for example, the instrument is called *gamenwudu* (play-wood) or *gleobeam* (mirth-tree), as well as *hearpe*.[8] It is usually mentioned in connection with the performance of the *scop* or *gleoman*. All these terms are invariably translated as "harp" in English versions of *Beowulf*. However, the term *harpa* generally meant a type of bowed lyre when used in Northern countries, so there is some question as to whether *hearpe* should refer to a harp or a lyre.

The first definite evidence of harps in Ireland dates to a period somewhere between the ninth and eleventh centuries. Carvings on stone crosses of that era show instruments that once were thought to be lyres but are now generally conceded to be harps because of the way they are shown as being held and played. From the eleventh century on, there are more pictorial examples, usually showing harps with an outward curve of the pillar. They had metal strings. The player rested the body of the harp against the left shoulder (see Plate 2). The left hand plucked the upper register and the right hand the lower. Usually the player had long fingernails used for the plucking. Most types of Irish bards probably used this kind of instrument in their performances.

The *telyn*, or Welsh harp, had horsehair or gut strings and more often a straight pillar rather than the curved, Irish type. But the harp served the same functions among the Welsh bards that it did among the Irish.

Harps are used in modern Africa as well as having been found there in ancient times. The *ardīn* is played only by females of Mauritania, of the bardic caste. This instrument is a harp with resonator made of half a calabash, covered with animal skin, and having ten to thirteen strings of gut, spaced out on the long, straight arm. In performance, the harp sound box is placed on the ground against the right leg, which is pressed close to the body. The handle rests against the left shoulder, and the left hand grasps it, while the right hand plucks the strings. Sometimes the *tīggiwīt* has partners who assist her by tapping on the skin of the sound box, so that there is percussion accompaniment as well. The narrators frequently do not do their own accompaniment, but perform facing the musicians. Norris has a very clear diagram of this unique type of harp.[9]

Lutes

Lutes, like lyres, have their strings parallel to the sound box. These strings pass along a neck, against which they are pressed by the player's one hand (to raise the pitch) while the other hand plucks, strikes, or bows (rubs) them over the sound box. There are short-necked lutes and long-necked ones.

There is also a harp-lute, with strings at right angles to the sound box. It is found only in West Africa. Among the Mande hunters' bards, it is called a *donso-nkoni*. This version has six strings and a calabash sound box. It takes the bard ten to fifteen years of apprenticeship to become a master of the *donso-nkoni* and of the narratives that are sung to it.[10]

Plucked lutes used for the enhancement of narration include the *tidīnīt*, played only by male Mauritanians of the *īggāwen* caste. The poet-narrator usually faces the musicians, which may include both male *tidīnīt* players and female *ardīn* players, as well as other instrumentalists. There are no objections to men and women participating in the same performance.[11]

The Japanese *samisen* is a form of lute. It was used by classical types of storytellers and later by *naniwabushi*, narrators of historical tales, who performed in public theaters.[12] An earlier form of Japanese lute was the *biwa*, a flat, short-necked lute used from the tenth to the fifteenth century by the *biwa-hoshi*. These were monks or persons in monks' clothing who wandered about singing songs or telling tales of war and folk heroes. The predecessor of the *biwa* was the Chinese *p'i p'a*, used by similar narrators in China.[13]

A single-stringed bowed lute is used by the Dagbon in Ghana. The body is made of calabash covered with taut skin, and the string is horse hair.[14] Chapter 13 summarizes the training of these musicians and how they perform in connection with oral narration.

A lute-like instrument resembling a guitar, called the *bandura*, was sometimes used by the *kalêki* of Russia. This instrument differed from the lyre already mentioned as being used by this itinerant type of religious narrator.[15]

Other Chordophones

Other chordophones used in different parts of the world as part of oral narrative sessions are the *dombra* and *balalaika*, the *saz*, the *gusle* and *gusli*, the *quyur*, the *rebab* and *amzad*, and various types of zithers and guitars.

The *dombra* was the forerunner of the *balalaika*, and the modern version still looks somewhat like the latter instrument. It was and is used in Russia and by the Kazakhs. Kazakh bards and ordinary persons use it to accentuate certain types of storytelling, especially to reproduce sounds of animals or nature that occur in the course of a story.[16]

The *balalaika* (as well as other stringed instruments) was used by some *byliny* singers in Russia, but not by those in Olonets, where the largest group of *byliny* singers was recorded and studied.[17]

Kazakh bards also use a *qobyz*, a two-stringed, bowed instrument with an alto pitch. The fingerboard curves upward, and thus the strings cannot be depressed to touch it. It is often adorned with bells and bits of metal that give off a tinkling sound during performances.[18]

The *saz* is a plucked, four-stringed instrument with a small body shaped rather like a pear and with a long neck. It is commonly played by minstrels in Turkey.[19] The *gusle* of Yugoslavia and the *gusli* of Russia are both used by narrators but are very different instruments. The *gusle* is a one-stringed instrument shaped somewhat like a ladle and played with a bow. It is the chief instrument of those who compose and perform oral epic narrative poems and can be likened in function to the *kitharis* of the Greek *aoidos*. However, Kirk believes that because the *gusle* is played by bowing this provides a continuous line of musical accompaniment, in contrast to the plucked *kitharis*. In his view, this results in a formulaic structure in the Yugoslav oral epics that is looser than that in the Homeric epics.[20] The *gusle* is called *lahuta* in Albanian.

The *gusli*, on the other hand, was a recumbent harp or psaltery, played on the lap. It once was used to accompany the singing of *byliny*, but in that form it became extinct some time ago. The modern folk version is different and not really related in function or form to the old *gusli*.[21]

The bowed chordophone used by Mongolian bards is called *quyur* or *quur*, or in Jarut, *hōr*. It is four-stringed. Its function appears to be similar to the *gusle*, since the Mongolian epic poems are also sung in a kind of rhythmic recitative, newly improvised with formulaic language at each performance.[22]

Spike fiddles are bowed instruments in which the arm or handle pierces the body or sound box and comes out the other side in a spike-like protuberance. Two types that are used to accompany storytelling are the *rebab* and the *amzad*. The *rebab* is among the instruments used by *penglipur lara* performers in Malaysia. These are oral folk romances usually known by the name of the hero or heroine who is the central character. Some performers in parts of Malaysia are so skilled and talented that they can make their living by these performances. Others perform only part-time or sporadically.[23]

The *amzad* is especially popular among the Tuareg, where it is most often played by women. The most frequent occasion for performance is at an *ahal*, a communal celebration of singing, oral recitation, and narration of various types. Generally, only unmarried men and women take part in an *ahal*.[24]

The *leqso*, used by the *azmaris* of Ethiopia, also appears to be similar to the spike fiddle. These professional poets and minstrels used instruments not only to accompany narration, but for all types of entertainment.[25]

The stick zither is a simple, straight stick to which is attached at either end a string, or possibly two. It usually has a gourd or calabash attached as a resonator. The *dakkalwars* of Maharashtra in India usually accompany their chanted myths with the *kingri*, a stick zither. During the recitation, they show their picture cloths on which are depicted episodes from the myths.[26]

Idiophones

An idiophone is any instrument that is made of material that vibrates and does not need a membrane, string, or reed to make it produce sound vibrations. Idiophones can be plucked, struck, shaken, scraped, or rubbed. There are relatively few idiophones used to accompany or accent storytelling.

Plucked idiophones are called linguaphones, and one type that is unique to Africa (and to parts of the Americas where Africans were dispersed) is the thumb-piano. This has almost as many names as there are languages in Africa. Not all types are used with oral narration. One important type that is used by professional narrators is the

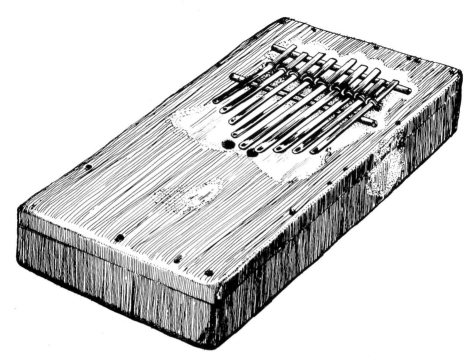

PLATE 22   An *asologun*. The names of the metal strips are (from left to right): 1 and 9, *ovbięho*, "a small voice, like that of a girl," 2–3 and 7–8, *enwanię*, "reply," 4–6 *ozi*, "strong wind." There are variations on this naming system. Reproduced with permission from Dan Ben-Amos, *Sweet Words* (Philadelphia: Institute for the Study of Human Issues, 1975).

asologun of the Benin region of Nigeria. It generally has nine la-mellae or strips made of metal or cane. Each lamella is tuned in a particular way and has a special name (Plate 22). The *asologun* is used to accompany oral narratives at an *okpobhię*, a communicative event to celebrate a rite of passage, a new social position or job, passing successfully through some danger, and similar events. One might assume that the *asologun* and its player thus had only a happy connotation, but this is not the case. The professional storytellers in Benin society have a socially marginal position and are merely tolerated, rather than having a distinct and honored position in society. The storytellers themselves consider their performances as psychological therapy, bringing release from unhappy and troublesome thoughts, but in an introverted fashion. Both the *akpata* (see the earlier part of this chapter) and the *asologun* are associated with evil spirits, so much so that they are banned in some parts of Benin.[27]

Central African groups seem to have happier associations with the thumb-piano. In Zambia, where it is used by boys and girls of the Tonga and Ila tribes to assist in composing and performing praise and story songs, the large type is called *kankobela* and the smaller type *ndandi.*[28] It is called an *mbira* by many of the Bantu-speaking peoples and is often used with narratives that are interspersed with songs and the playing of the instrument. Sometimes the sound box is made of a gourd or even of discarded sardine tins, but usually it is of wood. There are even some made of split cane (see Plate 32).

The Nyanga people of Zaire have an epic that is performed by bards who wear ankle bells and shake a rattle made from a dried gourd filled with seeds. Both can be considered idiophones of the shaken type. During their performances, three young men sometimes accompany parts of the epic on a struck idiophone, a kind of percussion stick resting on other sticks and beaten with drumsticks.[29]

Another form of struck idiophone is the *batil*, a brass bowl struck with the fingers and palms much like a drum. Some *penglipur lara* performers of Malaysia use this instrument to accent their storytelling.[30]

A scraped idiophone is found among the Mande hunters' bards. This is the *narinyo*, a ridged metal pipe scraped with a metal bar to provide the basic accompaniment and background rhythm of oral performances. The apprentice bards are the ones who must first master the use of the *narinyo* before going on to the *donso-nkoni*, described in the section on lutes.[31]

Membranophones

Membranophones are instruments in which sound is produced by striking, rubbing, or causing sound waves to hit a membrane or membrane-like material stretched over a frame or sound box. Three common types of membranophones are the tambourine, the drum, and the kazoo.

The drum is used extensively to accent or provide the rhythm of a performance of oral narrative, usually of the ceremonial type. Only a few examples will be mentioned here.

In the Dagbon area of Ghana, the court musicians and chroniclers use a closed drum of the hourglass shape, carved of wood and with skin covering both ends. For a description of the training involved in learning to play and perform with this instrument, see Chapter 13.[32]

In chanting *ijála*, the Yoruba of Nigeria like to have drum accompaniment provided by other musicians, and not by the chanter. The accompaniment is not necessary, however. Appropriate drums include the *dùndún*, a large hourglass drum, and many other types.[33]

A few of the *penglipur lara* performers in Malaysia use a *rebāna*, a frame drum shaped like a basin.[34] The wandering *areoi* performers of Tahiti used drum accompaniment of various kinds.[35]

Aerophones

Aerophones are instruments that produce sound by means of air vibrations. Not too many of these instruments have been used regularly in connection with storytelling. The Tahitian *areoi* mentioned in the paragraph above did use flutes as well as drums, but this was mostly for their danced narratives.[36] Winner mentions that the Kazakh bards of the past sometimes used a *čybyzga*. This was a primitive aerophone made of wood or leather.[37]

This chapter has by no means covered all the musical instruments associated in some way with storytelling. There are many places where there is a wide choice of music to accompany celebrations that include storytelling. For example, among the Nyanga of Zaire, drums, percussion sticks, horns, flutes, rattles, musical bows, zithers, thumb-pianos, and ankle bells have been and can be used.[38] This review has concentrated on those instruments known to have been used with some regularity in situations or events encompassing storytelling.

11

Pictures and Objects Used with Storytelling

While the majority of storytelling among the folk was and is accomplished without objects (other than musical instruments), there were and are important exceptions. This is especially true in the use of pictures to enhance the story or to sustain the audience's interest for at least part of it. The reports of some early experiments in North American schools and libraries with "picture" storytelling are often filled with the naive belief that they were trying something totally new. This was perhaps justified in view of the paucity of folkloristic or ethnographic research at that time concerning street storytelling in Europe and Asia.

An article in *Publishers' Weekly* in 1934, for example, describes the "new" technique of story hours with lantern slides devised by Julia Wagner and Ruth Koch after nine years of experimentation.[1] The method of projection may indeed have been new, but, in fact, Wagner and Koch were taking their places in a long line of picture storytellers, dating back to at least the Middle Ages. Another type of picture projection used with storytelling was the balopticon (Plate 23).

European Picture Scrolls and Sheets

In Europe the first evidence of narration accompanied by pictures appears to be in one of the *exultet* rolls, mentioned earlier in the chap-

PLATE 23 A storytelling hour at the Wylie Avenue branch of the Carnegie Library, Pittsburgh (1933), showing the use of a balopticon. Photo courtesy of Carnegie Library of Pittsburgh.

ter on religious storytelling (see Plate 14).[2] As was pointed out, although the text was usually the same, the various artists who illustrated the parchment rolls each selected different scenes to be emphasized and depicted. The roll illuminated in the eleventh century at the Abbey of Monte Casino, and now in the British Museum, has fourteen illustrations, each about a foot square. It begins with a figure of Christ, continues with two angels, and then shows a female figure personifying "Mother Church." Following this is a vivid portrayal of "Mother Earth," teeming with animal and vegetable life, and then scenes from episodes in the Old and New Testaments.

In his introduction to a set of plates reproducing the illuminations, Gilson writes: "The subdued tones of the olive-green and brown tints, and the dull pale gold, against which the blue and red of the principal figures stands out well, give a pleasing effect."[3]

Surely this must have provided fuel to fire the imaginations of many in the congregation, who probably had limited exposure to sequential visual story materials of such beauty and drama. For those children standing or seated close to the pulpit, it must have been an experience at least faintly resembling the picture-story hour of today, with its sequence of pictures on page or filmstrip, accompanied by the voice of the reader/narrator. It should be obvious that this experience would be quite different from the passive, introspective study of statues, altarpieces, mosaics, frescoes, or windows on view in the church, in which case the story would be provided partly by the artist and partly by the viewer, much the way a book stimulates a story only partly conceived by the writer and then completed by the reader.

It is just possible that these *exultet* rolls were the inspiration for the religious *bänkelsänger* that Brednich[4] and Schmidt,[5] among others, believe to have been the forerunners of the secular *bänkelsänger* (see Plate 15). Both of them have shown pictorial documentation for the sixteenth and seventeenth centuries that includes examples of religious and secular picture canvases separated into squares or rectangles so as to create a story by depicting a series of actions. The terms sometimes used for this are tessellated or tessellation.

Whether or not the *bänkelsänger* and his picture canvas stemmed directly from the earlier religious forms of picture storytelling, they probably were influenced by bardic or epic forms of narration, because the method of presentation was through song or chant. It must be remembered, however, that the *bänkelsänger* never achieved the status of the bard and often had to scrounge for a living by trying to collect coins for the performance itself, as well as through the sale of the cheap, printed versions of the ballads and stories they were singing.

Some of the *bänkelsänger* were regular employees of the printing companies whose wares were being sold. Others, perhaps the majority, were itinerants who had obviously developed some talent in presenting the stories in song, bought up supplies from various printers,[6]

PLATE 24   A picture sheet used by a German *bänkelsänger*. Photo courtesy of Fritz Nötzoldt.

made their own picture sheets (or possibly got a talented folk artist to do so), and then went on the road, stopping at towns on market days, when the crowds would be largest.

The technical term for these picture sheets is *schilder*.[7] In the paintings or etchings of the seventeenth through the nineteenth centuries in which *bänkelsänger* are depicted, the *schilder* appear to be either wood-block prints, copper engravings, or oil on canvas. These *schilder* are now extremely rare. The inexpensive ballad sheets, called broadsides in English and *flugblätter* in German, were printed in the hundreds of thousands, but they, too, are difficult to find today. It is no wonder, then, that the *schilder*, made in very few copies or in unique examples, are to be found in very few museums or in the hands of a few private collectors. Examples of nineteenth-century *schilder*, some printed and hand colored and others individually drawn and colored, are more common than those from previous centuries (Plate 24).

The picture sheets were large enough to be seen by a small crowd standing around and generally contained up to a dozen or so of the most dramatic scenes from the ballads or songs. A common size was roughly 1½ meters wide and 2 meters high. The example shown in Plate 24 depicts six scenes from the *moritatenlied* titled *Verstossen, oder der Tod auf den Schienen* ("Disowned, or Death on the Rails"). The text of this ballad is not extant but it obviously dealt with the love affair of a young girl, followed by her parents' rejection of this fact, their disowning of her, and her subsequent despair and suicide. The original is in color and measures about 1 meter by 1½ meters.[8]

Brednich points out that publishers were not the first to use large pictures and sticks or pointers for advertising their wares. Two examples among many that he cites are Hogarth's view of Southwark Fair and the church-fair scene of the Flemish *Imagerie Populaire*, both of which show the use of large picture sheets advertising various services or goods.[9] But it was in the *schilder* depicting story ballads that the specially displayed picture advertising sheet was most effective and long lasting.

That they had a powerful influence on the audience is attested to by many writers, among them Goethe. In his *Wilhelm Meister's Theatralische Sendung* he writes:

> The folk will be most strongly moved above all by that which is brought under their eyes. A daub of a painting or a childish woodcut will pull the attention of the unenlightened person much more than a detailed written description. And how many thousands are there who perceive only the fairy tale elements in the most splendid picture. The large pictures of the *bänkelsänger* impress themselves much deeper on the memory than their songs—although these also captivate the power of the imagination.
>
> Book 2, Chapter 5[10]

Their impact lasted until well into the twentieth century, as the text and photographs of Janda and Nötzoldt's *Die Moritat vom*

PLATE 25   Reproduction of a painting from the Kanora school, India, which is probably a
representation of Valmiki, teaching the meaning of the Vedas, or reciting
the text of the *Ramayana*, so that the young students can memorize it. New
York Public Library, Picture Collection.

Bänkelsang so clearly demonstrate.[11] Visitors to the Munich *Oktober-
fest* and to other similar yearly markets or festivals could still listen
and watch as the singer pointed his stick from picture to picture and
intoned the many verses of the ballads. But they were not able to
compete with films, and later radio. With the spread of these two
forms of mass media into all parts of Europe, the picture sheets of the
bänkelsänger disappeared from public view.

Earliest Uses of Pictures

A very early mention of the public exhibition of pictures, combined
with the recitation of a narrative, appears to be in a work called *Ma-
habhāṣya* (c. 140 B.C.) by Patañjali. In it, he refers to dramatic representations of the Krishna legend in pictures, pantomime, and words,
as performed by *śaubhikas*, or actors. There is quite a bit of disagreement among scholars about whether narration was involved.
The Indian scholar Coomaraswamy believes that it probably was.[12]
There are slightly later references to picture showmen, called *yamapaṭṭaka*, who showed scrolls on which there were series of pictures
representing legends. Some Brahmanical teachers were known to use
a portable frame on which they would have pictures drawn, showing
what would happen if one did this good deed or that evil one (Plate 25).
The later game of Snakes and Ladders probably developed from this.

These early forms of picture storytelling are the likely forerunners of modern Indian storytelling that employs pictorial devices. There is no readily accessible documentation to indicate how the practice was handed down from one era to the next. It is easier to find references to the ways in which this picture storytelling was carried by Buddhism to China and Java and other parts of East Asia than it is to find information on how such storytelling progressed in India. Chapter 4 reviewed the dramatic effect that Buddhist stories and pictures had on the Chinese, especially through the *pien-wen*.

It is known that picture storytelling made its way to Java also. A Chinese writer, Ying-yai Sheng-lan, wrote in 1416:

> There is a sort of men who paint on paper men, birds, animals, insects and so on; the paper is like a scroll and is fixed between two wooden rollers three feet high; at one side these rollers are level with the paper, whilst they protrude at the other side. The man squats down on the ground and places the picture before him, unrolling one part after the other and turning it towards the spectators, whilst in the native language and in a loud voice he gives an explanation of every part; the spectators sit around him and listen, laughing or crying according to what he tells them.[13]

This might have been the forerunner of the *wayang kulit*, the shadow-puppet play.

Picture Cloths in India

In India today there are narrators who use pictures, just as their ancient predecessors did. Unlike the *bänkelsänger*, the Indian bards have pictures on cloths that fold or roll up, rather than on paper or canvas sheets.

Among the types of storytelling cloths to be found today are the *kalamkari*, bard cloths of Madras and Andhra Pradesh; *pabuji kaa pat*, cloths from Rajasthan; Saurashtra temple cloths from Gujarat; and *badd* cloths used by the *dakkalwars* of Maharashtra.

The name *kalamkari* implies that the design is created by pen (Plate 26), but the process is really more complex than that. The Fergusons, who have observed the entire process in Andhra in South India, describe it thus:

> Essentially, the design is created by a master of the art who draws it on handspun-handloomed cotton cloth which has been bleached. Some of his design may be printed with clumsy-looking wooden printing blocks, and this is usually the case these days with the border designs. The details of the process are complex. Suffice it to say that the students of the master are responsible for filling his design with color. . . . But the heart of the *kalamkari* is the fresh design on each. . . . Thus, while to the untutored eye *kalamkaris* may seem to be alike, a few moments of study will show the individuality of each piece done by a single artist and his school. Different artists and schools create substantially different pieces. Yet all the themes and symbols are stylized and . . . the stories depicted are limited in number and quite familiar to all.[14]

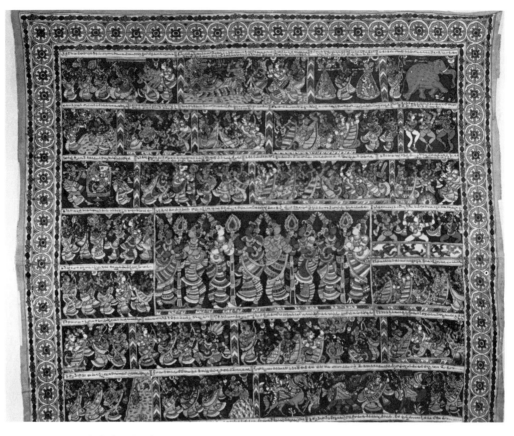

PLATE 26 A *kalamkari* storytelling cloth from Andhra Pradesh, India. Author's private collection.

The *pabuji kaa pat* are made by a completely different technique. *Pat* means scroll, and the *pabuji* are just that—large scrolls. They are generally about 1 meter high and from 2 to 4 meters in length. Traditional painters from Rajasthan, in the northwestern part of India, paint the pictures on canvas, using locally made colors, usually five. They paint episodes of the birth of the hero, his adventures, his marriage, his fight with the enemy, and his death, together with the death by self-immolation of his wife (Plate 27).[15]

The *mata ni pachedi*, already mentioned in the chapter on religious storytelling, comes from Saurashtra, a region of the state of Gujarat in western India. Just the preparation of the cloth for printing takes days, for it is boiled twice, buried once, soaked and rinsed many times, and dried in the sun. When it is finally received by the printer, it is a pale yellow. The printer applies the design by hand, using carved wooden blocks and a thick black ink. The sons or apprentices then fill in with various compounds the areas that will be red or black. After boiling, rinsing, blueing, and bleaching in the sun, the cloth is ready to be used in the religious ceremony. There are two standard sizes for

PLATE 27   Illustration of a *pabuji kaa pat* storytelling cloth from Rajasthan, India. Photo courtesy of InterCulture Associates, Thompson, Connecticut.

PLATE 28   Illustration from an educational pamphlet instructing how to use the *kami-shibai*. Reproduced with permission of the editors of *Kamishibai*, Tokyo.

the *mata ni pachedi*: a 6-foot square cloth used for a ceiling over a small temple or area of worship; and a rectangular cloth 3½ or 4½ feet high and 6 feet long. The finished cloths are all red, black, and white.[16]

No sample of the *badd* cloths could be obtained, but from the brief written description available, they would appear to be similar to the *kalamkari*.[17]

Kamishibai Picture Cards

The *kamishibai* of Japan, described earlier in the chapter on folk storytelling, also utilized pictures as a come-on, only in this case the articles being sold were candies or, in rare cases, books or medals showing popular heroes. The children who bought something were allowed to stay and listen to the story or stories and watch the pictures.[18]

The wooden holder for the *kamishibai* picture sheets was generally about 1 foot high and about 18 inches wide. On the top was a handle for carrying (see Plate 11). The front had flaps that opened out like a triptych or miniature stage. These wooden frames were produced by carpenters who specialized in building temples or altars, and each player bought his own, sometimes after arranging for a special design or adaptation.[19]

The picture cards were usually printed in color and contained the highlights of scenes from the stories. Some sets of hand-painted pictures can be found, but most were printed and sold for the express use of the *kamishibai*. In 1937 there were some sixteen of these publishers in Tokyo, and most of them reinstated their wares after the war.[20]

There were usually from 6 to 20 cards in a set, and these fitted into a slot on the side of the wooden carrier (Plate 28). The teller could see the text relating to the picture being shown, because it was printed on the back of the card preceding it. In other words, when the first picture card, which was usually a title card, was pulled out from the front position and slid into the back position, the text shown on the back of it related to the second picture card.

Considering the impact that the *kamishibai* had on children's literature and the fact that the same publishers who produced the cards were also later producing children's books, it is no wonder that one of the most popular formats for children's picture books in Japan is the horizontal style reminiscent of the *kamishibai*.

Picture Books

The picture-book story hour in libraries probably began soon after the regular story hours, at least in a few libraries. Yet there is little evidence that it was scheduled regularly prior to the Second World War. Professional journals make no mention of a "Picture Book Story Hour" before 1949. There are a few articles on the preschool story hour in the 1940s, but they still refer essentially to orally narrated stories unaccompanied by pictures. In one of them the librarian specifically mentioned that showing the pictures while telling or reading the story was attempted but proved unsatisfactory, and she concluded: "We have found it better to show the pictures after the story has been told."[21] This was probably an echo of the advice given in the most widely used storytelling manual of the time, *The Art of the Storyteller* by Marie Shedlock. In her first chapter, "The Difficulties of the Story," she states most clearly in Point 6:

> After long experience, and after considering the effect produced on children when pictures are shown to them during the narration, I have come to the conclusion that the appeal to the eye and the ear at the same time is of doubtful value, and has, generally speaking, a distracting effect. . . .[22]

However, internal reports in the New York Public Library indicated that in 1910 "there were 1,133 story hours including the extra story hours, *informal picture book hours* [author's italics], and story hour sessions held in connection with the playground association."[23] It was not until Eulalie Steinmetz became supervisor of storytelling (1945–1953) that the story-hour sessions were divided into two distinct types:

1. Story Hour for boys and girls third grade and above
2. Picture-Book Hour for those below the third grade[24]

The earliest article describing actual picture books and how they were used in a story hour appears in *Library Journal* and was written by Florence Sanborn. In it she suggests the use of picture books as a "vehicle for the hesitant, new storyteller to gain confidence." Since she gives explicit instructions on how to hold the book, turn the pages, and so forth, it would appear that she was writing about a new approach to library storytelling. Nowhere in the article does she suggest, though, that an entire story hour could be made up of picture storybooks.[25]

Such a suggestion is made in a little pamphlet written by F. Marie Foster and published by the Division of Adult Education and Library Extension of the New York State Education Department, some time in the mid-1940s. Foster recommended a short "picture book program" of from 20 to 25 minutes in length, and actually described (in text and photos) the kind of physical location needed, the manner of holding the picture book, the arrangement of the chairs, and many other factors. One of the main reasons she cites for such a program is that it "gives the librarian a real opportunity to see children's reactions to the books so carefully selected" for the public library children's room.[26]

In another article in *Library Journal* some years later, Adeline Corrigan implies by her title, "The Next Step—the Picture Book Hour," that this was not a widely scheduled practice in the public library. She does refer to the fact that children have enjoyed stories through pictures for hundreds of years. But she states that it is because of the recent increase in large picture books, clearly visible and understandable when shown to a group, that one can now have a picture-book hour as a regular storytelling session for groups of children.[27]

Obviously the publishers were listening and reading. The number of picture storybooks with illustrations selected, not for family or individual reading, but for their ability to stand out and be seen when held up in front of a group began to increase dramatically. The lavishly illustrated picture book had become too expensive for most individual buyers. In the institutional buyer, the publisher had a much steadier market for well-produced picture books.

Librarians adopted this new type of story hour very quickly once they discovered it and saw the steady stream of books being published to suit the programs. Also, they became much more adept at reviewing and criticizing the new picture books, not necessarily from an artistic point of view, but rather from the point of view of the library picture-book storyteller. To work well and hold the attention of a group of children already visually stimulated by films and television, the stories had to be very strong, with no unnecessary text. The pictures needed to strike a balance between showing too much and too little, and the most successful artists were clever and careful in building up suspense and surprise, just as the text did.

The more librarians used picture books successfully in the story hour, the more they realized how much easier this kind of program was, in relation to the long and difficult-to-learn tales they were expected to prepare for the regular story hour. The more the story hour came to be associated with picture books, the more the older children stayed away, believing such things were for "babies." By the mid-1960s, a familiar lament was voiced, exemplified by this statement by a children's librarian of the Toronto Public Library:

Almost all the librarians I have talked to report the same thing. Some of the enthusiasm has gone and what is more the older boys and girls have gone. Imperceptibly, week by week, their numbers dwindle until the librarian faces, on a Saturday morning, a sea of very young faces: little children who want *The Three Bears*, not the *Three Men of Power* and who thrill to the exploits of Mike Mulligan rather than Grettir the Strong.[28]

Beginning in the 1950s one can find in the professional reviews of children's picture books more and more frequent comments about the usefulness of the book in story hours, or, conversely, negative remarks about how difficult the pictures will be to see or how unnecessarily long the text is, making its use in the picture-book story hour limited. The reviewers were, for the most part, children's librarians who were reflecting their storytelling needs. It was not surprising, therefore, that in response to these reviews, an increasing number of trade picture books were published in the United States after World War II of the type suited to presentation in a group situation. They can almost invariably be differentiated from the European picture books of the same period, most of which have much greater detail in both text and illustration.

The picture-book hour (also called the preschool hour) is now an established routine in most public libraries in the United States, Canada, Great Britain, Australia, New Zealand, and the Scandinavian countries. Even continental European public libraries, slower in their development, now have this activity in many places. Well-developed public library systems in such places as Singapore and Japan also maintain the picture-book hour as a regular program.[29]

String Figures and Other Objects

Figurative drawings or art in a sequence are not the only ways to picture the main characters and events in a story. A much more abstract method can be found in the sequential sets of string figures commonly found in parts of Asia, the Pacific, and Africa.

Hornell discovered that a large number of the Fijian string games were originally meant to be worked out to the accompaniment of a chant. A year later Dickey recorded his researches in Hawaii and also found so many of the figures accompanied by chants that he suggested they might all originally have been devised as *aides memoires* to help keep alive the oral traditions of the people. His surmises were based mostly on the fact that the allusions in the chants were to legend and myth and to well-known stories. "Some of them," he stated, "are short extracts, many of them changed, from long, famous chants."[30]

In the December 1949 issue of *National Geographic*, an Australian aborigine, Narau, is shown in a photograph, composing string figures. The caption indicates that he "can tell 200 legends with a single strand of string."[31]

Lindblom found the same type of suggestive evidence in Africa that Dickey found in Hawaii, namely, that phrases with allusions to myths or tales were often said or sung during the formation of the figures.[32] The Leakeys, archeologists, while on a trip to Angola, were intrigued by the great number of string figures there. They wrote:

> One of the most interesting features of our brief study was the fact that in a number of cases the Tuchokwe natives of N.E. Angola have "serial" figures in which the successive stages seem to represent the illustrations of a story.[33]

Other objects are or have been used to accent storytelling style. The Japanese storytellers of the *yose* used a fan, called either *hakusen* (ringworm) or *kaze* (wind) in their jargon because of the sounds or actions it could simulate. A good storyteller is known for the distinctive ways in which he uses this fan, achieving sounds of great subtlety and effectiveness.[34]

The Chinese storyteller in the *shu-ch'ang*, the equivalent of the *yose*, similarly used a prop, a block of wood called *hsing-mu*. It, too, was introduced with great finesse and, when hit against a table properly, each time produced a different sound.[35]

For the Lepchas of Sikkim, everything in a story should be described minutely and precisely. They like to make their stories and descriptions clearer and more concrete by employing twigs or pebbles to represent the peoples and things described.[36]

Crowley mentions this same characteristic as being prevalent among Bahamian tellers. He noticed that quite a number reached out and spontaneously used props from their immediate environment (such as a pen, a shirt, a cockroach, and other objects) to represent human or animal characters, or some object important to their story.[37]

The Russian *skomorokhi* of the seventeenth century were described by a number of contemporaneous writers as wearing masks.[38] There does not seem to be any other reference to this custom among storytellers in other parts of the world, with the possible exception of *penglipur lara* performers in Malaysia.[39] The mask was generally used more as a theatrical device than as an aid to oral narration. The *skomorokhi* were definitely storytellers and not actors. There are no specific descriptions as to exactly the manner in which they used the masks in storytelling, or whether they used them only to disguise themselves as they went from place to place. They were the favorite targets of imitation. A number of *byliny* depict how one famous hero or another, disguised as a *skomorokh*, goes to a party or visits a court.[40]

Although the *skomorokhi* can be classed as bardic storytellers as the term is defined in this book, on the whole the bardic form of storytelling is much more formal than their style implied. The *shékárisi* of the Congo region are much more representative of this style in their use of objects. They consider it appropriate to occasionally hold a representation of one of the favorite symbols of the heroes of the epics they recount. During the Mwindo epic, this might be a conga scepter, since that is the major magical device that the hero uses in the epic.[41] For the bards of the ancient kingdom of Abomey, it was a spear, a baton, or a fly whisk that was used during the narration of the chronicles and epics.[42] The *omwevugi*, or bard, of the Bahima of Ankole (Uganda) also used a spear while reciting. It was held horizontally or planted in the ground.[43]

All of the above reinforce the notion that the use of the scepter conferred authority, even in very ancient times. The Greek *rhapsode*, however, used a staff, called a *rhabdos*, that more likely was originally a traveler's walking stick. It probably became associated in the public mind with this performer and thus began to be used as one of his symbols and prerogatives (see Plate 1).[44]

12

Closing of the Story Session

The closings to storytelling are, more often than not, determined by the type of story told. For *märchen*, we are most familiar with the satisfying "they lived happily ever after." This has many variations and expansions. Sometimes, it may be in rhyme:

> And soon was given to him a son and heir
> And they all lived happily without a care.
> > Luigi Capuana, *C'era una volta*,
> > Trans. from the Italian by Anne MacDonnell

> They had their wish fulfilled.
> Let's go up and sit in their seats.
> > Trans. from the Turkish by Barbara Walker[1]

Sometimes it describes the wedding of the protagonists in highly exaggerated terms:

> The marriage lasted nine days and nine nights. There were nine hundred fiddlers, nine hundred fluters, and nine hundred pipers, and the last day and night of the wedding were better than the rest.
> > Seumas MacManus, *Donegal Fairy Book*

> I was there too, but no one had time to think of me. All I got was a slice of cake with butter on it. I put it on the stove
> > And the cake did burn
> > And the butter did run
> > And I got back
> > Not a single crumb.
> > > Reidar Th. Christiansen, *Folktales of Norway*

So they looked for priest and bishop
Fresh potatoes, corn and peas.
Those who didn't come by wagon,
Made the trip in burlap bags.
                    Yolando Pino-Saavedra, *Folktales of Chile*

Humorous folktales often end with a catchy rhyme:

They lived in peace, they died in peace
And they were buried in a pot of candle-grease.

E lo ben
My story is end

Billy ben
My story end
                    All three found in the Bahamas[2]

I step on a thing, the thing bend,
My story is end.
                    Sea Islands of South Carolina[3]

I passed through a mouse hole
And my story is whole.
                    From the Languedoc area, France[4]

And then I leapt into a saddle and rode high and low
To tell others this story of wonder and woe.
                    Fairy Tales and Legends from Romania,
                    Trans. by Ioana Sturdza

Among some peoples, stories end with a rhyme or phrase that is not
necessarily nonsense and yet does not have any particular meaning,
although it may have had at one time. An example from the Thonga of
South Africa goes like this:

Tju-tju; famba ka Gwamba ni Dzabana.
(Run away; go to Gwamba and Dzabana) [which may refer to the first
man and woman, but this is speculative].
                    Henri A. Junod, *The Life of a South African Tribe*

Or the ending may be one terse word or phrase, a dramatic way of
indicating that "this is the end."

Kungurus kan kusu. (The rat's head is off.)
                    Frank Edgar, *Hausa Tales and Traditions*

Suka zona. (They remained.)
                    A. J. N. Tremearne, *Hausa Superstitions and Customs*

Dondo harai. (With this, it's sold out.)
                    Seki, *Folktales of Japan*

Mahezu. (Finished.)
                    Heli Chatelain, *Folktales of Angola*

Kiruskidits. (Untranslatable. The word is also used for the action of
drawing up the strings of a tobacco pouch.)
                    M. W. Beckwith, *Mandan-Hidatsa Myths and Ceremonies*

Le coq chanta et le conte fut fini. (The cock crowed and the tale was
ended.)
                    G. Massignon, *Folktales of France*

Among the Clackamas, as Jacobs reports, many stories closed with an epilogue that described the metamorphosis of the storyteller into an animal, fish, or bird, but the final brief phrase that ended the performance was always the same, and meant either "Myth, myth" or "Story, story."[5]

Among the longer endings are the "runs" common among Gaelic storytellers:

> It was long ago, and a long time ago it was.
> If I were alive then, I wouldn't be alive
> now. If I were, I would have a new story
> or an old one, or I mightn't have any story!
> Or I might have lost only my back teeth
> or my front teeth or the furthest back
> tooth in my mouth!
>
> Sean O'Sullivan, *The Folklore of Ireland*

Sometimes these longer endings are almost stories in their own right, as in the following examples:

> Thus my story ends,
> The Natiya-thorn withers.
> "Why, O Natiya-thorn, do you wither?"
> "Why does the cow on me browse?"
> "Why, O cow, do you browse?"
> "Why does the shepherd not tend me?"
> "Why, O shepherd, do you not tend the cow?"
> "Why does the daughter-in-law not give me rice?"
> "Why, O daughter-in-law do you not give the cow rice?"
> "Why does my child cry?"
> "Why, O child, do you cry?"
> "Why does the ant bite me?"
> "Why, O ant, do you bite?"
> Koot! Koot! Koot!
>
> Lal Behari Day, *Folk-tales of Bengal*

> I was there but they kicked me out, so I went to the stables and chose a steed with a golden saddle. His body was of steel, the legs of wax, the tail of tow, the head was a cabbage and the eyes two corn cockle seeds. I rode up a silex hill and the horse's tail began to melt, the tail to break and the eyes to pop. I rode astride a big blue fly and told you all a clever lie. I rode astride a ringing bell and told you all I had to tell.
>
> *Fairy Tales and Legends from Romania*,
> Trans. by Ioana Sturdza

> Were it not on account of the spider
> I should have greatly lied.
> As it is I have told an untruth.
> This lie is lucky for
> tomorrow morning when I arise from sleep,
> I will obtain a money-bag full of money
> behind my hut.
> A pile of silver

the spider has placed there.
If I do not get a money-bag
I shall at least get a bitter gourd.
A. J. N. Tremearne, Hausa Superstitions and Customs

Tremearne does not say so, but one wonders if the storyteller did not use this as a device to hint that payment by the audience was a hoped-for response.

Payment for Stories

Such a hint at recompense of some sort can be found in quite a number of tale conclusions:

There's my story, it isn't very long.
If it isn't worth a penny, it's maybe worth a song.
Anne MacDonnell, The Italian Fairy Book

It's not to drink beer! It's not to brew wine!
They were wedded and whirled away to love.
Daily they lived and richer grew.
I dropped in to visit, right welcome they made me.
Wine runs on my lips, nary a drop in my mouth!
Y. M. Sokolov, Russian Folklore

I came here and saw men quarreling and as I went to calm them one of them made for me at once and hit me hard, and as I cried out he took a bit of meat and put it in my hand, and I brought it and placed it on top of the doorway here; child, go and fetch it.
E. E. Evans-Pritchard, The Zande Trickster

This is meant to be a joke or trick, of course, and often if a child in the audience does not catch on, he or she may go to fetch it. This is meant as a device for concluding the tale decisively before beginning another. However, there could still be some hint of reward implied in the ending.

Three apples fell from heaven: one for the storyteller, one for he who listens, and one for he who understands.
Leon Surmelian, Apples of Immortality;
Folktales of Armenia

It is interesting to note that this last ending changed somewhat when the Armenians emigrated to the United States. Among the Detroit community of Armenians, the commonly heard ending is:

From the sky fell three apples: one to me, one to the storyteller and one to the person who has entertained you.
Susie Hoogasian-Villa, 100 Armenian Tales

Passing of Turn to Another Teller

In certain parts of the world, it is customary for the storyteller to add a kind of mock-serious disclaimer for the "lies" or exaggerations that have appeared. For example, Delargy reports that many Gaelic stories ended thus:

> That is my story! If there be a lie in it, be it so! It is not I who made or invented it![6]

Megas reports the following as an occasional ending for Greek folktales in the past:

> Neither was I there, nor need you believe it.[7]

From the Bahamas comes this blithe acknowledgment of untruth:

> Chase the rooster and catch the hen
> I'll never tell a lie like that again.[8]

In Polynesia, the exaggeration is eliminated or softened, and the disclaimer might be:

> Just a tale that people tell.[9]

In Japan, the teller tries to convince the audience that it is not necessarily his telling of the tale that makes it true or untrue by ending thus:

> No matter whether it is told or not, that is the way it happened.[10]

Occasionally, a final rhyme, phrase, or sentence will suggest that the storyteller has finished and now passes on the turn for telling to another:

> *Y entro por un caño roto y salgo por otro*
> *y quiero que me cuentes otro.*
>
> I enter through a broken pipe and leave through another
> And now I want you to tell me another.
> Howard T. Wheeler, Tales from Jalisco Mexico

> *Fola foletta, dite a vostra;*
> *a mea è detta.*
>
> Fable, little fable, tell yours;
> mine is told.
> G. Massignon, Folktales of France (Corsican)

> This story will have to do,
> For it went through a broken shoe,
> And came out in a little bean stalk
> So _____ can take up the talk.
> Yolando Pino-Saavedra, Folktales of Chile

According to Parsons, in the past the Taos Indians had a much more physical way of indicating whose turn it was next to tell a tale.

> As it grew toward daybreak if somebody was in the middle of a story, any one present who knew how would say, "Let's make him *lamopölu'na*." Then they spread a blanket on the floor, put him in it and bundled him up, tying him in. Four or five would carry him out to the refuse heap, the heap of the dead, and roll him down. If he could free himself and catch

somebody, that one in turn would be bundled down a slope, and the others would all run back to the house. While taking the "bundle" out from the house they had a song to sing which they kept up until they got to the refuse heap. [The song translates roughly as] "Deer hair bundle, pumpkin seed carving." [The concluding word is always] *"Kǫiw'ekima"* (You have a tail) or *"Tenkkǫiwe'ękim"* (So then, you have a tail).[11]

This is directed to the one whose turn is next and means that he must tell a story to take the tail off, so it won't freeze. The humor resulting from the homonym tail-tale in the English translation probably fits right into the spirit of the occasion!

If there has been a truly evil person in the folktale, sometimes the happy end is followed by the meting out of punishments:

> They were tied to the tails of wild jackasses who were whipped and driven over mountainous trails: the largest piece they found later was only an ear.
>
> Susie Hoogasian-Villa, *100 Armenian Tales*

> At once her brothers and her friends drew their swords and cut Mr. Fox into a thousand pieces.
>
> Joseph Jacobs, *English Folk and Fairy Tales*

> "Now, what doom does such an one deserve?"
>
> "No better than this," answered the false bride, "that she be put naked into a cask, studded inside with sharp nails, and be dragged along in it by two white horses from street to street, until she be dead."
>
> "Thou hast spoken thy own doom," said the old King; "as thou hast said, so shall it be done."
>
> Jakob and Wilhelm Grimm, *Household Stories*,
> Trans. by Lucy Crane

Among the Fōn people of Dahomey, the fairly standard ending for the folktale has a mysterious air of half threat, half joke:

> The words I told, which you have now heard, tomorrow you will hear a bird tell them to you.
>
> *or*
>
> Tomorrow morning you will hear the same story told you by a bird, but you had better not listen. If you hear it told by a bird, you will die.[12]

Other Closing Devices

After the last story was completed, most sessions came to an end. Sometimes this happened when all of the listeners had gone to sleep and no longer responded with their periodic expressions of assent and approval. In such cases the narrator, too, usually turned over and went to sleep. This custom is reported on the Indian subcontinent, among Native American groups, and in the Pacific Islands.[13]

Other sessions required a ceremony after storytelling. The Cowlitz, Native Americans of the western Washington region, often made their children take a swim after storytelling.[14] The Jicarilla Apache had different customs. After a night of storytelling they would all paint their faces with red ochre, even the children, and then leave this on through the next day as a sign that they had participated in the wisdom of the tribe. Sometimes the storyteller was required to give gifts to the listeners on the principle that a night had been "stolen" from them.[15]

The ceremonial ending for story hours in many public libraries is blowing out the candle that was lighted at the start. Some storytellers use a rhyme in which all the children are told to make a wish. Others simply have one child blow out the candle, to indicate it is time to file out of the story-hour room.

IV

The Training of Storytellers

13

A Brief History
of Training Methods

Storytellers in the past and in the present have received their training in one of five ways:

1. Through inherited office.
2. Through apprenticeship arranged by a guild or other professional group.
3. Through apprenticeship on an individually arranged basis.
4. At a school, university, or other formal institutional course.
5. By means of informal imitative learning from other narrators at home, in the community, or through books.

Storytelling is dependent on personality as well as on intelligence and experience. This would seem to make it a profession that is not too well suited to being passed on through inheritance. The storytellers whose positions tended to be rigorously limited to offspring or close relatives were those who were noted as bardic reciters of oral narratives that were not supposed to be changed. In other words, they were more historians than storytellers.

Inherited Positions

The earliest mentions of inherited positions in storytelling are in Chinese, Irish, and Welsh. In Chinese, the first record of storytelling schools appears in 1235. The tellers were called *chüan*, and invariably if the sons or daughters showed any talent or inclination toward the profession, they began their apprenticeship while still very young. One little girl of six, the granddaughter of a master storyteller, was entered formally into training at that age because "she was of a lively temperament, had large and expressive eyes, a strong voice and clear enunciation."[1]

The guilds were responsible for the entire training process, which could last several years. It consisted of stages very similar to the modern storytelling schools in the Japanese *yose*. We will return to these later. Suffice it to say that in the end, the social standing of the professional storyteller in medieval China was somewhat higher than that of the actor.

For the Irish and Welsh, the bards that we know most about are the *fili*, *ollam*, and *pencerdd*. The Chadwicks cite sources that seem to indicate there was a tendency for these professions to become hereditary.[2] Corkery agrees with this. It was, he writes, "a profession that was hereditary, a rich, strongly-organised caste, an over-elaborated catechism of art." His description of the bardic schools does not cite any contemporaneous sources, but it agrees with those found in Toland and other writers:

> It is not probable that we shall ever discover the origins of the bardic schools.... They were ancient when St. Patrick came amongst us.... When the schools did at last become Christian they did not become monastic; and they are not to be confused with the famous monastic schools. The Bardic Schools were lay, officered by laymen.... The Studies of the students were chiefly: history, law, language, literature.[3]

In the second tract on poetry in the Book of Ballymote, dating to the eighth or ninth century, there are a number of passages relating to the training of bards, *filid*, and *ollam*. Depending on the rank or grade, training lasted seven, ten, or twelve years and consisted of learning many sagas, the composition and recitation of all types of poetry, and oral lore of all kinds.[4] Obviously, when their ranks began to be filled entirely through inheritance, the bardic schools began to produce those who could write academic poetry but were probably more interested in maintaining their rank and privileges in society. This was bound to cause a decline in the quality of performance, for as Corkery remarks, "in art who does not fear privilege and organisation?"[5] The hereditary bard in Ireland and Wales died out, and the folk storyteller lived on.

There are still hereditary bards today in Africa. They are known under such terms as *diaré, gawlo, gêwel, griot, īggīw, lunga, mugani wa lugano, shékárịsị,* and *tīggiwīt*. The blood relationship is sometimes strictly insisted upon; in other cases, it is loosely interpreted.

One of the stricter groups practicing hereditary bardship is the Dagbon in northeastern Ghana. In *Growing Up in Dagbon*, Christine Oppong translates the term *lunga (lunsi)* as drummer(s), as indeed

they are. But they are also the chroniclers of the past and the record-
ers of the present. "They play an important part in all rituals involving royals including those performed at installation, naming and
funeral ceremonies. The unbroken historical narrative and royal
genealogy which they remember and recite is the charter of the political structure of the kingdom, and the story of the origins of the
people."[6] In short, they are bards, as we are defining the term in this
book.

The social and cultural constraints requiring the Dagbon child
whose father is a drummer to be, in turn, a drummer are very great:

> He is compelled to assume the role at least in the nominal sense, while
> drummers' daughters, since they are not eligible to assume the role
> themselves, must give at least one of their offspring to replace them in
> the next generation. On the other hand strong sanctions also operate to
> prevent those unrelated to drummers from playing. Thus a drummer's
> sons stay at home to be taught by their father or are taught to play by a
> brother or father's brother. It is considered unthinkable for a drum-
> mer's son to stay in his father's house and not learn to play. Should he
> object very violently to learning his father's profession, however, then
> he may go to live elsewhere, escape by running away, and no evil should
> befall him so long as he always keeps his drum and plays it symbolically
> on Mondays and Fridays. But if a son learns when small and later goes
> south without taking his drum then it is said misfortune and even death
> will pursue him. Difficult as it is for drummers' sons to escape becoming
> drummers, when they grow up, it is still more difficult for a daughter's
> son to escape learning, for he must replace his mother. The particular
> child who is to represent his mother and siblings with his maternal kin is
> chosen by divination and then "adopted" by his mother's brother or ma-
> ternal grandfather.... Even on the day that a drummer's daughter is
> married her husband is told that one day one of their offspring will be
> claimed for this purpose. It is usually after a daughter has born one or
> two children that one is taken at the age of four or five.... Should a
> drummer's daughter only bear female children then she must send a
> daughter who will later be given in marriage to a drummer, or to anoth-
> er man on the understanding that one of her sons will be given to learn
> to play. Thus it is a strongly sanctioned rule that any drummer's daugh-
> ter, wherever she is, must send a child back to her natal family, other-
> wise illness and death ... will visit her children, in the form of insanity,
> leprosy or other misfortune.[7]

To learn the massive body of oral material is an arduous and pains-
taking task. The young pupils learn to drum and to recite narratives
and genealogies. The length of time it takes to become a good performer depends on the ability of the individual child.

> Learning is thought to be a very difficult process accompanied by ear-
> pinching and pulling and beating from the teacher. Wisdom is consid-
> ered very hard to acquire. A typical teaching situation is for the teacher
> to recline in his entrance hall after supper in the evening, while the chil-
> dren gather round him, sitting and kneeling upon the floor. On one occa-
> sion witnessed, the teacher was rhythmically massaged by his eight

pupils. While they sang songs they rocked back and forth rubbing their teacher's legs and backs as they sang.... The senior and most competent pupil sang the leading phrases which were repeated in unison by the rest, without drum accompaniment.[8]

Oppong also describes the training of children who become "fiddlers." That is, they play a single-stranded bowed lute, made of calabash covered with a taut skin, and at the same time they sing praises for their patrons:

A child can begin to learn to play the fiddle when he is quite small, about five or six years old. The first step is simply to learn to move the bow up and down while sitting next to the father or other teacher, who performs the finger movements with his left hand. Words and music are always learnt simultaneously, so that if the player does not sing aloud while he plays he tends unconsciously to mouth the words at the same time. As in the case of drummers, talents differ so that while one has a good memory for songs and praises, another has a sweet voice and a third may be a skillful player. Some boys born into fiddlers' families are said to be able to play in a matter of months, while another takes years to become a mediocre performer. For example one boy, Abu, was sent to his mother's older brother for training at about twelve, because he was misbehaving at home and had refused to stay with his father. He learnt to play with considerable competence in a mere five months, his performance being better than that of many pupils after three years' training. A boy practises playing at any time when he is free and if his father or teacher is at hand and hears him playing badly he will call him and demonstrate the correct way. By the age of nine or ten a boy with aptitude may be quite a competent player and be called by neighboring musicians to accompany them to play at celebrations in neighboring villages, as well as going to play with his father or teacher.[9]

This position of fiddler is also hereditary, but it does not carry with it the extreme obligatory force that the drummer's position has. Most sons do learn to play, and daughters are expected to learn to play rattle accompaniments. As in the case of the drummers, one of the daughter's sons is expected to learn the art, but it is much easier for the boy who does not wish to play to escape his responsibility without retribution.[10] Unfortunately, we do not know which of these two types (if either) can be considered the equivalent of the other main classes of West African bards, especially the *griot* or *īggīw*.

The bard commonly known by the term *griot* is also trained by inheritance. Some of the names for this bardic group in different parts of West Africa are *gêwel* in Wolof (Senegal), *diaré* in Soninké (Senegal), *gawlo* in Toucouleur (Mauritania), and *īggīw* or *tīggiwīt* in Shinqiti (Mauritania). Norris is the only writer so far to have described the training of this type of bard, albeit sketchily.[11] Most of these bards accompany themselves on a musical instrument.

The art of playing both these instruments requires years of training and instruction, and it is not uncommon to find miniature models of both instruments in the houses and tents of the *īggāwen*. Their sole purpose is to instruct children in the technique of the instruments they are learning to play.[12]

Since most of the Mauritanian families never marry outside their class, they have been able to maintain their musical and oral traditions for generations. Many families can trace their ancestry back for several centuries. Thus it is only natural that a child growing up in such a family would learn these arts as automatically as he or she might learn to talk and walk.[13]

There are a few cases of strict training by inheritance that are not exactly bardic forms of storytelling. In some cultures, family stories can be passed on only to descendants. But this usually means that all in the culture are oral-tradition carriers. Such would be the case in a number of Polynesian groups. Handy described how children in the Marquesa Islands were trained. Their father built a special house for this purpose, called *oho au*, and then hired a *tuhuna* or bard to instruct them. Usually, around thirty men and women from the same family group would also participate in the teaching, which lasted one month. All other work was suspended during the period of learning. After it was over, the house was destroyed.[14]

The Maori equivalent of such a house was called *whare wananga*; the bard was called a *tohunga*. Seemingly, not all youngsters were chosen to participate, but only those of noble birth. Such persons would not necessarily become storytellers except that they would have to relate the traditions a sufficient number of times so as to keep them fresh in their memory. Some would later become *tohuna* or *tohunga*.[15]

There is also the individual inheritance of certain stories, respected as the sign of the artistry of one individual who is able to tell them particularly well or because each story is considered as property to be bequeathed or sold. The latter occurs with the *waikan*, a type of sacred story among the Winnebago.[16] To a certain degree it was also practiced among the *byliny* performers in Russia.[17] Malinowski wrote of a Trobriand Island chief who gave food and other goods to the descendants of a certain person in exchange for a dance, a song, and a story owned by them.[18] But this kind of situation does not describe the inherited "position" or "caste" of the storyteller, with all of its ramifications relating to lack of choice and duty.

Among the many brief descriptions available of ancient Greek and Indian bards, there is none indicating that they held hereditary posts, although the likelihood is certainly there. Nor do we know much about their training. We know a great deal about the performance and position in society of the Anglo-Saxon *scop* or *gleoman*, but we know nothing about his training and whether or not he passed on his position to his sons,[19] regardless of their talent. The same is true of the positions of the *cuicapicque* and the *amauta* among the Aztecs and Incas, respectively, although we do know that the latter were carefully trained in special schools.[20]

Formal Apprenticeship

Formal apprenticeship that is not hereditary is the more usual kind of training given to bardic storytellers and to a few other kinds of storytellers too. The term "formal apprenticeship" means here a pre-scribed course freely chosen by the student and generally paid for in some monetary way, during which the apprentice usually lives for a time with the master and performs other duties as well as learning. In some cases the course has a prescribed length of years, and in other cases it can be cut short or expanded, depending on the individual abilities of the students.

The most formal training of this type today is probably that of the *zenza*, who are preparing to become master storytellers in the *yose*, public halls in Japan. They must be classed as folk storytellers, as pointed out earlier. Hrdličková gives an excellent account of their training, and the following description is taken from her two articles on the subject.[21]

The training of the *zenza* is essentially the same as it was in feudal times, except that it has been shortened somewhat, and the apprentices now join the master while still children or in their early teens. This change occurred at the end of the eighteenth century or the beginning of the nineteenth, when formal schools for carrying out the apprenticeship were established. Prior to that, the students had worked individually with masters, starting when they were somewhat older.

The act of "entering the gate of apprenticeship" is called *nyūmon*; as soon as this happens the master gives the apprentice his artistic name. The first period of apprenticeship now lasts from six to twelve months, and during this time, the young student is called *minarai*. He spends this time observing and also performing menial chores.

The second period of apprenticeship lasts two to three years, and the apprentice is now called a *zenza*. During the teaching period, the *zenza* must kneel in front of the master. He is orally given stories with "jaw-breaking passages" to learn. He may not write anything down and is usually required to repeat exactly what the master has recited until he has learned the "secret" of the story. At the same time, he usually must learn to play some traditional musical instrument, such as the drum.

Once he has mastered a few stories and is considered good enough to begin interpreting them in his own way, the *zenza* is occasionally allowed to perform. He even earns a small salary. But most of his time is spent in service to the master storyteller, preparing the stage and keeping the record books up to date. These are kept in the dressing room, and it is here that the *zenza* records the date, the stories told, and by whom, because the program gives only the storytellers' names, not the titles of the stories. After three or four years, the *zenza* in turn becomes a master storyteller.

There were public halls similar to the *yose* in parts of China and Mongolia. Virtually all of the storytellers who performed in these halls received training similar to that offered in Japan. There do not appear to be any such schools in present-day China or Mongolia. The main differences between the Chinese schools of the past and the Japanese seem to be that the Chinese were more strongly hereditary than those of Japan and seemed to specialize in teaching only one type of story performance.[22]

Cejpek writes that at one time there were storytelling schools in Persia, but that they no longer exist, with very few exceptions. He notes, however, that the *kitabcha*, a prompt book used by Persian professional narrators that is similar to the one used by the Chinese, is now being replaced in modern Iran by cheap lithographic folk prints that the narrator uses as his *aides memoire*.[23]

Another type of long apprenticeship is that served by the hunters' bard among the Mande people of West Africa. This lasts from ten to fifteen years. The young apprentice must first master the *narinyo*, a rhythm instrument, until he becomes a *nara*, or master singer. Then he must learn to play the *donso-nkoni*, a six-string harp-lute. Once he can perform well on this, and learns to sing the traditional narratives, he can call himself a *donso-jeli*, or hunters' bard.[24]

Informal Apprenticeship

The *oníjălá*, who performs in Yoruba in Nigeria and in neighboring countries, is also a hunters' bard. He begins chanting *ijála* under a master during late childhood or early adolescence. Some men are married before they start their apprenticeships. All the *ijála* chanters interviewed by Babalola gave as their main reason for going to a master "that they wanted to do it beautifully."[25]

In the first stage, the apprentice to the *oníjălá* listens as the teacher performs in his own house or at social gatherings where he has been invited to entertain. During the second stage, the pupil imitates the teacher word for word, repeating the narratives privately. He is also permitted to go along to public performances where he repeats the master's words simultaneously. If there are two or more such apprentices practicing in this way, it often makes the *ijála* performance sound like a group chant, but this is only due to the teaching method. The master is definitely considered the storyteller.

The third stage occurs when the master gives the pupil a chance to perform on his own. On the average, the whole process takes about ten years. There is no final test, and the apprentice leaves his master's service either without notice (if he fears the teacher will not approve of his departure) or with the blessings of his master, because the student has now been recognized as a master in his own right.

In a number of places the apprenticeship is carried out much less formally. The Nyanga of Zaire call their bard *shékárĩsĩ*. According to

Biebuyck and Mateene, young men who are relatives or friends of the bard accompany him as he performs and thus learn the epic and how to present it orally.

> They are usually about three in number, but not all these young men will ultimately be expert in narrating the epic. It is likely that only one of them—the more energetic, intelligent, assiduous, better-liked one—will be fully instructed by the bard in the performance in all its complexity.[26]

During the performance, the tasks of these young men are to beat the percussion instruments and to lead the refrains of the songs, in which the audience joins.

If one of these young apprentices falls sick or has other things go wrong in his personal life, this is usually interpreted as a sign that the spirits are angry at the slow and negligent way he has been learning the epic. In order to set this right, he must speed up his learning and make ceremonial offerings of banana beer.[27]

Ben-Amos describes the training of two types of professional storytellers in Benin[28] and points out that this can be accomplished by formal or informal apprenticeship. Of the nineteen storytellers he interviewed, eight had learned informally from their fathers, uncles, or older brothers; four were instructed by friends; and six had been formally apprenticed to professional players outside their immediate family. In all cases, the instruction was direct and indirect. The student was given special musical patterns to practice, sometimes for hours, and the teacher corrected his mistakes. The verbal parts were usually listened to several times, and then the student, after asking the teacher to repeat a number of details, felt ready to assist in performing in public. Just as in the case of the *shékárisi* of Zaire, there is a group of three or four apprentices, called *igbesa* in Ẹdo, who support the storyteller in his performance. They learn to watch for the special signals that tell them when to join in the singing or when to stop.

The period of learning lasts from one to three years, during which time the apprentice may visit his teacher once or twice a week. The master also teaches the student how to make his own musical instrument before he graduates and makes his first professional appearance at a coming-out party.

The training of the young *ntsomi* teller appears outwardly to be very informal indeed. Scheub was fortunate to be able to observe and listen to fairly young performers who were in the initial stages of learning, as well as to slightly older and more experienced *ntsomi* tellers and to accomplished artists. This enabled him to conclude:

> The "apprenticeship" of the young performer is quite casual, but this should in no way suggest that no period of apprenticeship is involved.... Nor does that apprenticeship lack rigorous standards.... She may receive some coaching in the very early stages from her parents and other sympathetic members of the family.... She learns, watches, listens, experiments, adopts, and adapts. She toys with new ideas, with nuances,

idioms, songs, gestures, movements.... She begins with episodes and isolated details, with a few gestures, some clichés. She memorizes nothing, she remembers many things.[29]

This last point is extremely important because the good *ntsomi* teller must show originality and contemporaneity, even within the framework of core plots that often stay the same. Scheub reports that it is not uncommon to hear the youngest children, just learning to talk, conciously using ideophones for animal sounds and actions, with great flair and originality.[30]

With regard to Serbo-Croatian tale singing, Lord distinguishes between the mere performers who carefully learn to present old, memorized versions in an authentic manner, and the real poet-singers, who create new versions each time they perform.[31] The latter generally began to learn their art starting at the age of fourteen or fifteen. The young boy starts by listening carefully to one or more singers of note whose style appeals to him. Sometimes he might go off by himself to practice the songs, first trying to remember them word for word out of admiration for the master. After he has built up enough confidence and learned the basic fingering of chords on the *gusle*, he might perform for his companions. The more his competence increases, the more he realizes that he must use the formulaic phrases in his own manner, and the more confidence he has then in adding his own ornamentations and variations. Finally, he builds up his own repertoire of favorite songs, but in each performance he tries to improve the quality by a smoother delivery, better organization of the themes, and complete mastery of the formulaic expressions. Some singers never reach this stage no matter how hard they try.[32]

Another informal type of apprenticeship is that of the *aqyn*, or Kazakh bard. It was only after competing successfully at several *ajtys* (singing competitions) that the *aqyn* could finally claim to have become a professional. There were usually two "opponents" in the *ajtys*, and after the first had spontaneously composed a verse to one of the basic melodies used, the second had to reply, using the same type of formula. In most cases there were no fixed rules, but there was general agreement among listeners and "duelists" as to who had won.[33]

Library School Courses

The modern substitute for the formal system of apprenticeship in many fields is the trade, technical, or professional school. As was pointed out earlier, the public library perceived one of its functions to be that of purveyor of oral literature for children. It is not surprising then that the early library schools, many of them operated by library systems and not by universities, included course work in storytelling. The first to do so were the Carnegie Library Training School for Children's Librarians in Pittsburgh, which opened in 1900,[34] and the Pratt Institute, which began a specialist course in children's library work in the fall of 1899.[35] The training offered in Pittsburgh was two years in length and included courses in "Storytelling and Reading Aloud" both years.[36] At Pratt Institute, there was no special course, but one of the theses assigned to all students in the children's specialist program was "Storytelling and Reading Aloud in the Children's Library."[37]

Some of the other library schools that added storytelling courses (or parts of courses) were: Library School of Western Reserve University, 1904[38]; Wisconsin Library School of the State Library Commission, 1909[39]; New York Public Library, Library School, 1912[40]; St. Louis Public Library School, 1917[41]; Columbia University Library School, 1927.[42] The years given are not necessarily the first year of operation of the schools, but the first year for which a course description including storytelling could be located.

The last-named university described its first storytelling course, taught by Alice Hazeltine, in this manner:

> A study of source material for the storyteller, with emphasis on folk and epic literature. Selection and adaptation of stories for children of different ages, especially cycles of stories for older children. Methods of learning and of presentation and practice in telling stories.[43]

This trend continues to the present day. Those library schools that give special courses on aspects of children's literature and library work with children also tend to offer a course in storytelling or oral narration. In addition, quite a number of universities or institutions of higher learning have placed such courses in the department of education or in the speech and drama department. If the library school does not offer such a course, the student can usually get credit for taking it in another department. By 1960 there were at least 211 institutions of higher learning in the United States offering some instruction in storytelling.[44]

A modern variation on the storytelling course is one that combines storytelling with other program techniques. Such courses concentrate on the planning and directing of film, picture-book, and story-hour programs, as well as covering the techniques of managing the content through selection and various forms of presentation.

In-service Training

In addition to the formal courses that were part of a curriculum leading to a professional degree or certificate, many public libraries also established short, in-service training seminars for their own staff. Some of these courses, such as those offered by the New York Public Library and the Enoch Pratt Free Library of Baltimore, remain to this day a requirement for all new children's librarians entering the system. The New York Public Library in-service seminars were begun in 1951, under the direction of Eulalie Steinmetz.[45]

These in-service seminars usually consist of a series of four to eight lectures, spread out over as many weeks. The seminars are followed by active planning in several story hours. First might come several "shared" story-hour programs in which a previously trained person does some of the telling and the new librarian may tell only one story. This number is then increased gradually until the novice storyteller arranges to tell a full program.

By the end of the season, the training specialist, operating out of the central administrative offices, will have observed all the new storytellers in action. In some library systems, the best of them are then selected to tell in a symposium or showcase of storytelling. Such a custom has been practiced annually in May by the New York Public Library. This has a precedent from the distant past. The medieval storytelling guilds in China often selected their best tellers after an apprenticeship of anywhere from three to twelve years to perform in a public display. Sometimes there were contests among the various guilds, to show off what each could accomplish in training.[46]

Other Training Groups

Two other organizations that influenced the training of storytellers in the United States were the Chautauqua Institution and the National Story League. The former was at first a church-related summer school. Later it incorporated as a service organization providing adult education during the summer, a lecture bureau, social clubs, and many other social and educational services. Their summer school in Chautauqua had a storytelling course for many years. In 1904 it was taught by Marie Shedlock and in the decade of 1910 by Mabel C. Bragg.[47] Many librarians and others working with children were trained in these courses.

The National Storyteller's League was founded in 1903. Among its original purposes were:

> To encourage the art of storytelling and the use of classic and folklore stories in schools and other educational centers; to foster creative work in the arranging and re-writing of stories from various classic and historic sources; to serve as a medium of exchange of stories and experiences in the use of the story; to discover in the world's literature, in history, and in life the best stories for education, and to tell them with love and sympathy for the children, and to bring together in story circles those who love to hear and tell a good story. . . .[48]

Richard T. Wyche, an educator, was the prime mover and organizer. The members were not only educators, but also librarians, kindergartners, playground workers, and ordinary interested persons. Wyche was determined to get the art of storytelling accepted as part of the programs of all kinds of organized work with children. He also stressed the importance of storytelling in the home. Although the league did have impact, it was never to be as strong as Wyche had hoped. The magazine he began, associated with the league, lasted only two issues. The most important contribution of the league was that it provided an opportunity for storytellers of different styles and from different disciplines to hear and see each other.

In 1923 the name and the purpose of the league were changed. It became the National Story League and its purpose is to "encourage the appreciation of the good and the beautiful in life and literature through the art of storytelling." It still operates voluntary storytelling sessions in many public institutions, through local chapters in many cities. Courses for storytellers, if any are offered, are very informal. Most of the groups simply get together and compare storytelling techniques.[49]

Training Manuals

To cater to the needs of all these courses, formal and informal, there has been a constant stream of manuals and handbooks on storytelling. Usually these contained tips on the methods of selecting good stories to tell, on learning and reciting the stories, and on how to set up a story-hour session. Often this was followed by a collection of favorite stories to tell. The breakdown of the number published, by decade, gives a pretty fair idea of the steady demand for such material. Many remained in print for five or more decades.

Decade	No. of Storytelling Manuals Published[50]
1890s	2
1900s	1
1910s	11
1920s	8
1930s	3
1940s	4
1950s	5
1960s	4

Richard Alvey, in his dissertation on organized storytelling in the United States, gives an excellent analysis of the different approaches to storytelling that were to be found in many of these manuals. He documents some of the ways in which they proved to be important in the training of storytellers. Of special interest are his comments contrasting the manuals of Marie Shedlock and Angela M. Keyes. In Alvey's view Keyes had expressed in print five years before Shedlock "one of the most sophisticated of all models for storytelling to children in organized contexts." He cites the remarkable similarity of Shedlock's philosophy to that of Keyes, and speculates as to why the Shedlock book proved to be so much more popular and influential than the Keyes manual.[51]

Training Outside the United States

Training for children's librarians in England, Australia, New Zealand, Sweden, Denmark, the Netherlands, Spain, and the socialist countries of Eastern Europe all generally include some brief training in storytelling, either in separate courses or as a part of courses on introducing literature to children. In Japan, Momoko Ishii and her assistant, Kiyoko Matsuoka, have made a specialty of training librarians who are in the home library movement in the art of storytelling. Miss Ishii used as her model the in-service courses of the Toronto Public Library, which she had observed on an extended visit.[52] Shigeo Watanabe, who received his in-service training at the New York Public Library, returned to teach in Japan and included some storytelling in his courses at Keio University.[53]

Still another Japanese person who was influenced by library storytelling in the United States is Mitsue Ishitake. After seeing the preschool and picture-book hours in the Westchester Public Library system and in the Weston Woods traveling caravan, she returned to Japan and began the training of a staff that could function in a mobile unit specializing in programs for young children. This caravan, sponsored by the Hakuho Foundation, travels now throughout Japan, to day-care centers, parks, libraries, and other places, giving programs that are a mixture of storytelling, puppetry, films, and music. In addition to the trained leaders, there are always some persons in training who go with the caravan, learning as apprentices do.[54]

Informal Training in the Home

By far the majority of storytellers are trained in informal situations in their homes or communities. They learn by imitating the older tellers they admire, or occasionally they learn from their peer group. Oftentimes, they learn in secret as children who are not supposed to be present at an adult session. Delargy mentions an old man telling about this.

> The other boys thought I was too young to go with them to the house where Diarmuid the storyteller was staying, but I would give them the slip, and would hide under the table, where I could listen to the tales, undisturbed. There is not a word the storyteller would say that I had not off by heart the next morning.[55]

On the other hand, in some places they learn as children because training in storytelling is considered part of every child's upbringing, as in parts of Polynesia or of Africa. Sometimes they learn easily, as did the Eskimo teller, Paul Monroe, who said: "When I heard stories they got in my head and I couldn't forget them."[56]

There does not seem to be any worldwide pattern of male parent, grandparent, or elder exclusively teaching the sons, and female parent or grandparent teaching the daughters, as seems to be the case in most apprenticeships. There are many reverse situations mentioned in folk storytelling. Tirabutana as a girl in Thailand lived with her grandmother, but it was her father who told her stories and taught them to her.[57] Peig Sayers, the famous Irish storyteller from the Blasket Islands, also learned mostly from her father:

> ... he was the best teller of a tale that ever was in this countryside. ...
> My father had more tales than any man of his time, and if you had heard
> him telling them you would have wondered, for he never forgot any-
> thing. ... .[58]

She speaks of only boys coming over to listen to the tales, but obviously she was also allowed to listen and learn.

Henssen, on the other hand, mentions that the Dutch German storyteller that he recorded, Egbert Gerrits, learned from the wife of the
farmer to whom he was apprenticed as a young boy of eleven. In the
evenings, she would sew, rock her child, and sing ballads or tell
märchen.[59]

Our most complete picture of the way in which a group of similar
folk tellers from one small area form their repertoires comes from the
fine research of Linda Dégh, particularly in her book *Folktales and
Society: Storytelling in a Hungarian Peasant Community*. In it she
shows how one family came to be famous for its three generations of
storytellers, and how at the same time and in the same area individuals who came from families with no particular history of storytelling talent could develop the art by listening to the rich body of oral
narrative presented on many occasions.[60]

The kind of talent that seemed to pass from one generation of a
family to the next cannot be considered as conveying a hereditary
position of storyteller in folk communities. It is true that the children
of great storytellers will certainly have the advantage, so that if they
have natural ability, they will then have the means of developing it by
hearing outstanding story material told with frequency by a master.
But often it will be the neighbor's child, or the outsider's, or a distant
relative, who will carry forth the tradition of a well-known teller in
the community. The children might express little or no interest in becoming narrators. The community often expects good telling to run in
families, but if it does not there are no sanctions. In fact, it seems as
though it is considered *too* unusual when *many* members of the same
family have exceptional narrative talent. In the Hungarian community of the Szeklers in Kakazd, the villagers tried to explain the unusual talents of the Zaicz family by saying their origins were from
outside, or that "their grandmother was a Jewess, and the gift of storytelling came from her."[61]

Those who have access to the tales often hear them repeated on
such frequent occasions that they unconsciously almost learn them
by heart. They become tale-bearers whether they actually tell stories
or not. This was the case of Mrs. Palkó, who did not tell stories while
her brother was still living, because he was known to be the best storyteller around and it was unthinkable for her to infringe on his position. Yet when he died and she did begin to tell stories at large in the
community, she told only some of the tales for which he had been famous and added others he had not told at all. As Dégh writes, "She
must have heard hundreds of tales during her long life; still, she

adapted only a handful of them. The first encounter with these was so memorable, however, that she recalled it all her life."[62]

The remarkable memory of some storytellers is attested to over and over again. Apparently, quite a number of them could hear a story once and, if they liked it, it was "theirs" for life, for they remembered it in great detail. It would be easy to think that this was an exaggerated boast on the part of the storytellers, but it is a phenomenon reported in so many of the areas of the world and by so many different types of storytellers that one has to discount "bragging" as the reason behind the statement, "I heard it once and then I could tell it." The only conclusion one can draw is that memory is an extraordinarily important factor in the training of a good storyteller.

Training via Story Collections

Informal training could often take place via books as well. Some purists, such as O'Sullivan, expressed the belief that once a folk storyteller learned from a book, his or her stories no longer had validity as oral tradition. "Be very cautious in dealing with a storyteller who can read," he warned.[63] Fortunately, most modern folklorists recognize the fact that it is inevitable in the modern world, just as it was in the past, that the storytellers will use any sources at their disposal to find stories that please them and spark their talent. This includes material from books, other printed matter, films, and even television.

Dégh believes it is often the storybook collection that has inspired tellers to create new versions. In one part of her book *Folktales and Society*, she gives an excellent summary of the opinions of various folklorists concerning the impact of the written literature on the oral tale. Later she lists all of the origins of the more than sixty tales recorded from Mrs. Palkó, at least insofar as she could remember them (Plate 29). Six of the tales Mrs. Palkó had heard first from someone who read them in a book. In her retellings she of course changed them into her own style.[64]

Other collectors whose informants mentioned that they got stories from reading books or listening to others read were Edwin Hall and H. R. Lynton. Hall recalled that one time, after the Eskimo storyteller Paul Monroe had recited a particularly dramatic and unusual story, he asked where Monroe had first heard it. Monroe's answer was that it had come from a copy of *True Confessions* magazine![65]

Lynton reported that the story appetite of the Nawab Fakhr ul Mulk Bahadur, a Moslem noble who lived in Hyderabad at the turn of the century, was so great that one of the four night attendants, who was a storyteller, spent her days reading books so as to "increase or refresh her stock in trade."[66] On the other hand, Anna Liberata de Souza, an informant from India of the same period, did not like the book versions of the stories at all, calling them inferior and "all wrong." She believed they left out "the prettiest parts," and could not be counted on as good sources.[67]

PLATE 29 Zsuzsánna Palkó, gifted storyteller from the village of Kakasd, Hungary; reprinted, with permission, from Linda Dégh, *Folktales and Society* (Bloomington: Indiana University Press, © 1969).

Perhaps what Anna did not like was the same kind of thing objected to by modern Native Americans. Ella Clark writes:

> College-educated Indians ... have told me or written me that they had been shocked by the caliber of many of the stories published from their own and other tribes. Such tales were never related around their firesides in their youth and, in their opinion, give an unfair impression of the literature of their people.[68]

The words of a recorded oral story without the accompanying actions, expressions, gestures, and voice of the teller, and without the mood of the intimate occasion of storytelling, often do sound bald and not at all effective or beautiful.

Asbjørnsen must have believed that at least some storytellers would get their materials from the collections he recorded, because he left a special legacy for his editors. They were to be sure to change the language of the tales to correspond to the currently spoken Norwegian whenever a new edition appeared.[69]

Finally, the Chinese tradition must be mentioned once again because, although the medieval storytelling guilds taught their apprentices through completely oral means and continued to do so even up to modern times, it was not long before the best stories were put down in writing. These collections continued to be enriched so much over the centuries that it became obvious that the storytellers no longer were learning only from oral tradition, but from oral tradition that had been written and rewritten after many retellings. The more common modern word for storytelling in Chinese, *shuo-shu*, literally means "to recite books."[70] For many storytellers of today, this would be the correct interpretation.

14

Suggestions for More Authentic Storytelling

The earlier chapters in this book were designed to introduce the storyteller to some of the methods and styles of telling used in the past and in the present, and to show where and when story sessions have taken place. The reader may wonder why so little attention has been paid to the content of the stories. There are several reasons for this, the main one being the sheer amount of story matter that would have had to be considered in order to give a balanced view. It seemed better to call attention to the works of specialists who have spent years working with the content of specific story material and to concentrate on the outward aspects of telling style. By going directly to the works cited in the bibliography and the notes and to many others that can be found by consulting standard indexes, the student will get a much more accurate picture of the literature that is used in each type of oral narration. Furthermore, such an exercise can be of great help in determining how to judge the authenticity of stories that appear in edited versions, especially for children. This will be discussed later in greater detail.

Another reason why the author has avoided including more about story content, or even a list of favorite stories, is that the student is then subtly led to a belief that such stories are "the best" or the kind to look for when searching out new tales to tell. If one lesson can be learned from the earlier chapters, it is that each person must learn to recognize for himself or herself what kinds of stories are best to tell. This is something no teacher or guidebook can hope to do well—to select stories for others to tell—except perhaps as a classroom exercise to prove some point.

The Art of Listening

Since storytelling is an oral art, the best method for learning about new stories, or new ways of telling old stories, is to listen. This is, seemingly, the most obvious kind of advice and should not have to be mentioned. The fact remains that, based on this author's experience, most students of storytelling who wish to learn so they can tell in libraries, schools, parks, museums, and the like come to a course expecting to get most of their information, help, advice, and even all their stories from books.

To learn better storytelling techniques one does not necessarily have to listen to entire stories told under formal or informal conditions in group sessions. Some of the most effective devices (pauses, gestures, phrasing, and so forth) can be observed and learned by watching and listening to the animated conversationalist at a party, on a crowded bus, or even in a family gathering. Such persons are often called "born storytellers" by their friends and relatives, as indeed they probably are. Dorson makes the point that there is probably no community, however small, that does not have its storyteller.[1]

Above all, the student teller must watch for devices that she or he can pick up and use comfortably and unselfconsciously. It is all very well to admire the techniques of a master storyteller, but if the master uses a highly exaggerated and dramatic style with much mimicry and the student is reserved, soft-voiced, and not adept at mimicry, it would not be a good idea for the student to directly imitate the master. What the student can watch out for are the more subtle aspects of the good storyteller's style, such as which words are paused over or what parts are sped over quickly or what kind of core phrases are used again and again. If the student is not sure of using these successfully in storytelling, they can first be tried out in conversation. This not only makes good practical sense, it can also be an aesthetically pleasing and satisfying experience. Our everyday language has become so repetitious and devoid of personal flavor that it can only be an improvement to inject into it some of the wonderful wit and vividness of folktale language.

In the Home

Fewer and fewer parents of today narrate stories to their children. This is becoming as prevalent in village-oriented societies as it is in urban areas. It is a great pity, since there is now widespread agreement among educators, psychologists, and child-development theorists that listening to stories of the traditional type provides great emotional satisfaction to children and helps them come to terms with their psychic and intellectual growth. Some parents who feel ill at ease putting a story into their own words turn to reading aloud to their children. This can be quite effective, but it is by no means a complete substitute for the personal stories that only a family member can compose and tell.

The stories of this type that please children most are those that have to do with the childhood of their parents, grandparents, or other elders, but only if these are presented in such a way that the child can relate to them in some way. That is, they must deal with the dramatic or naughty or puzzling events of the older person's childhood, but related as they were experienced by that person as a child, and not as they are remembered in retrospect. Some of the finest examples of this kind of storytelling can be found in the books of Laura Ingalls Wilder,[2] and any parent who would wish to learn better how to tell such stories would do well to study the parts where Pa and sometimes Ma tell Laura and her sisters about the funny, naughty, scary things they did as children. Note that invariably these are put into the third person, a much more effective voice for storytelling than the first person.

Such stories are far more successful with children than tales about famous persons in the family or events in the lives of ancestors so far removed that the children cannot experience or imagine them. If a family has such stories in its history, then it is better to connect them in the telling with some unusual object or an old photograph or book, so as to give a concrete dimension to them. Above all, if there is a moral to the story, it should be allowed to speak for itself. Too many adults allow the stories from their past to become a justification or an excuse for moralizing about the future. They let the moral take over and control the story, rather than vice versa.

Other stories that children enjoy are those related to their birth and the first year of their life. These are short stories, but each one is unique, and the clever parent remembers just enough silly or important details in each telling to make each child feel he or she was an interesting individual from the moment of arrival. Again, it is good to put these in the third person, using the child's real name. They should be told like a story, however short.

Traditional stories from the world's folklore are often more difficult to tell because they have complex plots. They appear to use flowery and ornate language, and adults are often fearful that they cannot capture it in telling. Elaborate and wordy versions of folk and fairy tales have invariably been worked over by adapters with literary pretensions. Most of the great folktales in all parts of the world use language that is very direct and unadorned. The poetic and dramatic effects are achieved by the use of formulaic expressions (see Chapters 8 and 9), through carefully placed repetition of key phrases or rhymes, and through the use of striking and vivid similes. The successful modern storyteller is the one who can use these conventions in a manner that is clear and direct and understandable to ordinary speakers of everyday language.

For the parent who is fearful of attempting to tell these tales orally, there is the comforting device of the folktale picture book. Fortunately, there are many of these to choose from. Reading a number of them aloud several times gives invaluable practice in the timing and phrasing necessary for good storytelling. If the adult reads them a sufficient number of times to almost know them word for word from memory, he or she will know whether creative oral storytelling is possible. The confidence will either be there to tell them alone, without aid of the book, or it will not.

Such books can rarely be found in inexpensive format in the supermarket or chain store. It is better to borrow them from a library or school if they cannot be purchased. The popularized versions, especially those based on films, are not at all effective as training for the storyteller. In order to suit the medium of film, the directness of the narration has had to be embellished with much more descriptive matter. The repetition of events that sounds so natural in oral form is not particularly effective on film, so it is usually dropped. This does not mean that the parent should not let children go to see these films. Rather, it is a recommendation that both film and original book versions be introduced, and, if possible, a completely oral version. This gives the child the opportunity to develop his or her own preferences in taste, style, and medium.

Families wishing to introduce stories from parts of the world with which they are not familiar can follow some of the suggestions included in the remaining parts of this chapter. However, it is a good idea to search for institutions in their area that have storytelling programs. Sometimes the quality of these programs in public places is no better than that in the home. In other cases, it can be exceptionally good because the nature of the programs has attracted the person with talent to work in them. Parents should never pass by the opportunity to let their children and themselves hear stories told by first-rate tellers. This is especially important if the stories are from another cultural group. Children should not be forced to go to such programs if their interests lie elsewhere, but they will generally show their interest and delight if the parent does.

In Institutions: Libraries, Museums, Schools

There are many excellent manuals and guidebooks related to general storytelling techniques, so they will not be covered here. This section is concerned only with devices or methods to use when introducing or using stories from a source that is not thoroughly familiar to the audience.

The experience of hearing stories told is universal. The content and form of that experience are not. It is difficult, if not impossible, to describe or recreate something one has not seen, heard, or felt. To attempt to tell stories "in an African style" or "in an Indian style" after reading only this book would be problematic. The intent of the author is not to be a substitute for the opportunity to see and hear stories told firsthand.

The teller can, however, learn enough to become more skilled at recognizing authenticity in stories. Let us say, for example, that a book of Yoruba tales is to be reviewed. It consists of long tales that have themes similar to European *märchen*, couched in very poetic language, but definitely set in West Africa. The compiler has given no source for the stories, except that they were written down in the last century. A check through the index and dictionary of this book will show that this style of tale is not one of the common Yoruba types, mentioned by folklorists and anthropologists. Let us further assume that in the collection there are a few stories that strongly and immediately appeal to the teller. In such a case, it would be better to review the collection as an original work, pointing out that the contents may or may not represent traditional Yoruba literature.

In telling tales from such a collection, it is better to introduce them, not by saying: "Here is a story from the Yoruba of West Africa," but rather: "Here is a story that is somewhat like many of the same stories you know from Europe, but the author has set it in West Africa; she (or he) has imagined what it would be like if it happened there." This allows the teller to use stories that are appealing, even though they are not authentic in the sense that they do not represent the oral traditions of the people with whom the editor has identified them. When feasible, the work should be checked with the major studies carried out in the same area, but this is seldom possible since such materials tend to be only in scholarly libraries.

If the text appears to be so completely changed from the oral traditions where it originated, it is better to remove all place names and treat the story as coming from no particular region.

For the stories that do appear to have authenticity, it is still challenging to create a storytelling scene that will even suggest the ambience of the original sessions. This is especially the case if one has not been present at such a session. In such a situation the teller should try to describe briefly the atmosphere and occasions that might surround the tale if it were being told in its place of origin. Many such descriptions can be culled from this book. Following this, he or she should say something to this effect: "I cannot tell you the story in that way, because I have never been there. But I like the story, so I will tell it for you in my own way."

If the story has been taken down from a master storyteller and the book or other source gives some information about this person, or perhaps even a photograph, it is a good idea to share this with the audience. The same would be true for original stories that do not pretend to be anything but that. If there is no explanation about the original teller or creator, write to the publisher to see if they have further information.

Sometimes, an unusual object mentioned in the story can be obtained from the country of origin and shown to the audience. This is most successful when the object looks intriguing and unlike anything the audience may know. Plates 30 and 31, for example, show a series of Japanese items that the author has used many times in telling stories from that country. In Plate 32 are shown a variety of thumb-pianos, used to accompany storytelling in a number of African countries. After telling a story that might be accompanied by the music of this type of instrument, it is a good idea to let the audience try out the thumb-pianos, so as to see what sounds they can make. Plates 33 and 34 contain a variety of other objects that have all been tried out by the author in storytelling sessions.

Materials such as these must usually be bought in the country of origin. They are not the typical kinds of export gifts. But in these days of extensive travel, one can generally find someone who will watch out for specific objects that can give the extra touch to a storytelling session. Museums, of course, can select objects from their collections and use them. It is important to select at least some that are not too precious so that they can be handled by the audience.

There are some materials available in this country that can be used to inject a bit of color or an authentic new shape to the story hour format. Wooden *kamishibai* are a perfect way to introduce a special Japanese style of storytelling. Story cloths (see Plate 26) are available for a number of the Indian myths or for stories from the *Ramayana*. A list of sources for these and other items is given at the end of this chapter.

More ordinary items often provide just as much interest as do unusual ones. For a series of programs on the origins of foods and the meaning of certain foods in specific cultures, the author gathered a collection of plastic containers full of wheat, rice (raw), corn, oats, barley, palm nuts, cocoa beans, and many other cereal grains, legumes, and nuts. An origin story for each one was located. The children in the audience could pick out the items one by one each time the relevant story was narrated, indicating which culture it had come from.

Picture books and other books that show the language of origin of the stories used are also of much interest to children, particularly if they are in other alphabets. They do not necessarily have to be the books containing the precise stories being told. It is also good if the teller can say a few words in the language, to indicate what it would sound like. Or a song in the language can be played between stories.

The best way to learn new techniques for authentic telling is by observing storytelling in its natural milieu. This demands careful preparation. All of the written materials on folklore and storytelling

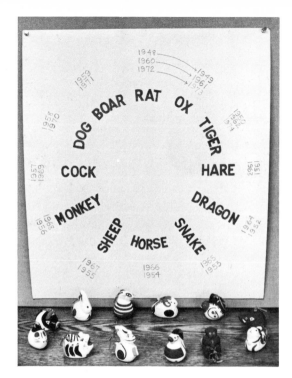

PLATE 30   Ceramic animal year figures, handmade and hand-painted in Japan, together with a chart used in telling the story, which has several versions, of why the year is named after animals. Collection of the Information Center on Children's Cultures.

PLATE 31   A *daruma* (wishing figure or good luck figure) and a *tengu* mask from Japan, used in a number of folktales. Collection of the Information Center on Children's Cultures.

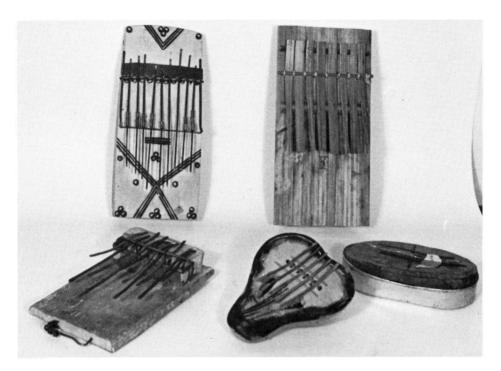

PLATE 32 Thumb-pianos from five different regions of Africa, used to accompany certain kinds of storytelling. Collection of the Information Center on Children's Cultures.

PLATE 33 A collection of raw cereals and grains used to accompany tales about the origin of corn, rice, wheat, etc. They are alphabetically arranged, clockwise, starting from the lower right: alfalfa, barley, clover, corn, millet, oats, rice, rye, and wheat. Collection of the Information Center on Children's Cultures.

PLATE 34   Examples of three armadillos from Brazil, Venezuela, and the Amazon region, typical of those used during storytelling to help young children visualize
the unusual animals that are the characters in folktales from other parts of
the world. Collection of the Information Center on Children's Cultures.

that have to do with the area for the proposed visit should be read well
in advance. Corresponding with a folklorist or anthropologist who has
done work in a specific area can often lead one to the best places for
observing and participating in storytelling sessions. But persistent
questioning once one is in the area can also bring results and should
not be overlooked as a means of getting to know and hear new tellers.

For more formal places, such as the *yose* in Japan, one should go
with a guide or at least learn the proper etiquette. The same would be
true of coffeehouse storytellers in Iran or some of the Arabic-speaking
countries.

Knowing the language is an enormous help, but lack of it should not
deter the student from observing and listening. One can learn a great
deal about the ambience and feeling of a storytelling session without

understanding a word. It is better not to have a guide attempt a step-by-step translation as the story progresses, but to hear a resumé either at the beginning or at the end. It should be remembered that the rules for recording the folkloric material for later study and possible publication demand very careful notes and an in-depth knowledge of the discipline of folklore. On the whole, it has been the author's experience that the storyteller gains more by simply observing and absorbing the atmosphere than by attempting to note down story variants or other matter.

For very informal sessions with groups of children, it is a good idea to be prepared with one or two stories to tell in return, for this is sometimes expected as a courtesy. The author's particular favorites for such situations are short tales with nonsensical, tongue-twisting language, such as "Master of All Masters" or the Appalachian ballad version of "There Was an Old Woman All Skin and Bone."[3] The latter has been told now to children in many countries, from Nigeria to Nepal to New York, and with resounding success whether the English is understood or not.

In Publishing

Much as we might like to see more stories passed on through oral means, it is not likely that a great number will reach the next generation in that manner, at least not in the United States. The majority will certainly be inherited, directly or indirectly, through some recorded form. In the chapter on training it was briefly pointed out that a number of peoples believe stories to be inheritable property. Robert Lowie cites even more examples and points out that for many non-literate societies, ownership of stories and other privileges corresponds directly to the system of patents and copyrights in force in most of the literate world.[4] Linda Dégh mentions that among the storytellers in the Hungarian villages where she recorded and observed a storytelling milieu there was enormous respect for the story version that was identified with a specific person. It would have been unthinkable for one storyteller to perform a story in public that was identified with another teller.[5]

On the whole, this respect has not been forthcoming from those who have retold, edited, and published folk stories for popular, commercial sale. Rare is the collection, or the individual picture-book folktale, that mentions the name or circumstances of the original teller, even when that was known. This is partly the result of selecting stories from out-of-print nineteenth-century compilations that did not record the names of the original storytellers. Mostly, it is out of fear that if a source is cited, the copyright cannot be claimed by the reteller or the publisher.

This situation could be remedied a great deal if editors and publishers insisted that every modern reteller or editor provide at least a brief paragraph listing the specific sources of the stories. Some indication would also have to be given as to whether the tales have been edited or changed extensively, and how. There is nothing intrinsically wrong about taking a story and making it one's own through retelling. This is part and parcel of the folk storytelling process. What is dishonest, professionally if not legally, is to pretend that the story is close to its originally recorded version. Thus it can be claimed as being typical or authentic of a country or group, all the while leaving out mention of the original source.

Such a phrase as "Loosely based on a tale found in . . . or heard from . . ." can go a long way to helping the reader and user identify how much of the story is newly invented and how much is traditional. It should also be made clear when illustrations are fantasy and when they are based on actual artistic motifs coming from the same cultural base as the story. The Blair Lent illustrations for *Why the Sun and the Moon Live in the Sky* are an excellent example of this. The artist points out that they are his fantastic imaginings, based only on a limited access to African art of the region of Nigeria from which the story comes.[6] This, in fact, makes for a perfect method of introducing the book to children, by mentioning that this illustrator imagined the story would be acted out and told, as a masked pageant, in Africa. They might dream up other ways of picturing the tale. This has been successful with audiences of children in North and South America and in Africa, as experienced by this writer.

Some Sources of Objects Used in Storytelling

1. Indian storytelling cloths can be purchased from:

InterCulture Associates
Box 277
Thompson, Conn. 06277

This company has a selection of *kalamkari* and *pabuji kaa pat* cloths. Write for description and price.

2. The hand-painted Japanese animal figures can be ordered from:

Hirano
2-48-7
Kaenji-Minami
Suginami-Ku
Tokyo, Japan

Occasionally, better Japanese gift shops in the United States will have *darumas, tengu* masks, and other appropriate pieces.

3. Musical instruments used to accompany some forms of storytelling in other countries can sometimes be purchased through:

Classical Instruments   House of Musical Traditions
133 Gateway Building   *or*   305 S. Washington St.
New Orleans, La. 70130   Berkeley Springs, W. Va. 25411

4. Thumb-pianos from Africa can usually be purchased through:

International Program
  for Human Resource Development
Box 316
Bethesda, Md. 20014

5. "Sources of Children's Books from Other Countries" gives addresses of book dealers who have children's books in different languages. For a free copy, send a stamped, self-addressed, legal-size envelope to:

Information Center
  on Children's Cultures
331 East 38 St.
New York, N.Y. 10016

The important thing to remember is to select carefully for quality and authenticity. Do not use cheap tourist objects, dolls, etc., just for the sake of having an object. Make sure the item is truly and closely connected to the story.

V

A Multilingual Dictionary of Storytelling Terms

Dictionary

This dictionary includes terms that are used in many languages to describe the storyteller; the occasions, sites or buildings used for storytelling; the musical instruments and objects employed to accompany storytelling; and the types or genres of stories told. The singular form, if known, is the main entry, with the plural form in parentheses. Terms within a definition that are followed by an asterisk (*) have their own entry. Whenever possible, at least one printed source is given for each entry, so that those seeking further information can find it readily. Differences in definitions and variations in spelling are noted, if two or more authorities disagree. Author(s) and page number(s) only are cited for the majority of source entries. Full information on each source can be located in the bibliography. If an author has more than one entry in the bibliography, the first key word or two from the title indicates the particular work used as a source. The definitions in most cases have been condensed, rather than quoted directly. The author apologizes for any misinterpretations that may have occurred and would like to be informed of them.

There are many inconsistencies in the transliteration of terms from non-Roman alphabets and in the use of diacritic marks. The terms are reprinted here as given in the sources cited. No attempt was made to check dictionary spellings or definitions, except in the few cases noted.

Names for characters, or for gods, goddesses, and other supernatural creatures common to folktales, myths, and legends, are not included here since they are extensively indexed and defined in the *Standard Dictionary of Folklore Mythology and Legend* edited by Maria Leach and Jerome Fried (Funk and Wagnalls, 1972). That dictionary should also be consulted for more complete definitions and discussions of the common terms in English for oral narrative, for example, ballad, fable, folklore, folktale, fairy tale, legend, myth. It was impossible to give sufficient time and space to the numerous and differing opinions of scholars in regard to these terms.

abateekerezi   In Rwanda, memorialists whose task it was to remember and recite the most important events of each reign; similar are *abiiru*, preservers of the secrets of each dynasty; *abasizi*, reciters of panegyrics regarding the kings; *abacurabwenge*, the person responsible for memorizing genealogies and historical tales (Vansina, p. 32).

abuwab   See *uwa*.

ada'ox   The Tsimshian Indian term for myth, as distinct from *ma'lesk**; the Kwakiutl equivalent is *nu'yam*; the Chinook equivalent is *ik!anam*; the Thompson Indian equivalent is *speta'kl* (Boas, p. 565). The Crow Indian equivalent is *bá-itsitsiwà* (Lowie, p. 13).

aefintýri   The Icelandic equivalent of *märchen** (Simpson, p. 3).

aeventyr   The Danish equivalent of *märchen** (Bolte and Polivka, vol. 4, p. 1).

afsâneh   The Persian equivalent of *märchen**. Alternate term: *dâstân** (Bolte and Polivka, vol. 4, p. 1).

aggadah   In Hebrew, oral narration (Gerhardsson, pp. 181–189; Schwarzbaum, p. 19). The Hebrew term for legend (Oring, p. 19). The Hebrew term for story, talk, narrative, or homily (Nahmad, p. 17). Alternate spellings: *agada; haggadah*.

ahal   Evening parties among the Tuareg at which poetry reciting, storytelling, and witty conversation are the chief entertainment; generally attended only by unmarried girls and young men; alternate term: *diffa* (Chadwick and Chadwick, vol. 3, p. 666).

ahanjito   In the Fōn language of West Africa, the king's professional minstrel-rhapsodist (Herskovits and Herskovits, p. 21). Rouget (p. 48) disagrees with this use of the term, believing that Herskovits was referring to an alternate term for *kpanlingan*, or reciter of praise names.

ahli cherita   See *penglipur lara*.

'ai-ni-mae   Among the Lau in Melanesia, sacred epics that cannot be performed by just anyone; when recited for their informative value they are told; when used in ceremony they are sung (Maranda, pp. 11–13).

ainos   Among the ancient Ionian Greeks, the term used when referring to the type of *logos** known in English as a fable* (Thomson, p. 19).

airneán   In Gaelic, a women's gathering to spin or card wool; also, a session for winter storytelling (Delargy, p. 18).

ajtys   A Kazakh singing competition between two individuals or two groups, in which the words comprise improvised stories, debates, or mock love duels, praise songs, etc.; men and women could take part; professional bards usually began their careers by performing well in the *ajtys* (Winner, pp. 33–34).

akalaŵi   See *ulusimi*.

akasimi   See *ulusimi*.

akhbār   In Arabic, fabricated narratives, i.e., those that do not stem from Koranic or accepted oral Islamic tradition (Ibn al-Jawzī, p. 104).

âkhyânavidah   In Sanskrit, one versed in stories (*Kaushitaki-Brahmana-Upanishad*, S.B.E., III, 25). Alternate spelling: *ākhyānaçīla* (Chadwick and Chadwick, vol. 2, p. 617).

akhyayika   In India, a story rooted in the basic facts of history, as contrasted with *katha** (Upadhyaya, p. 225). Alternate spelling: *ākhyāna* (*Encyclopaedia Britannica Macropedia*, vol. 8, pp. 927–932).

akin   Traveling minstrels or saga tellers of the Kirghiz people who generally perform at feasts; probably the same as *aqyn** (Chadwick and Chadwick, vol. 3, p. 178).

akpalo kpatita   In Yoruba, one who makes a trade of reciting stories, but distinguished from the *arokin** by not being attached to any court; often used a drum as accompaniment (Chadwick and Chadwick, vol. 3, p. 647).

akpata   In the Ẹdo language, a seven-stringed bow-lute used by the professional storyteller in Benin society (*ọkp'akpata**) to accompany himself at a "communicative event" called *okpobhiẹ** (Ben-Amos, pp. 25–29). See Plate 21.

alheghia   The Basque equivalent of *märchen** (Bolte and Polivka, vol. 4, p. 1).

alim   Among the Ifugaos of the Philippines, a series of ballads in jocular, romantic vein that may be chanted only by the wealthy (Barton, p. 3).

alo apagbe   In Yoruba, a popular or entertaining folktale (Chadwick and Chadwick, vol. 3, p. 647).

amauta   One who taught and protected oral tradition in the Inca culture (Rowe, p. 183).

amzad   Tuareg one-stringed instrument generally played by women at an *ahal** or at any time to accompany poetry or song; composed of half a calabash over which a skin is stretched and pierced with one or two holes; played with a curved bow (Chadwick and Chadwick, vol. 3, pp. 559ff.).

aoidos (aoidoi)   The term for poet-singer used in Homer, as contrasted to the *rhapsode** who performed only already-composed epic poetry, and as contrasted to the prose teller of tales; accompanies himself on the lyre (Kirk, *Songs*, pp. 38, 56).

aqyn   A Kazakh wandering bard (Winner, p. 26). See also *akin**.

ardīn (irdīwen)   A harp played by the *tīggiwīt** in Mauritania (Norris, p. 61).

areoi   Groups of highly organized Tahitian strolling performers who told stories, acted out dramas, sang, danced, usually using erotic themes; they decorated themselves with elaborate tattooing, wore costumes, and generally accompanied themselves with drums and flutes; alternate spelling: *'arioi* (Chadwick and Chadwick, vol. 3, p. 423).

àrò   In the Yoruba language of West Africa, an oral folk narrative told by children and adults for self entertainment; there are two main types, the cumulative tale and the tall tale (A. Babalola, p. 179).

arokin   A chronicler or ballad singer in a Yoruba king's court; the head *arokin* is called *ologbo** (Johnson, pp. 125–126; Ellis, p. 243).

ashoughs   Wandering Armenian singers or minstrels (Hoogasian, p. 21). Compare with *ašyq** and *aushek**.

asologun   In the Edo language, a thumb-piano used by professional storytellers in Benin society (*okp'asologun**) to accompany themselves in their storytelling at a "communicative event" called an *okpobhię** (Ben-Amos, pp. 26–29). See Plate 22.

ašyq   An Azerbaijani or Armenian bard (Winner, p. 27). Compare with *ashoughs** and *aushek**.

ata ngke   See *mbuk*.

atoga   The Mangarevan word for all oral literature, such as myths, legends, folktales, chants, songs, historical narratives, etc. (Luomala, p. 777).

aushek   Professional minstrel, saga teller or storyteller among the Turkomans; also called *khan* (Chodzko, pp. 12–13). Compare with *ashoughs** and *ašyq**.

azmari(-s)   In Ethiopia, professional poets or minstrels who dance, sing, tell tales, do improvisations, etc.; they could be compared with the Russian *skomorokhi**; use a *leqso** as accompaniment; female equivalent is called *mungerash* (Chadwick and Chadwick, vol. 3, pp. 524–526).

babalawo   Ashanti priest diviners who told the traditional stories associated with the divinities; similar in many respects to Irish *fi-lid** (Chadwick and Chadwick, vol. 3, p. 646).

babi stariny   A type of Russian *bylina** narrated mainly by women (Chadwick and Chadwick, vol. 2, p. 45).

báchora   See *pohádka*.

badd   In Maharashtra, a large piece of cloth folded up to appear the size of a book, containing pictures from mythological tales; used by the *dakkalwars** to tell tales (Mande, p. 71).

bá-itsitsiwà   See *ada'ox*.

bajka   The Masurian term for *märchen**; see also *básń** and *kazka** (Bolte and Polivka, vol. 4, p. 1).

bakhar(-i)   Term for a storyteller in ancient Russia; alternate term: *bayany* (Sokolov, pp. 381, 457).

ballad   A form of folksong that tells a story, usually with economy and impersonality (Clarke and Clarke, *Concise Dictionary*, p. 4).

bandura   A stringed musical instrument resembling a guitar, used by Russian *kalêki** to accompany their oral narratives (Chadwick and Chadwick, vol. 2, p. 271).

bänkelsänger   From the end of the seventeenth century to the beginning of the twentieth, itinerant performers in German-language areas who set up a stand on which they usually hung a large picture sheet, next to which they set a bench on which they stood to perform in town squares, usually during market season; they sang or chanted stories based on recent events such as family tragedies, robberies, ships sinking, fires, etc., which were printed in the *flugblätter** and *flugschriften** that they expected to sell to the audience; alternate terms: *moritatensänger, marktsänger, ständlisänger, schildersänger*; there were similar performers throughout Europe (*Reallexikon*, vol. 1, pp. 128–129). See Plates 12 and 13.

baqsy   A Kazakh bard who also carries out shamanistic functions; alternate spellings: *baksha, bajan* (Winner, p. 26).

bard(-i)   Term used commonly in England, Ireland, and Wales from the twelfth century onwards to denote a poet-narrator or saga teller; alternate spellings: *bardd* (*beirdd*) (Chadwick and Chadwick, vol. 1, pp. 492, 602; Jackson, *Oldest*, p. 24; Williams, pp. 4–15).

In this book, *The World of Storytelling*, the term bard (plural, -s) is used to mean a storyteller whose function is to create and/or perform poetic oral narrations that chronicle events or praise the illustrious forebears of a social, cultural, or national group.

bardd teulu (beirdd teulu)   In twelfth-century Wales, a house bard in a princely court, lower than a *pencerdd** but of equal rank to all twenty-four other officers of the court (Williams, pp. 7–8; Wade-Evans, p. 167).

barē'-tsiwe-tā're   See *ma'lesk*.

basma   The Romanian equivalent of *märchen** (Bolte and Polivka, vol. 4, p. 1).

básń(-ie)   The Polish equivalent of *märchen**; alternate terms: *powieść, bajka*, gadka, klechda, opowiadanie, przypowiadka, podanie* (Bolte and Polivka, vol. 4, p. 1). The following distinctions can be made: *podanie*—village legends; *klechda*—old wives' tale; *gavęda*—tall tale; *básnie* and *bajki*—*märchen** (*Polish Folklore*, vol. 5, 1960, unp.).

basna   See *pripovijetka*.

basnička   The Wendish equivalent for *märchen** (Bolte and Polivka, vol. 4, p. 1).

berneteltje   See *teltje*.

bhopa   Wandering bards of Rajasthan who use large scrolls called *pabuji kaa pat** to illustrate their tales (Ferguson and Ferguson, n.p.).

biwa-hoshi   In Japan, from the tenth to fifteenth centuries, itinerant monks or persons in monk's clothing who composed and performed songs of war and folk heroes; accompanied by a lute called *biwa* (Barth, p. 3).

bla madong   In the Gola language, a teller of many stories, usually humorous; often presents himself as a caricature of the elders (d'Azevedo, p. 23).

bobe-ma'asses   A Yiddish term for tales of wonder and magic (Schwarzbaum, p. 21).

bothántaiocht   See *céilidhe*.

broadside   A handbill or sheet of paper on which was printed a ballad, intended to be sung and sold in the streets or vended through the country by "flying stationers" (Motherwell, xli–xlii). Could contain any advertising or message (Clarke and Clarke, *Concise Dictionary*, p. 6).

bugarštice   Serbo-Croatian and Albanian anonymous oral epic narrative poems similar to the *narodne pjesme** but having a different meter; survived to some time during the eighteenth century (Chadwick and Chadwick, vol. 2, p. 303; Skendi, p. 26).

bukad   Among the Ifugaos of the Philippines, the recitation of myth (Barton, p. 4).

bylina (byliny)   Anonymous, unrhymed, Russian oral poems concerning secular subjects, often grouped into cycles; performed chiefly for entertainment in large homes and in the court (Chadwick and Chadwick, vol. 2, p. 3). A scholarly term introduced by Sacharov in the 1830s to describe the above type of narrative poem; narrators themselves used the terms *stáriny* or *starinki* (Sokolov, p. 128).

cantor da feria   The Spanish equivalent of the *bänkelsänger** (*Real-lexikon*, vol. 1, p. 128).

caso   See *conto*.

céilidhe   In Gaelic, a social gathering held for the purpose of story-telling (Delargy, p. 18). Alternate spellings: *celidh* (Chadwick and Chadwick, vol. 1, p. 603); *ceilidh* (Carmichael, vol. 1, p. xxii). Also known in different parts of Ireland under the following terms: *scoraiocht, bothántaiocht, cuartaiocht, ránaiocht.*

cerddor (kerddorian)   A minstrel in the court of Welsh princes in the twelfth century; lower in rank than a *pencerdd** or *bardd teulu** (Williams, pp. 7–8). See also *cyfarwyddyd**.

chansons à toile   Women's narrative lyric poems sung or chanted while working at the loom, in France (Holmes, p. 195).

chansons de geste   Old French epic poems of the eleventh to thirteenth centuries, of moderate length, and having a theme related to the glory of the Franks, the Christian religion, or the deeds of certain famous knights; see also *geste du roi** (Holmes, p. 66).

chantefable   In medieval French, a story with alternating sections of prose and verse, usually recited by *jongleurs** (Holmes, p. 250).

chascarillo   See *cuento*.

chastushka   Folk rhymes with two or four verses, often used as part of Russian folk narratives, or before or after them (Sokolov, p. 128).

chatigan   A kind of zither with five to eight strings, used by various Tartar tribes in the past to accompany oral narration; alternate spelling: *jädigän* (Chadwick and Chadwick, vol. 3, p. 22).

chizbat   See *ha-chizbat*.

chorchok   In Russian, a rhythmical folktale (Chadwick and Chadwick, vol. 2, p. 272).

chüan   An early Chinese name for professional storytellers (Průšek, "Narrators," p. 376).

ch'uon   See *chwoh*.

chwedl   See *ystor*.

chwoh   The Chinese equivalent of *märchen**; alternate terms: *sz tsih, ch'uon, kú sz, hwáng tán* (Bolte and Polivka, vol. 4, p. 1).

çifteli   An Albanian *tambura**.

ci-ndzano   See *ka-labi*.

ci-ximi   See *ka-labi*.

cler (clerwr)   In Wales, from the sixteenth to eighteenth centuries, a wandering poet of the lowest order; counterpart of the continental *cleri, clerici vagantes, goliardi* (Nash, p. 33; Williams, pp. 12–15).

conseja   See *cuento*.

conte   The French equivalent of *märchen**. Alternate terms: *conte de fées, conte bleu, récit, legende* (Bolte and Polivka, vol. 4, p. 1).

conte courtois   See *romance*.

conte de fées   See *conte*.

conto   The Portuguese (also Italian) equivalent term for *märchen**; alternate terms: *fabula, historia, caso, exemplo, lenda, patranha, dito, facecia* (Bolte and Polivka, vol. 4, p. 1).

cuartaiocht   See *céilidhe*.

cuento   The Spanish equivalent term for *märchen**; alternate terms: *cuento de hadas, fábula, hablilla, chascarillo, conseja, patraña* (Bolte and Polivka, vol. 4, p. 1). Lenz (p. 1) prefers the term *conseja* as being closest to *märchen**.

cuhüdhor   See *whethlor*.

cuicapicque   In the Nahuatl language of the Aztecs, composers and performers of songs and chants in praise of heroic ancestors, gods, etc. (Durán, p. 299).

curces   See *suptses*.

čybyzga   Primitive woodwind instrument made of wood or leather and used by Kazakh bards to accompany their storytelling (Winner, p. 29).

cyfarwyddyd   In old Welsh, an oral tale once told by the *cerddor** who later came to be known by this term because of being associated always with this type of tale (*Encyclopaedia Britannica, Macropedia*, vol. 10, pp. 1114–1115).

dabteras In Ethiopia, educated men, intermediate between clergy and laity, whose chief duties are to chant psalms and hymns; also compose *qene** and other narrative poetry and are sometimes known for their secular prose and poetry recitations (Chadwick and Chadwick, vol. 3, p. 507).

dakkalwars A group of beggars of the Mang caste in Maharashtra who sing, dance, and narrate mythological stories; they live off alms but accept them only from their own caste; see also *badd** and *kingri** (Mande, p. 69).

dalang The narrator in the *wayang kulit*, the Indonesian form of shadow-puppet performances; strictly speaking, a dramatist rather than a storyteller (McVicker, p. 596).

danével See *hekiats*.

dāstān(-s) In Persian, an intermediate form of oral literature, between epic and folktale; the main story is interspersed with episodes and interludes; the best-known example is the *Thousand and One Nights* (Cejpek, p. 642). Bolte and Polivka list this as an equivalent term for *märchen**.

densetsu The Japanese tales that are legendary in nature, as distinct from the folk or fairy tale type known as *mukashi-banashi** (Seki, p. vi).

diaré (diarou) The Soninké word for *griot, gêwel** or *bard** of the hereditary type; see also *īggīw** (Norris, pp. 53–54). Alternate spelling: *diali* (Diop, p. xviii). Alternate spellings and alternate terms: *diari (diaru); geseri (geseru)* (Jablow, *Gassire's*, p. 7).

diffa See *ahal*.

dikoma In the South Sotho language, secret songs, chants, and other oral material recited during the initiation ceremonies of boys and girls (Guma, p. 3).

dit See *romance*.

dithoko See *lithoko*.

dito See *conto*.

dombra Kazakh plucked string instrument used by bards and ordinary storytellers to accompany themselves or to reproduce sounds of animals or nature as they occurred in the story; somewhat similar to the balalaika; alternate spelling: *domra* (Winner, p. 29).

dong In the Gola language, stories that are meant to be true but that are told for entertainment, in *kabande** form (d'Azevedo, p. 23).

donso-jeli Among the Mande people of Africa, a hunters' bard; position is gained by apprenticeship, as opposed to the hereditary *griot*; see also *nara*, narinyo*, donso-nkoni** (Bird, p. 278).

donso-nkoni Among the Mande people, the six-stringed harp-lute used by a hunters' bard to accompany himself as he narrates; it has a calabash resonator (Bird, p. 279).

do-wa See *hanashi*.

dudunap See *tuttunnap*.

dukhovnie stikhi Oral religious narrative poems recited by Russian *kalêki*** (Chadwick and Chadwick, vol. 2, p. 272).

dziad In Polish, a storyteller (*Polish Folklore*, vol. 3, no. 1, March 1958, p. 16).

džyršy A Kazakh bard who specializes in epic songs (Winner, p. 26).

eachtra See *seanchas*.

eventyr The Swedish equivalent of *märchen***; alternate term: *saga* (Bolte and Polivka, vol. 4, p. 1).

exemplo See *conto*.

exemplum (exempla) A classic fable or more popular anecdote, the content of which could form the basis of a sermon, during the Middle Ages in Europe; the German term is *exempel* (Bødker, p. xix). The Hebrew equivalent is termed *mashal* (Oring, p. 30).

exultet rolls Parchment scrolls used during the Easter vigil service; they contained pictures placed upside down so that the worshipers could see the scenes as they were unrolled by the deacon, who stood in the *ambo* (pulpit) and chanted the text; most were produced in South Italy, during the eleventh and twelfth centuries, but they were found in churches throughout Europe (Gilson, p. 5).

fabla See *parevla*.

fable An animal tale told with an acknowledged moral purpose (Thompson, *Folktale*, p. 10).

fabliau Versified folktale or droll story (not a fable) in medieval French, common mostly in the thirteenth and fourteenth centuries; the closest equivalent English term is beast epic; the *Roman de Renart* is the best-known example (Holmes, p. 200).

fábula See *cuento* or *conto*.

facecia See *conto*.

fagogo See *tala*.

fairy tale One of the equivalent terms in English for *märchen*** (Bolte and Polivka, vol. 4, p. 1). A fictional prose narrative drawn from oral tradition; the commonly used English term for a folktale* conceived as fiction (Clarke and Clarke, *Concise Dictionary*, p. 12).

fáith Probably the Irish term for *vates*, Latin term for prophet or seer; *vates* and *fili** were originally synonymous terms (Chadwick and Chadwick, vol. 1, pp. 613–614). A female type of *fili** (Jackson, *Oldest*, p. 25).

fananga In the Tonga language, stories used to lull people to sleep (Fanua, p. 7). An entertaining piece of fiction (Luomala, p. 777).

fârsā Among the Galla of Ethiopia, a tribal praise song; a personal praise song is called *giērársā* (Cerulli, pp. 58, 100).

favola See *fiaba*.

fiaba The Italian equivalent of *märchen**; alternate terms: *favola, conto**, *racconto, storia, novellina, rosaria, pastocchia, panzanega, romanzella* (Bolte and Polivka, vol. 4, p. 1).

fiannaiocht In Gaelic, the Finn cycle in prose or verse told by Gaelic storytellers (Delargy, p. 18). Any long prose narratives in Gaelic (Bruford, p. 61).

fili(-d) Early medieval Irish reciters of stories, poetry, ballads, non-heroic sagas, etc.; training lasted from six to twelve years; sometimes attached to courts of kings or princes (Chadwick and Chadwick, vol. 1, p. 603). Alternate spellings: *filea (filidhe)* (Joseph C. Walker, p. 14).

finnscéal An individual tale in the Finn cycle (Bruford, p. 61). Alternate spelling: *fionnsgeul*; the equivalent of *märchen** (Bolte and Polivka, vol. 4, p. 1).

flugblatt (flugblätter) A sheet printed on one side, usually containing one picture plus a very simple text; every possible subject was covered; sold by many types of vendors, but frequently by itinerants who sang or chanted the text as a come-on; the pictures were usually woodcut prints; common from the sixteenth through nineteenth centuries (Fehr, p. 3). See also *bänkelsänger**.

flugschrift(-en) The German term for pamphlets of up to fifty pages containing the same type of material as *flugblätter*, only in more expanded form and with fewer pictures; those in story-ballad form were frequently sold by itinerants such as *bänkelsänger** (Fehr, p. 4). See also broadside*.

folklore A science that studies a specific that is primarily characterized as anonymous, noninstitutionalized, and eventually as being old, functional and prelogical (Carvalho-Neto, p. 110). Popular, informal arts and skills shared by the folk, as distinguished from formally acquired knowledge and practice (Clarke and Clarke, *Concise Dictionary*, p. 16).

folktale A prose narrative that is regarded as fiction; the equivalent of *märchen** (Bascom, p. 4). In the broad sense, all forms of prose narrative, written or oral, that have come to be handed down through the years (Thompson, *Folktale*, p. 4).

fös monomon   Among the Trukese in Micronesia, the term for parables (Mitchell, "Study," p. 165).

fowolo   Among the Bandi in northwest Liberia, the oral narrative form concerned with matters of olden times, as distinct from *gbengi*, the entertaining folk tale (O'Connell, p. 1).

futatsume   The rank achieved by a Japanese storyteller after completing apprenticeship, often taking up to five years (Hrdličková, "Japanese," p. 173).

gačica   See *pripovijetka*.

gadka   See *básń*.

gammalt snak   See *soge*.

gaoulo   See *gêwel*.

gatka   See *pripovijetka*.

gawęda   See *básń*.

gawlo   The Toucouleur word for *griot* or bard; see also *iggīw** and *gêwel** (Norris, p. 53).

gbengi   See *fowolo*.

geseri (geseru)   See *diaré*.

geste du roi   A *chanson de geste** that treats of a king (usually Charlemagne) (Holmes, p. 73).

gêwel   The Wolof word for *griot* or bard; see also *iggīw** (Norris, p. 53). Alternate spelling: *guewel* (Diop, p. xix). Presumably, *griot* is a translation of this term or its Fulani equivalent, *gaoulo* (Finnegan, p. 96).

giērársā   See *fârsā*.

gissa   In Arabic-speaking Sudan, the nonfictional type of narrative or tale, as distinct from the *hujwa**; alternate term: *hikaya* (Hurreiz, p. 159).

gleoman   See *scop*.

gli (gliwo)   In the Ewe language of Ghana, animal stories for children, with moral examples of obedience, kindness, courage, honesty, etc. (Egblewogbe, p. 47).

goliardi   See *cler*.

gonob   Among the Ifugaos of the Philippines, an invocation of the names of characters in myth, recited before the myth (Barton, p. 4).

griot See *gêwel*.

guewel See *gêwel*.

guslar(-i) A Serbo-Croatian male minstrel who performed oral narrative poems, *junačke pjesme**, accompanied by the *gusle**; could be Christian or Moslem; alternate term: *pjevači* (Chadwick and Chadwick, vol. 2, pp. 239, 436).

gusle Serbo-Croatian one-stringed instrument with long neck and narrow body, covered with parchment and played with a bow; used to accompany *junačke pjesme** (Chadwick and Chadwick, vol. 2, p. 435).

gusli Russian recumbent harp, played on the knees and used to accompany *bylyny** in the past; now extinct (Chadwick and Chadwick, vol. 2, p. 22).

hablilla See *cuento*.

ha-chizbat In Israel, a term derived from Arabic referring to a humorous folktale, based on a kernel of truth, told among the Palmakhniks (a kind of paramilitary group) during an evening get-together called a *kumsitz* (Oring, pp. 30–49).

hadisi See *nagano*.

hadith In Arabic, a term meaning tale or communication; in a religious context, a parable, tale, saying, or proverb associated with Mohammed (Goldziher, p. 17).

haggadah See *aggadah*.

halk hikâyeleri Minstrel epics or popular narratives in Turkey, similar to the *chantefable** of France; told in prose, interrupted by verses sung to the accompaniment of a *saz**; last from one to twenty or more hours; recited at meetings of ordinary men in small towns in tea- or coffeehouses, or at weddings (Eberhard, *Minstrel Tales*, p. 1).

hanashi The Japanese equivalent of *märchen**; alternate terms: *ofogibanashi, do-wa, monogatori* (Bolte and Polivka, vol. 4, p. 1). The generic term in Japanese for all types of stories; see also *mukashi-banashi** (Adams, p. 6).

hanashi-ka In Japan, narrators of folktales that were generally humorous (Brinkley, vol. 8, p. 286; Post Wheeler, p. 1).

heho For the Fōn in Dahomey, the folktale, as distinct from traditional history, *hwenoho**; not limited to narration within one family or group (Herskovits and Herskovits, p. 15).

hekiats (hekiatner) In Armenian, the *märchen** or extended fairy tale (Hoogasian, p. 14; Surmelian, p. 11). Bolte and Polivka (vol. 4, p. 1) do not list this term but give the following as equivalents of *märchen** in Armenian: *danével, konchou, nôjen, kel*.

hikâjet   See *khirâfet*.

hikaya   See *gissa*.

hikâye   In Turkey, the general term for oral stories (Eberhard, *Minstrel Tales*, p. 3).

hira   Among the Hausa of Nigeria, storytelling sessions held only at night, and including narrations of all types as well as conversation, gossip, etc. (Edgar, p. xvi).

historia   See *conto*.

hoge   In the Mandan language (Native American), the term for story; the equivalent of *māshī**; the term for a holy story is *hohohopini'i*, which is the equivalent of *māshī aruhopa* (Beckwith, p. xvi).

hua-pen   In Chinese, literally, the "root of the story"; general term for the vernacular short story; also applied to a special type of prompt book as developed by professional storytellers of the Sung (960–1279) and Yüan (1279–1368) dynasties; written in colloquial language, often using slang; prose alternates with poetic passages; heroes are ordinary people; see also *pien-wen* (Průšek, *Origins*, pp. 7–22). Not used as prompt books by storytellers, but for reading (Hrdličková, "Professional," p. 234; "Some Questions," pp. 211–212).

hujwa (huja)   In Arabic-speaking Sudan, the fictional type of folktale, as distinct from *gissa** (Hurreiz, p. 159).

hula   Originally, a rhythmical Hawaiian dance, religious in nature, accompanied by songs, chants, tales, pantomimes and even occasional puppet plays; was considered a source of religious experience, as well as artistic and social pleasure; term also referred to the young women performers (Chadwick and Chadwick, vol. 3, pp. 384ff.).

hwáng tán   See *chwoh*.

hwenoho   For the Fŏn people of Dahomey, traditional history, including myths, clan chronicles, and the like; told only at family councils; distinct from *heho** (Herskovits and Herskovits, p. 15). *Hwenukhodoto* or *wenukhodoto* are bards of either sex who perform *hwenoho* (Rouget, pp. 39–41). See also *ahanjito** for disagreement on meaning of the above terms.

ibisigo   In Rwanda, oral dynastic poems composed in a distinctive style, different from pastoral and warrior's epic poems (Vansina, p. 57).

ibota   In the Edo language of Benin, Nigeria, a "communicative event" in which the narrators are not professional artists; primarily a family event in which children, youth, wives and the head of

the household (male) participate; there is much audience participation; see also *okpobhie** (Ben-Amos, p. 23).

icisimikisyo   Among the Lamba of Zambia and Zaire, the term for a
prose story; see also *ulusimi** (Doke, p. xiv).

igbesa   In the Ẹdo language of Benin, Nigeria, a "choir" of three or
four supporters used by professional storytellers; usually also informal apprentices to master storyteller (Ben-Amos, p. 49).

īggīw (īggāwen)   A male, Mauritanian folk poet or bard who accompanies himself on the lute while performing *leġna**; he must be a
member of the hereditary caste of musicians and bards; see also
tīggiwīt, gêwel, gawlo, diaré, na<u>shsh</u>ād (Norris, pp. 51–53).

igiteekerezo   In Rwanda, popular tales enjoyed by all because of their
entertaining and artistic qualities (Vansina, p. 167).

ijála   In the Yoruba language of West Africa, oral poetic compositions of varying lengths (a dozen to several hundred lines), con-
forming to specific rules in use of themes, metrics, and language;
mythically and ritually associated with worship of Ogun; performed on such occasions as child naming, weddings, burial, and
other important days (S. A. Babalola, p. vi).

ik!anam   See *ada'ox*.

imbongi (iimbongi)   In Xhosa or Zulu, a bard or praise poet who traditionally performs *izibongo** (Jordan, *Tales from*, p. 2; Mafeje,
p. 193; Scheub, *Xhosa*, pp. 22–23; Cope, p. 25).

imilando   In the Xhosa language of southern Africa, a term for historical tales (Jordan, *Tales from*, p. xvii).

immram(-a)   Celtic legend type in which the hero sails out on a difficult quest, meeting many adventures; possibly inspired by classical sources. Alternate spelling: *imrama* (Holmes, p. 44; Saul, p. 52).

impango   In Rhodesia, one of a group of numerous praise songs or
story songs for women and girls, often composed while still very
young; masculine term for those composed by and for men and
boys is *ziyabilo*; often accompanied by a large thumb-piano called
kankobela or a small one called *ndandi* (Jones, pp. 15–29).

intsomi   See *ntsomi*.

irdīwen   See *ardīn*.

iro   Among the Igbo of West Africa, tales that are sung (Okeke, p. xi).

iro-ita   Among the Igbo, tales that are sung and spoken (Okeke, p. xi).

ita   Among the Igbo, tales that are spoken (Okeke, p. xi).

ìtan   In Yoruba, an oral narrative that is a myth or legend (*Dictionary
of the Yoruba Language*, p. 126).

itang   See *uruwo*.

itihâsa   See *kalhâ*.

itnangniksuit   According to the Eskimo, young stories that happened not very long ago; compare with *ulipḳuḳ** (Hall, p. 39).

izibongo   In the Xhosa language, heroic, orally chanted praise poems performed by an *imbongi** (Jordan, *Tales from*, p. 2; Scheub, *Xhosa*, pp. 22–23; Cope, p. 25).

izinganekwane   See *ntsomi*.

jädigän   See *chatigan*.

jathum   Among the Luo of East Africa, the person who plays the *nyatiti** and performs lament songs or chants (Anyumba, pp. 187–190).

jongleur   French term for a public singer of a higher type who performed in France and Norman England in the twelfth century and later moved into Italy and Spain; were often men of some clerical training (Holmes, p. 36). Were victims of denunciation and decrees against them from the eleventh to fourteenth centuries (Faral, pp. 18ff.). While *troubadour** performed in courtly style, *jongleur* used a popular style; often reinterpreted *troubadour's** works in more popular manner; to a certain extent, the *jongleur's* tasks were taken over by gypsies (Leach, p. 557). The apprentice or servant of the *troubadour** or *trouvère** who was eventually replaced by the minstrel* around the fourteenth century (*Columbia Encyclopedia*, 2nd ed., pp. 1022, 1290).

junačke pjesme   Serbo-Croatian anonymous oral narrative epics, usually accompanied by the playing of the *gusle** or the *tambura**; always performed by males for males (Chadwick and Chadwick, vol. 2, p. 303; Lord, p. 4).

jutt   The Estonian equivalent of *märchen**; alternate term: *muinasjutt* (Bolte and Polivka, vol. 4, p. 1).

kabande   In the Gola language of Liberia, parables or episodic stories offering moral comments on human behavior; they are anecdotal, and can encompass all forms of oral narrative, including myths and legends (d'Azevedo, pp. 22–23).

kabys   See *qobyz*.

kahānī   The Hindustani term for fable; incorrectly, sometimes spelled *khaunie* (Meer Hasan Ali, pp. 251–252).

ka-labi   In the Bwine-Mukuni language, a folktale containing two parts, one of narrative prose and the other a sung dialogue or monologue and chorus; term literally means "it opens a little one's eyes"; equivalent terms in neighboring languages include: *kâno*, in Tonga; *ci-ximi*, in Ramba; *ci-ndzano* in Ñungwe (Torrend, p. 3).

kalamkari   A cloth with a series of pictures on it, used by wandering storytellers in Andhra Pradesh of southeastern India; may vary in size from small rectangular panels to approximately eight feet square (Ferguson and Ferguson, n.p.). See Plate 26.

kalêki   A confraternity of itinerant professional religious singers and storytellers in Russia, generally crippled, blind, or beggarly; could be male or female; some groups lasted until early in twentieth century (Chadwick and Chadwick, vol. 2, p. 270). See Plate 16.

kalhâ   The Sanskrit equivalent of *märchen**; alternate term: *itihâsa** (Bolte and Polivka, vol. 4, p. 1). Probably refers to *katha** but spelled incorrectly.

kamishibai   In Japan, a traditional storytelling art form practiced by performers descended from *kabuki* and shadow-play tradition; performances of stories were to children, in streets and squares, accompanied by picture cards held in wooden frame; common from about 1920 through the 1950s; term means "paper theater" (Kako, p. 6). See Plate 11.

kankobela   See *impango*.

kâno   See *ka-labi*.

kapa   A Hawaiian evening feast of earlier times, combining entertainment of dance, song, stories, and mimetic action, held in honor of one or more of the gods; it was held in a long booth under a canopy of green leaves; men and women took part; required a year of preparation (Chadwick and Chadwick, vol. 3, pp. 372ff., 418ff.).

kâpchemosin(-ik)   Among the Nandi people of Africa, the term for story or tale (Hollis, p. 300).

kárịsị   In the Nyanga language of the Congo region, an epic; also, the bard who narrates the epic; see also *lugano** (Biebuyck, "Epic," p. 261; Biẹbuyck and Mateene, pp. 11–14).

katha(-s)   In Hindi, the general term for story or tale (Chaudhury, p. xi). A story that is the product of the fertile mind of its author, as distinguished from *akhyayika** (Upadhyaya, p. 225). In Assam, generally called *sadhu katha*, because it is the *sadhu* who narrates them (Pakrasi, p. 13).

kathakas   In Hindi, the term for traditional storytellers who moved from place to place; alternate term: *bhats* (Chaudhury, p. xvi).

kazalica   See *pripovijetka*.

kazka   The Byelorussian name for *märchen**; alternate term: *bajka**
(Bolte and Polivka, vol. 4, p. 1). Alternate term: *kazochiki* (Bain, p.
10).

kel   See *hekiats*.

këngë pleqërishte   An Albanian term for ancient songs of heroes,
composed and performed orally; alternate term: *këngë trimash*;
equivalent of *junačke pjesme** (Skendi, p. 85).

khan   See *aushek*.

khaunie   See *kahānī*.

khirâfet   The Arabic equivalent of *märchen**; alternate terms:
hikâjet, kissa (Bolte and Polivka, vol. 4, p. 1). Compare with *qaṣaṣ**
and *qiṣṣa-khwān**.

kibare (kibeyan)   Among the Mossi people of Upper Volta, the term
for legends (Guirma, pp. ix–xi).

kingri   In Maharashtra, a stringed instrument used by the *dakkalwars** to accompany their singing, dancing, and tale telling
(Mande, p. 70).

kishambaro   In the Nyanga language of the Congo region, "true" stories told orally (Biebuyck, "Epic," p. 261).

kishimikijyo (bishimikijyo)   In the Sanga language of Central Africa, a simple tale that is narrated without any accompaniment or
song; the same as *lufumo** (Centner, p. 352).

kissa   See *khirâfet, qaṣaṣ* and *qiṣṣa-khwān*.

kitabcha   In Persian, a kind of folk-book in manuscript form, used by
professional storytellers as an *aide-memoire* (Cejpek, p. 666).

klechda   See *básń*.

kobuz   See *qobyz*.

kodan   In Japanese, long narrative tales, mainly of a historical nature; persons who are trained in telling these tales are called *kodan-shi*; the halls where they perform are called *kodanseki* or
koshakuba (Hrdličková, "Japanese," pp. 172, 185–187).

komus   See *qobyz*.

konchou   See *hekiats*.

kōrero   Among the Maori of New Zealand, the general term for all
kinds of prose narratives; can also mean news, discussion, tell;
very short tales with dialogues are called *kōrero tara* or *whakataukī* (Orbell, p. x–xi).

koshaku-shi   In Japan, raconteurs who performed in public halls
called *yose**; they usually used a fan or a small flat baton of paper

to accompany and extend their gestures (Brinkley, vol. 8, p. 286). Compare with *zenza**.

kpanlingan　See *ahanjito*.

kramářský zpěvák　The Czech equivalent of the *bänkelsänger** (*Reallexikon*, vol. 1, p. 128).

kú sz　See *chwoh*.

kudem'dé　Among the Mossi people of Upper Volta, the term for tales about their history and ancestors (Guirma, pp. ix–xi).

kukwanebu　In the Trobriand Islands, entertaining folk or fairy tales recited most frequently right after planting time (Malinowski, "Myth," p. 102).

kule　For the Ijo of the Niger delta, praise songs of a bardic nature, recited in a singsong fashion, accompanied by a drum; Yoruba equivalent is *oriki* (Alagoa, p. 410).

kumsitz　See *ha-chizbat*.

kwadwumfo　Chroniclers in the Ashanti king's court (Rattray, *Religion*, p. 143).

labari (labarai)　In Hausa, historical and other oral traditions, as distinguished from *tatsuniya** (Edgar, p. xxiii).

láed　See *romance*.

lafofua　See *tala*.

lahuta　An Albanian one-stringed instrument similar in construction and function to the *gusle** (Chadwick and Chadwick, vol. 2, p. 456).

lai　See *romance*.

lebôkô (mabôkô)　In the Tswana language of Botswana, oral praise poems; equivalent of *lithoko** and *izibongo** (Schapera, p. 1).

legend　A prose narrative, like myth, that is regarded as true by the narrator and audience but set in a period less remote than myth (Bascom, p. 4). Not the same as *sage** in German; a narrated tale with a characteristic spiritual tone (Gunkel, pp. 6–7). Unconscious fiction in the field of history (Thomson, pp. 20–21). Primarily a literary form, not an oral one; the term is sometimes used to refer to stories connected to the lives of saints (Thompson, *Folktale*, p. 10).

leġna　The Mauritanian name for folk-epic poetry, both recited and sung, in the western Sahara (Norris, p. 5).

lenda　See *conto*.

leqso　A one-stringed instrument used by the *azmaris** in Ethiopia (Mondon-Vidailhet, p. 3181).

libwogwo   In the Trobriand Islands in Melanesia, the term for legends, historical accounts, and hearsay tales, all regarded as "true" (Malinowski, "Myth," p. 102).

liliu   In the Trobriand Islands, myths or sacred tales (Malinowski, "Myth," p. 102).

lipitso   See *lithoko*.

lithoko   In the Sotho language, praise poems that are somewhere between an ode and an epic; they were performed at assemblies called *lipitso* or work-parties called *matsema* (Damane and Sanders, pp. vii, 24). Alternate spelling: *dithoko* (Guma, p. 3).

logos (logoi)   Literally, "what is said"; among the ancient Greeks, the term used to refer to any traditional story or narrative; see also *muthos** (Thomson, p. 13).

lufumo (mfumo)   In the Luba language of central Africa, a simple tale that is narrated without any accompaniment or songs (Centner, p. 352).

lugano   In the Lega language of the Congo region, an epic; the same as *kárìsì** (Biebuyck, "Epic," p. 262).

lunga (lunsi)   A drummer in the Dagbon society of northeastern Ghana who is also a chronicler and performer of historical narratives (Oppong, p. 54).

lungano (ngano)   In the Venda language of Rhodesia, a story that is related formally and includes a song; term may also refer only to the song; performed in evening by adults or older children, for boys and girls, but not during hoeing time; young children join in on responses (Blacking, p. 24).

maase   In Yiddish, a term referring to any and all forms of oral tales or narratives (Schwarzbaum, p. 89).

ma'aseh   The Hebrew equivalent of *märchen** (Bolte and Polivka, vol. 4, p. 1; Gerhardsson, p. 181; Oring, p. 30). The equivalent of *exemplum** (Schwarzbaum, p. 21).

māgadha   In the Mahābhārata and in Sanskrit scriptures, a narrator or minstrel attached to a king's court; named after the region in India from which they came (Law, pp. 1–3).

maît' contes   In Haiti, a storyteller of especial renown (Courlander, *Drum*, p. 170).

maka   In Kimbundu language of Angola, the term for legends or stories reputed to be true; entertaining or instructive anecdotes (Chatelain, pp. vii, 21).

ma-ko'u   In Hawaii in the past, court retainers who told stories, gossiped and played games with the chiefs (Luomala, p. 774).

ma'lesk The Tsimshian Indian term for true or historical tales, based on experience (Boas, p. 565). The Crow Indian equivalent is *barē'-tsiwe-tā're* (Lowie, p. 13).

ma-lunda In the Kimbundu language of Angola, the term for historical narratives; alternate term: *mi-sendu* (Chatelain, pp. vii, 21).

ma'mūr In Arabic, someone commissioned by an *imām* to tell stories, but only if they conform to Islamic teaching (Ibn al-Jawzī, p. 114).

märchen Narrative tales of original (native) peoples and their surroundings (Gunkel, pp. 6–7). The equivalent of folktale* (Bascom, p. 3). A tale of some length involving a succession of motifs or episodes that occur in an unreal world without definite locality or definite characters, and filled with the marvelous (Thompson, *Folktale*, p. 8). Unconscious fiction in the field of custom or ordinary life (Thomson, pp. 20–21).

ma'rika In Persian, a gathering of people in a public place that often served as an occasion for storytelling (Cejpek, p. 652).

marknadsångere The Swedish equivalent of the *bänkelsänger** (*Reallexikon*, vol. 1, p. 128).

marktsänger See *bänkelsänger*.

maroki (maroka) One of an organized group of praise singers attached to emirates of the Hausa in northern Nigeria; female of the group was known as *marokiya* (M. G. Smith, p. 27).

masal The Turkish equivalent of *märchen** (Bolte and Polivka, vol. 4, p. 1).

mashal See *exemplum*.

māshī In Hidatsa (Native American) language, the term for story; includes myths and legends having to do with creation of the earth, origin of customs, etc., but not with religious customs or ceremonies; the term for this latter type is *māshī aruhopa*, meaning holy story (Beckwith, p. xvi).

mata ni pachedi Cloth with pictures depicting episodes connected with Mother Goddess, used in worship and religious storytelling in parts of India (Erikson, p. 3).

matsema See *lithoko*.

maysele The Yiddish equivalent of *märchen**; alternate spelling: *mayselekh* (Gimblett, p. 71).

mazarlyk-dji A storyteller among certain nomadic Turkish tribes (von Kamphoevener, p. 7).

mbali (amabali) In Xhosa, a legendary tale that can verge on the fabulous. Alternate term: *siganeko* (Jordan, *Tales from*, p. xvii).

211

mbano   See *wano*.

mbom mvet   See *mvet*.

mbongi   See *imbongi*.

mbuk   In the Efik language of Nigeria, the general term for all types of oral narratives; *ngke* is the specific term for folktales, proverbs and riddles; *ata ngke* is the term used for myths and legends (Simmons, pp. 417–418).

meddah   In Turkish, a master entertainer and storyteller (Barbara K. Walker, "Folks," p. 639).

mese(-fa)   The Hungarian equivalent of *märchen**. Alternate terms: *népmese, rege, monda* (Bolte and Polivka, vol. 4, p. 1).

minarai   In Japan, the first period of apprenticeship of a storyteller in the *yose**, often lasting about a year (Hrdličková, "Zenza," p. 34).

mingaco   In Chile, a community work project at the end of which food and drink and storytelling were often shared (Pino-Saavedra, p. xliii).

minnesänger   The German equivalent of the *troubadour** (Brandl; La Rue; many sources).

minstrel   One of a guild of traveling performers, including acrobats, jugglers, instrumentalists, and storytellers; probably were originally *jongleurs** who settled down in one court as *ménétriers* or *ménéstrels*, having also an advisory capacity to the court; eventually became wanderers again (Faral; Holmes; La Rue).

mi-sendu   See *ma-lunda*.

mi-soso   In the Kimbundu language of Angola, the term for a fictitious type of folktale used for entertainment; always have special formulae for opening and closing (Chatelain, pp. vii, 21).

monda   See *mese*.

monogatori   See *hanashi*.

moritatensänger   See *bänkelsänger*.

mudhakkir   See *qāṣṣ*.

mugani wa lugano   In the Lega language of the Congo region, a narrator of epics; see also *shékár̨ṣ̨* (Biebuyck, "Epic," pp. 261–262).

muinasjutt   See *jutt*.

mukashi-banashi   One of the Japanese terms for *märchen** or fairy tales (Seki, p. vi; Adams, p. 6). Compare with *hanashi** and *densetsu**.

mungerash See *azmari*.

murā'i In Arabic, one who tells stories with a religious context without being commissioned by an *imām* to do so; alternate term: *mukhtāl* (Ibn al-Jawzī, p. 114).

mushíngá In the Nyanga language of the Congo region, a tale in which the supernatural element stands in the foreground (Biebuyck, "Epic," p. 261; Biebuyck and Mateene, p. 9).

muṣinjo In the Nyanga language, eulogistic recitations for chiefs or headmen, given on state occasions by elders, without musical accompaniment, but with some rhythm and gesture (Biebuyck and Mateene, p. 8).

muthos (muthoi) The term preferred by Homer and other Greek poets and writers to describe any traditional story; see also *logos** (Thomson, p. 17).

mvet In southern Cameroon and northern Gabon, the term for an epic song or chant; also, the name of the instrument used to accompany its performance; the person who performs it is called *mbom mvet* (Towo-Atangana, pp. 163–173).

mvngrung ka Ballad speech used by Burmese *rawangs* to chant special myths for special feasts (Lapai, p. 277).

mwitabizia In the Nyanga language, an apprentice bard (Biebuyck, "Epic," p. 262).

myth A prose narrative that, in the society in which it is told, is considered to be a truthful account of what happened in the past (Bascom, p. 4). A narrated tale in which the highest forms of the great gods play the leading role (Gunkel, pp. 6–7). A tale laid in a world supposed to have preceded the present order; intimately connected with religious beliefs and practices of the people (Thompson, *Folktale*, p. 9). A piece of unconscious fiction in the field of religion, i.e., the unknown, magic, philosophy, etc.; a *logos** that has its origin in some belief or practice in religion or explains the natural by the supernatural (Thomson, pp. 20–21, 74).

nagano The Swahili equivalent of *märchen**; alternate term: *hadisi* (Bolte and Polivka, vol. 4, p. 1).

naniwabushi Storytellers similar to the *kodanshi* except that they were accompanied by the music of a *samisen* (Meissner, pp. 240–241).

naqqāl bāshī In Persian, a court narrator (Cejpek, p. 652).

nara Among the Mande people of Africa, an apprentice to a hunters' bard (*donso-jeli**), after he has achieved master singer status and is entitled to accompany the bard on the *narinyo** (Bird, p. 279).

nareguyap   Among the Shoshoni Indians, the single term encompassing all types of prose narratives (Hultkrantz, p. 554).

narinyo   Among the Mande people, the rhythmic instrument that an apprentice to a hunters' bard (*donso-jeli**) must use to accompany his master bard, after the apprentice himself has become a master singer; it is made of a ridged metal pipe and played by scraping with a metal bar; it provides the basic background rhythm for the narration (Bird, p. 279).

narodne pjesme   In Serbo-Croatian, anonymous oral narrative epic poems having a uniform decasyllabic line with caesura after the fourth syllable (Chadwick and Chadwick, vol. 2, p. 300).

nashshād   In Mauritania and other parts of the Sahara, a bardic singer who is not of the *īggāwen**, or hereditary caste of musicians and bards (Norris, p. 51).

nathaiocht   Extempore disputative dialogue in verse, as told by Gaelic storytellers at a *céilidhe** (Delargy, p. 18).

ncok   Among the Bushongo of Burundi, the term for artistic, historical, narrative songs of the Bushongo, sung while the persons taking part in a masked dance are dressing; also sung at other times, not predetermined (Vansina, pp. 43, 119, 189).

ncyeem ingesh   Among the Bushongo, the term for dynastic songs that are sung once a month, at the new moon (Vansina, p. 43).

ndandi   See *impango*.

népmese   See *mese*.

ngano   See *lungano*.

nganuriro   In the Nyanga language of the Congo region, the narration of extraordinary events (Biebuyck, "Epic," p. 261). "True" stories about remarkable personal experiences, partly true and partly imaginary (Biebuyck and Mateene, p. 10).

ngewa   See *ukewa*.

ngke   See *mbuk*.

nithan kuhog   In Central Thailand, the common term for tales or oral narratives; literally means "tales of lies"; also called just *nithan* (Attagara, p. 234).

nôjen   See *hekiats*.

novella (novelle)   German term for a tale similar in structure to *märchen** but taking place in a real world with definite time and place; marvels occur but differently from *märchen** (Thompson, *Folktale*, p. 8).

novellina   See *fiaba*.

n'siring Among the Toucouleurs of Mali, the general term for all oral tales (N'Diaye, p. 9).

ntsomi In Xhosa, a fictional type of folk narrative, as distinct from the *siganeko* or *mbali**; performed potentially by every member of Xhosa society, not by professionals; correct spelling is *intsomi (iintsomi)* but the tales are most commonly referred to under this simplified spelling; Zulu equivalents are *nganekwane (izinganekwane*)* (Jordan, *Tales from*, p. xvii; Scheub, *Xhosa*, pp. 3, 12).

nursery tale *See* fairy tale, folktale.

nu'yam See *ada'ox*.

nyatiti The lyre used by the Luo of East Africa to accompany laments or chants at burials, weddings, etc. (Anyumba, pp. 187–190).

nyūmon In Japan, the act of entering apprenticeship as a storyteller in the *yose**; at this point the master gives the apprentice his artistic name (Hrdličková, "Zenza," p. 33).

o'deshi In Japan, an apprentice storyteller in the *yose** (Hrdličková, "Zenza," p. 33).

ofogibanashi See *hanashi*.

okalugtuak An Eskimo equivalent for the term *märchen**; alternate term: *okolualârut* (Bolte and Polivka, vol. 4, p. 1).

okp'akpata In Benin, Nigeria, a professional storyteller who accompanies himself on the *akpata** (Ben-Amos, p. 25). See Plate 7.

okp'asologun In Benin, Nigeria, a professional storyteller who accompanies himself on the *asologun** (Ben-Amos, p. 25).

okpobhie In Benin society, the Edo-language term for a "communicative event" that differs from the *ibota** in that the storytelling is always done by a professional narrator who always accompanies himself on a musical instrument. "The event must have a ceremonial significance that warrants an extravagant celebration in a family circle" such as a naming ceremony for a newborn child, a marriage ceremony, etc. (Ben-Amos, pp. 24–25).

ollam In Gaelic history, the highest grade of *fili**; position was usually hereditary; wore a special dress of feathers (Chadwick and Chadwick, vol. 1, p. 603; Cormac, p. 127). Alternate spelling: *ollamh* (Saul, p. 53).

ologbo The head ballad singer or chronicler in a Yoruba king's court; the office was hereditary; see also *arokin** (Johnson, pp. 125–126; Ellis, p. 243).

omwevugi In the Runyankore language of Uganda, a bard who recites praise poems for warriors, animals, famous persons, etc. (Morris, p. 21).

oníjălá   In Yoruba, those who perform *ijála** (S. A. Babalola, p. 3).

opowiadanie   See *básń*.

oriki   See *kule*.

oriori   In Polynesia, lullabies full of historical allusions that a mother would sing to a child (son) so as to have him learn about his ancestors and their deeds (Luomala, p. 777).

o'shisho   In Japan, a master storyteller (Hrdličková, "Zenza," p. 33).

pabuji kaa pat   Storytelling canvases from the Rajasthan area, used by wandering bards known as *bhopa**; alternate spelling: *pabuji ki phad* (Ferguson and Ferguson, n.p.). See Plate 27.

panzanega   See *fiaba*.

paramythion   The Modern Greek equivalent of *märchen** (Bolte and Polivka, vol. 4, p. 1).

parevla   Swiss Romansh equivalent of *märchen**; alternate term: *fabla* (Bolte and Polivka, vol. 4, p. 1).

pāsaka   The Lithuanian equivalent of *märchen**; without diacritic mark, the Lettish equivalent; alternate terms in Lettish: *stahsts*, *teika, teiksma* (Bolte and Polivka, vol. 4, p. 1).

pastocchia   See *fiaba*.

patraña   See *cuento*.

patranha   See *conto*.

pauraṇika(-s)   In India, tellers of ancient stories, especially at festivals and fairs; modern equivalent of *sûta** (*Encyclopaedia Britannica, Macropedia*, vol. 8, pp. 927– 932).

pencerdd   The chief bard attached to a princely house in Wales; corresponds roughly to the Irish *ollam** (Chadwick and Chadwick, vol. 1, p. 604; Wade-Evans, pp. 179–180). Alternate spelling: *penkerdd*; position was protected by law (Williams, pp. 5–7).

penglipur lara   Oral folk romances in Malaysia; term also refers to narrators and to the occasion; storytellers are also known by the name of the hero of the most popular story in their area or by other local terms (Sweeney, pp. 47–53).

pevci   In the South Slavic languages, the equivalent of *bänkelsänger** (Skendi, p. 41).

pien-hsiang   In Chinese, literally, "pictures of incidents"; series of pictures in Chinese Buddhist temples, either on the walls or in scrolls, illustrating wondrous events in the scriptures (Demiéville, p. 186; Waley, *Ballads*, p. 245).

pien-wen Chinese manuscripts found in a cave near Tun-huang, dating to the T'ang dynasty (618–907) or a bit later; they contained stories in colloquial language, in a mixture of prose and verse similar to the *chantefable**, and were probably used by Buddhist monks or by secular storytellers as a guide or memory aid; they may or may not have been used with pictures painted on the back of some of the scrolls, or on the temple walls; alternate term: *tun-huang pien-wen*; see also *hua-pen* (Demiéville, pp. 185–187; Hrdličková, "Some Questions," pp. 211–225; Průšek, *Origins*, pp. 18–22).

p'ing-hua Anonymous, popular-language stories based on prompt books of paid, professional narrators (Eberhard, *Folktales*, p. xxiv).

p'ing-shu Prose tales without musical accompaniment, interspersed with verse; performed with extreme simplicity. Alternate term: *p'ing hua** (Hrdličková, "Chinese," p. 103).

pjevači See *guslar*.

pjóthsagnir The Icelandic term for folk legends (Simpson, p. 3).

ploshchadnoi pevetz The Russian equivalent of the *bänkelsänger** (*Reallexikon*, vol. 1, p. 128).

pobyvalshchiny Russian heroic sagas narrated in prose as contrasted to *byliny**, narrated in poetry (Chadwick and Chadwick, vol. 2, p. 268).

podanie See *básń*.

pohádka The Czech equivalent for *märchen**; alternate terms: *povídka, povést, báchora, báchorka* (Bolte and Polivka, vol. 4, p. 1).

povest' The Slovakian equivalent of *märchen**; the same term is used, but with other diacritic mark, in Czech (see entry above) and with no diacritic mark in Slovenian; alternate term in Slovakian: *rozprávka* (Bolte and Polivka, vol. 4, p. 1).

povídka See *pohádka*.

powieść See *básń*.

prală The Albanian equivalent of *märchen**; alternate term: *cafsă* (Bolte and Polivka, vol. 4, p. 1).

pravljica The Slovenian equivalent of *märchen**; alternate term: *povest* (Bolte and Polivka, vol. 4, p. 1).

priča See *pripovijetka*.

prikazka The Bulgarian equivalent of *märchen** (Bolte and Polivka, vol. 4, p. 1).

pripoviest See *pripovijetka*.

pripovijetka The Serbo-Croatian equivalent of *märchen**; alternate terms: *priča, pripoviest, gatka, gačica, basna, kazalica* (Bolte and Polivka, vol. 4, p. 1).

przypowiadka See *básń.*

pulhoeitekya In the Kiowa (Native American) language, a fictional story (Parsons, *Kiowa,* p. xvii).

qaṣaṣ In Arabic, storytelling in the religious sense, i.e., the stories must conform to Koranic teaching (Ibn al-Jawzī, p. 99).

qāṣṣ (quṣṣāṣ) In Arabic, a storyteller who tells only tales that stem from Koranic teaching; alternate spelling: *qaṣṣaṣ* (singular) (Ibn al-Jawzī, p. 101). Alternate terms: *wā'iz, mudhakkir* (Goldziher, p. 152).

qene Short, witty poem composed and recited by *dabteras** in Ethiopia (Chadwick and Chadwick, vol. 3, p. 514).

qiṣṣa-khwān The Persian term for folktales (Phillott, p. 376).

qiṣṣa-qū The most common Persian term for storyteller or narrator (Cejpek, p. 652).

qobyz Two-stringed instrument with an alto pitch, round body (open at the top), and a fingerboard that curves upward so that the strings cannot be depressed to touch it; often adorned with bells and pieces of metal; used most frequently by Kazakh bards to accompany storytelling that had shamanistic functions; alternate spellings: *kobus, kabys, komus* (Winner, p. 29).

quipu-kamayoq Among the Incas, a professional interpreter of the *quipu* (knotted cord) who memorized historical data, legends, genealogies, etc.; alternate spelling: *quipomaoc* (Rowe, pp. 183–330). See Plate 6.

quyurčin In Mongolia, the term for a bard (Kara, p. 50).

racconto See *fiaba.*

rakugo Short humorous tales, episodes or narratives, usually lasting from 10 to 20 minutes, as opposed to *kodan** which lasted an hour or more; persons who perform this type of tale are called *rakugokas* (Hrdličková, "Japanese," p. 172).

ránaiocht See *céilidhe.*

récit See *conte.*

rege See *mese.*

regle See *soge.*

remse See *soge.*

rhapsode(-s)   In ancient Greece, a person who performed Homeric poems but, in contrast to the bard, did not compose new forms or alter the old ones; generally carried a staff, called *rhabdos*; alternate term: *rhapsodist* (Bowra, p. 431; F. Young, p. 3; Kirk, pp. 314–315). See Plate 1.

rianaiocht   Discussions on such matters as genealogies, current news, and local, national, or international events, as recounted by Gaelic storytellers at a *céilidhe** (Delargy, p. 18).

rispe   See *soge*.

roko   The craft of praise singing as practiced by the *maroki** attached to the emirates of the Hausa in Nigeria; it is accompanied by drums, gongs, trumpets, or horns, each used for special occasions (M. G. Smith, p. 27).

romance   From the thirteenth century on, a fictitious narrative in verse, with subjects of chivalry and love; shorter forms include the *lai**, the *conte courtois**, and the *dit** (all Old French), the *láed** (Celtic), and the *nouvelle* (Holmes, p. 133).

romanz   Originally, a translation from Latin into the vulgar tongue; after the twelfth century, the term became *romance** with a new meaning (Holmes, p. 133).

romanzella   See *fiaba*.

rondalla de la bora del foch   The Catalan equivalent of *märchen** (Bolte and Polivka, vol. 4, p. 1).

rosaria   See *fiaba*.

rozprávka   See *povest'*.

sadhu katha   See *katha*.

saga (sögur)   Literally, "something said," in Icelandic; prose tales of the heroic age from the middle of twelfth century to beginning of fifteenth, from Scandinavian region and Iceland; should not be confused with German *sage** (Craigie, pp. 1–11; Thompson, *Folktale*, p. 10).

sage(-n)   In German, a narrated tale in which historical or taken-as-historical persons are the subject (Gunkel, pp. 6–7). In German, an account of an extraordinary happening believed to have occurred; a local legend; usually contains a single narrative motif (Thompson, *Folktale*, p. 8).

saráu   See *serão*.

satu   The Finnish equivalent of *märchen**; alternate term: *tarina* (Bolte and Polivka, vol. 4, p. 1).

saz   Turkish guitar used to accompany the telling of *halk hikâyeleri**
(Eberhard, *Minstrel Tales*, p. 1).

sazşairleri   Turkish minstrels who are professional but usually work
on their farms during the growing season; they are *not* blind and
are not in the service of one family or group (Eberhard, *Minstrel
Tales*, p. 1).

scéal   See *sean-sgéal*.

scélaige   A medieval Gaelic storyteller (Delargy, p. 9).

schilder   The term used for the large picture sheets, usually depicting six to ten scenes from the story ballads sung and sold by
bänkelsänger* (Janda and Nötzoldt, p. 9).

schildersänger   See *bänkelsänger*.

scop   The old Anglo-Saxon term for a minstrel or bard at a court;
used in *Beowulf, Deor*, and other early literature; alternate term:
gleeman (Chadwick and Chadwick, vol. 1, p. 596). Alternate spelling: *gleoman* (L. F. Anderson, pp. 2–6). One of two words in Anglo-
Saxon used to describe singer-performers at a court; *scop* referred
to a bardic type who composed and sang only; *gleoman* referred to
a singer-juggler; later terms used in Anglo-Saxon as the equivalent of *scop* were: *harpour, sautreour, rymour, sangere*; later terms
used for the *gleoman* included *japer, jangler, juglour, tregetour*;
see also minstrel* (Brandl, pp. 873–878).

scoraiocht   See *céilidhe*.

seanchai(-dhe)   In Gaelic, a man or woman who makes a specialty of
telling local tales, family sagas, short realistic stories, etc., called
seanchas* or *eachtra*; alternate term: *seanchasai* (Delargy, p. 6).
Alternate spellings: *shannechas* (Thompson, *Folktale*, p. 450);
seanacha (seanachaidhe) (Joseph C. Walker, p. 14). Commonly referred to in English as shanachie.

seanchas   Irish oral tradition in the form of local tales, family sagas,
short realistic stories, all similar to the German *sage**; also called
eachtra (Delargy, p. 4).

sean-sgéal   In Gaelic, a folk story of a complex and intricate nature,
similar to the *märchen** (Delargy, p. 6; Raine, p. vii). Alternate
terms: *sgeul, scéal* (Bolte and Polivka, vol. 4, p. 1).

se'pt   See *siele'pt*.

serão   In Brazilian folklore, an evening gathering of the family
circle, during which time stories are told; alternate spelling: *saráu*
(Gorham, p. 53).

seroki (liroki) A praise poet in the Sotho language who composes and performs *lithoko** (Damane and Sanders, p. 18).

sgéal See *sean-sgéal*.

sgéalai A Gaelic storyteller who specializes in telling *sean-sgéal**, as contrasted with the *seanchai** who specializes in *seanchas**; alternate spelling: *sgéaltoir* (Delargy, p. 6).

sgeul See *sean-sgéal*.

sgeulachd In Welsh, a folk story or tale; similar to the Irish *sean-sgéal** (Jackson, *International*, p. 54; Bruford, p. 66).

shanachie See *seanchai*.

shannechas See *seanchai*.

shékárįsį In the Nyanga language of the Congo region, a master bard who narrates epics; the equivalent of the *mugani wa lugano** (Biebuyck, "Epic," pp. 261–262).

shin-uchi Term sometimes used for the highest rank of storyteller in the Japanese *yose** (Meissner, p. 236).

shu-ch'ang In China, halls similar to the Japanese *yose** where storytelling was performed; common in latter half of the nineteenth century, especially in Shanghai (Hrdličková, "Chinese," p. 98).

shuo-ch'ang wen-hsüeh A general term in Chinese for literature to be narrated and sung; often of epic character; *pien-wen** and *hua-pen** are two of many forms (Průšek, "Shuo-ch'ang," p. 161).

shuo-shu In Chinese, a broad term covering most forms of post-medieval storytelling (Hrdličková, "Chinese," p. 97); Průšek, "Creative," p. 253).

siele'pt The Upper Chehalis (Native American) term, among the western Washington Salish, for tales from the time "when all the animals were people"; the Cowlitz language equivalent is *se'pt* (Adamson, p. xii).

siganeko See *mbali*.

skáld(-s) The Icelandic word for poet, but generally used to refer to the specific group of Norwegian and Icelandic oral poets of the ninth to thirteenth centuries who composed in a syllabic verse different from that of the *Eddas*; the best-known example of the type is *Egil's Saga* (Craigie, pp. 1–11).

skazitel(-i) A Russian amateur bard or storyteller, usually of peasant origin; feminine: *skazitelnitsy* (Chadwick and Chadwick, vol. 2, p. 239).

skazka (skazki) A Russian folktale or story; the equivalent of *märchen** (Bolte and Polivka, vol. 4, p. 1).

skomorokh(-i) A Russian bard, performer or entertainer, commonly found from the late Middle Ages to the late seventeenth century; sometimes used masks, and often accompanied themselves on the *gusli** (Bowra, p. 415; Chadwick and Chadwick, vol. 2, p. 261).

skylls In Manx, the term for tales in the old days (Killip, p. 23).

soge The Norwegian equivalent of *märchen**; alternate terms: *regle, rispe, remse, gammalt snak* (Bolte and Polivka, vol. 4, p. 1).

solemde (soalema) Among the Mossi people of Upper Volta, the term used for funny, entertaining tales (Guirma, pp. ix–xi).

sou fös See *uruwo*.

sourneto The Provençal equivalent of *märchen** (Bolte and Polivka, vol. 4, p. 1).

speta'kl See *ada'ox*.

spielmann The German equivalent of minstrel* or *jongleur**; a wandering performer who collected and recited heroic songs based on popular legends and began to link them together to form longer epic narratives, of which the best-known example is the *Nibelungenlied* (Brandl, pp. 873–875).

sprookje The Dutch equivalent of *märchen**; alternate terms: *zeisel, vertellinge, vertelsel* (Bolte and Polivka, vol. 4, p. 1).

stahsts See *pāsaka*.

ständlisänger See *bänkelsänger*.

stáriny or *starinki* See *bylina*.

storia See *fiaba*.

suptses The Lapp equivalent of *märchen**; alternate term: *curces* (Bolte and Polivka, vol. 4, p. 1).

sûta In the Brahmanas (sacred Hindu texts), a royal herald and minstrel (Chadwick and Chadwick, vol. 2, p. 617). Panegyric bards for the Kshatriya caste who later became popular narrators of myth and legend (*Encyclopaedia Britannica, Macropedia*, vol. 8, pp. 927–932).

sz tsih See *chwoh*.

tagatupu'a A Polynesian term from the Rennell and Bellona Islands, used for all types of stories and tales, but not for ritual formulas and songs; alternate term: *tautupu'a* (Elbert and Monberg, p. 29).

takhles In Yiddish, didactic tales that point out some moral (Schwarzbaum, p. 21).

tala   The Samoan equivalent of *märchen**; alternate terms: *fagogo, lafofua* (Bolte and Polivka, vol. 4, p. 1).

talatupua   In Polynesia, a tale of the gods (Luomala, p. 777).

tale   *See* fairy tale, folktale.

tallol (tali)   Among the Fulani of Northern Nigeria, the term for folktales of a fictional nature, as contrasted with *tindol** (Lestrange, pp. 6–7).

tamaschahuts   The Kabyle (Tuareg) equivalent of *märchen** (Bolte and Polivka, vol. 4, p. 1).

tambura   A two-stringed, plucked instrument used by Serbo-Croatian oral epic singers in Yugoslavia (Lord, p. 4).

tarina   See *satu*.

tassunja   See *tatsuniya*.

tatsuniya (tatsuniyoyi)   In Hausa, fables and tales of fancy, as distinguished from *labari** (Edgar, p. xxiii). Alternate spelling: *tassunja*; the equivalent of *märchen** (Bolte and Polivka, vol. 4, p. 1).

tautupu'a   See *tagatupu'a*.

teika   See *pāsaka*.

teiksma   See *pāsaka*.

tekerleme(-ler)   In Turkish, a nonsense jingle or rhyme that introduces many stories or is used in the body of the story to create interest (Walker and Uysal, p. 3).

teltje   The West Friesian equivalent of *märchen**; alternate term: *berneteltje* (Bolte and Polivka, vol. 4, p. 1).

tendi or *tenzi*   See *utenzi*.

tetok   A small hammer used by the *dalang** in Indonesia to separate speeches of the different characters appearing as shadow puppets; strictly speaking, part of the theater form, and not storytelling (McVicker, p. 600).

thyle (thylir)   Among the ancient Anglo-Saxons, the term for a cult-orator whose function was both sacred and literary; the Old Norse equivalent was *thulr* (Huizinga, p. 121).

tial   The North Friesian equivalent of *märchen**; alternate term: *staatje* (Bolte and Polivka, vol. 4, p. 1).

tīdīnĭt (tidānaten)   Four-stringed, plucked lute, used by *īggīw** (Norris, pp. 54, 62).

tīggiwĭt (tīggāwāten)   A female, Mauritanian folk poet or bard who accompanies herself on the harp; she must be a member of the hereditary caste of musicians and bards; see also *ĭggĭw** (Norris, pp. 51–53).

tindol (tindi) Among the Fulani of Nigeria, the term for legends or myths (Lestrange, pp. 6–7).

tohunga(-s) Polynesian intellectuals who were responsible for guarding, remembering and narrating genealogies, praise songs, sagas, geographical information, and many other types of oral narratives (Chadwick and Chadwick, vol. 3, part 2; Luomala, p. 774; Best, vol. 1, pp. 57–84).

toigh áirneáil In Ireland, a house where storytelling was practiced regularly (Delargy, p. 10).

troubadour(-s) In southern France, northern Spain and northern Italy, from the end of the eleventh century to the end of the thirteenth, a poet-musician who composed and performed in the Provençal language for the entertainment of a court or wealthy household; strictly speaking, not a storyteller since the compositions were rarely story poems; related to storytelling in that the life and work of some *troubadours* became subject of storytelling activities of *jongleur** (Bonner; Faral; Holmes; La Rue; many other sources).

trouvére(-s) In northern and central France and in Norman England, during the twelfth and thirteenth centuries, a poet-musician who copied the style of the *troubadour** but used the *langue d'oc*, or medieval French dialect; died out shortly after the *troubadour* (Bonner; Faral; Holmes; La Rue; many other sources).

tshomo (ditshomo) The collective term in the South Sotho language meaning all myths, legends, fables and folktales (Guma, p. 4). Alternate spelling in Sotho: *tsomo (litsomo)* (Postma, p. 3).

tugen A cloak or toga of feathers worn by the *ollam** as a sign of rank; alternate spellings: *tuighean, taeidhean* (Cormac, p. 160; *Leabhar na g-ceart*, n.p.).

tun-huang pien-wen See *pien-wen*.

tuttunnap Among the Trukese of Micronesia, the term for story, folktale, or fable, told chiefly for amusement; alternate spelling: *dudunap* (Mitchell, pp. 166–169).

tze-ti During Ch'ing dynasty in China (1644–1911), a professional balladeer who performed in wealthy homes, but never received remuneration (Hrdličková, "Chinese," p. 103).

tz'e-tze Handbook or manual of secrets handed by master reciter to student upon completion of apprenticeship, in old Chinese storytelling guilds; alternate terms: *ti-pen, chiao-pen* (Hrdličková, "Professional," p. 233).

uano   In the Nyanga language of the Congo region, the term meaning any type of tale (Biebuyck, "Epic," p. 261; Biebuyck and Mateene, p. 9).

ukewa (ngewa)   In Kikamba, in Kenya, stories and incidents told from personal experience (Mbiti, p. v).

üliger kelekü tangkim   In Mongolia, a public hall where bards and storytellers perform; alternate term: *üliger-un ger*; in the Jarut language: *ulgerīn ger* (Kara, p. 8).

üligerčin   In Mongolian, the general term for a storyteller (Kara, p. 50).

ulipḳuḳ   Old, true stories that happened a long time ago, according to the Eskimo; see also *itnangniksuit** (Hall, p. 39).

ulogho   In Benin, long traditional stories told only by men, accompanied by the *akpata** (Sidahome, jacket copy).

ulusimi   Among Lamba of Zaire and Zambia, a prose story interspersed with song; alternate terms: *icisimi, akasimi, akalaŵi*; see also *icisimikisyo** (Doke, p. xiv).

umugani   In Burundi, the term that refers to all historical and nonhistorical tales, proverbs, local stories, personal recollections, etc.; in Rwanda, the same term refers only to nonhistorical tales and proverbs (Vansina, p. 165).

umwes   In Trukese (Micronesia), the term for crazy, foolish, or silly tales; noodle tales; alternate spelling: *umes* (Mitchell, "Study," pp. 166–168).

upakathas   In Bengali, the general term for stories (Day, p. 88).

uruwo   The Trukese (Micronesia) term for legend or history; often chanted in a special language called *itang*; must be learned and told exactly; considered as sacred property of the family; often has entertainment as well as sacred value; the skilled narrator of *uruwo* is called *sou fós*; alternate spelling: *uruo* (Mitchell, "Study," pp. 168–176).

utenzi (tenzi)   In Swahili, a long epic-type narrative poem containing either homiletic material or the narrative of deeds of Moslem heroes; originally meant to be performed orally for entertainment and inspiration; in recent years, the form has come to mean written poetry of this type, covering such themes as the life of Christ, the lives of political leaders, etc.; alternate spelling: *utendi (tendi)* (Harries, p. 24).

uwa   Among the Ifugaos of the Philippines, the term for myth; alternate term: *abuwab* (Barton, p. 4).

vertellinge   See *sprookje*.

vertelsel   See *sprookje*.

virarautua   In the Papuan language, the term for folktales and folklore in general (Ker, p. x).

waikan   Among the Winnebago Native Americans, a sacred tale that always ended well; its heroes were spirits or deities; each *waikan* belonged to a particular family or individual and passed, through purchase or inheritance, from one gifted raconteur to another (Radin, p. 122).

wā'iz   See *qāṣṣ*.

wano (mbano)   In Kikamba (East Africa) a story, fable, myth, or narrative of a remote or fictitious nature (Mbiti, p. v). Compare with *uano**.

warai-banashi   The Japanese term for anecdotes (Adams, p. 6).

wędrowiec   In Polish, a wandering storyteller (*Polish Folklore*, vol. 3, March 1958, p. 16).

wenukhodoto   See *hwenoho*.

whakataukī   See *kōrero*.

whare wananga   In the Maori language, a house built for the special teaching of oral tradition to the young (Best, p. 57; Luomala, p. 774). Alternate term in Marquesa Islands: *oho au* (Handy, *Marquesan*, p. 20).

whethel (whethlow)   In Cornish, a story or tale (Nance, p. 167).

whethlor   In Cornish, a storyteller. Alternate term: *cuhüdhor* (Nance, p. 167).

wiy-nù   Among the Shilluk people of Sudan, the term for story or tale (Westermann, p. 304).

worak   For the Winnebago (Native Americans), a secular tale, as distinct from the sacred *waikan**, that could be told at any time; it often ended unhappily; its heroes were human beings (Radin, p. 118).

yamapaṭa   Scrolls used by early "picture showmen" in India to illustrate religious legends or the like; the showmen were called *yamapaṭṭaka* (Coomaraswamy, pp. 182–184).

yaquṣṣu   In Arabic, traditional stories that conform to orthodox Islamic teaching (Ibn al-Jawzī, p. 109).

yose   Public halls in Japan where *koshaku-shi** were performed; at the end of the nineteenth century, there were 180 *yose* in Tokyo (Brinkley, vol. 8, p. 286). For description of twentieth-century *yose* see Hrdličková ("Zenza," pp. 31–41).

ystor   Welsh equivalent of *märchen**. Alternate term: *chwedl* (Bolte and Polivka, vol. 4, p. 1).

zeisel   See *sprookje*.

ženske pjesme   Types of Serbo-Croatian *narodne pjesme** performed chiefly by women, without accompaniment, at weddings and social occasions (Chadwick and Chadwick, vol. 2, p. 439).

zenza   In Japan, the second period of apprenticeship for storytellers in the *yose**, lasting from two to three years (Hrdličková, "Zenza," p. 35).

zibongo   See *izibongo*.

ziyabilo   See *impango*.

Notes

Note: Full reference citations for *The Sacred Books of the East*, F. Max Müller, ed., and the Loeb Classical Library can be found by consulting the Bibliography.

Chapter 1

1. "Tales of the Magicians," in *Egyptian Literature*, ed. and tr. by Epiphanius Wilson (London and New York: The Colonial Press, 1901), pp. 159–169.

2. Ibid., pp. 173–176.

3. K. Ranke, "Volkserzählung," in *Die Religion in Geschichte und Gegenwart*, 3rd ed. (Tübingen: J. C. B. Mohr, 1965), vol. 6, p. 1451.

4. H. Munro Chadwick and Nora Kershaw Chadwick, *The Growth of Literature*, vol. 2 (Cambridge: Cambridge Univ. Pr., 1932–1940), p. 753.

5. *The Sacred Books of the East* (S. B. E.), vol. 12, p. xxiv.

6. S. B. E., vol. 29, pp. 246–248.

7. S. B. E., vol. 30, p. 29.

8. S. B. E., vol. 36, book 4, chap. 7, 1–7, pp. 92–96.

9. Euripides, *Complete Greek Tragedies*, vol. 5 (New York: Modern Library, n.d.), p. 312.

10. Aristophanes, *The Eleven Comedies*, vol. 1 (New York: Liveright, 1943), p. 267.

11. Ibid., vol. 2, pp. 61–62.

12. William Chase Greene, ed., *The Dialogues of Plato* (New York: Liveright, 1927), p. 295.

13. Loeb Classical Library (L. C. L.), no. 257, 1932, p. 203.

14. L. C. L., no. 42, 1916, p. 181.

15. L. C. L., no. 49, 1917, pp. 67–69.

16. L. C. L., no. 268, 1933, p. 93.

17. New York: Everyman's Library, 1911, pp. 206–207.

18. New York: Modern Library, 1950, pp. 5ff.

19. L. C. L., no. 56, 1915, p. 329.

20. Greene, *The Dialogues of Plato*, p. 123.

21. S. B. E., vol. 41, p. 60.

22. L. C. L., no. 340, 1939, pp. 177–179.

23. L. C. L., no. 49, 1917, p. 65.

24. Johan Huizinga, *Homo Ludens* (Boston: Beacon Press, 1955), p. 1.

25. Ibid., p. 129.

26. Chadwick and Chadwick, *Growth of Literature*, vol. 3, pp. 706ff.

27. Arthur Ransome, *A History of Storytelling: Studies in the Development of Narrative* (London: T. C. & E. C. Jack, 1909), pp. 6–7.

28. Albert B. Lord, *The Singer of Tales*, Harvard Studies in Comparative Literature, 24 (Cambridge: Harvard Univ. Pr., 1960), pp. 137–138.

29. L. C. L., 1920, p. 157.

30. *The Panchatantra*, tr. from the Sanskrit by Arthur W. Ryder (Chicago: Univ. of Chicago Pr., 1956), p. 16.

31. Diego Durán, *Book of the Gods and Rites* and *The Ancient Calendar*, ed. and tr. by Fernando Horcasitas and Doris Heyden (Norman: Univ. of Oklahoma Pr., 1971), pp. 398–399.

32. Dan Ben-Amos, *Sweet Words: Storytelling Events in Benin* (Philadelphia: Institute for the Study of Human Issues, 1975), pp. 30–31.

33. Linda Dégh, *Folktales and Society: Storytelling in a Hungarian Peasant Community*, tr. from the German by Emily M. Schossburger (Bloomington: Indiana Univ. Pr., 1969), pp. 79, 171.

34. Isabelle Jan, *On Children's Literature* (New York: Schocken, 1974), p. 32.

35. Edwin S. Hartland, *The Science of Fairy Tales* (New York: Frederick A. Stokes [c. 1891]), pp. 18–21.

36. Ellin Greene, "Storytelling," in *World Book Encyclopedia*, vol. 18 (Chicago: Field Enterprises Educational Corporation, 1976), p. 718.

37. Axel Olrik, "Epic Laws of Folk Narrative," in *The Study of Folklore*, ed. by Alan Dundes (New York: Prentice-Hall, 1965), pp. 129–148 (first pub. in 1908).

38. William Hugh Jansen, "Classifying Performance in the Study of Verbal Folklore," in *Studies in Folklore*, ed. by W. Edson Richmond (Bloomington: Indiana Univ. Pr., 1957), pp. 110–118.

39. Harold Scheub, "The Art of Nongenile Mazithathu Zenani," in *African Folklore*, ed. by Richard Dorson (Bloomington: Indiana Univ. Pr., 1972), p. 115.

40. Dell Hymes, "Models of the Interaction of Language and Social Life," in *Directions in Sociolinguistics*, ed. by J. J. Gumperz and Dell Hymes (New York: Holt, Rinehart and Winston, 1972), pp. 35–71.

41. Robert A. Georges, "Toward an Understanding of Storytelling Events," *Journal of American Folklore* 82 (1969): 313.

42. Ibid., p. 317.

43. Dégh, *Folktales and Society*, pp. 50–52.

44. Mia I. Gerhardt, *The Art of Storytelling* (Leiden: E. J. Brill, 1963), p. 41.

Chapter 2

1. *The Sacred Books of the East* (S. B. E.), vol. 44, p. 370.

2. Bimala Churn Law, *The Magadhas in Ancient India*, Monographs, no. 24 (Calcutta: Royal Asiatic Society, 1946), pp. 1–3.

3. S. N. Kramer, *Sumerian Mythology*, Memoirs, 21 (Philadelphia: American Philosophical Society, 1944), p. 63.

4. Henri Frankfort, *The Art and Architecture of the Ancient Orient* (Baltimore: Penguin Books, 1969), pp. 35–36.

5. Christiane Desroches-Noblecourt, *Ancient Egypt* (Greenwich, Conn.: New York Graphic Society, 1960), plate 23.

6. H. Munro Chadwick and Nora Kershaw Chadwick, *The Growth of Literature*, vol. 2 (Cambridge: Cambridge Univ. Pr., 1932–1940), pp. 252ff; Albert B. Lord, *The Singer of Tales*, Harvard Studies in Comparative Literature, 24 (Cambridge: Harvard Univ. Pr., 1960), pp. 19ff; Wolfram Eberhard, *Minstrel Tales from Southeastern Turkey*, Folklore Studies, 5 (Berkeley and Los Angeles: Univ. of California Pr., 1955), p. 2.

7. Loeb Classical Library (L. C. L.), no. 50, 1917, p. 245.

8. Baltimore: Penguin, 1957, p. 38.

9. L. C. L., no. 208, 1928, p. 195.

10. *Leabhar na g-ceart* or *The Book of Rights*, tr. by John O'Donovan. Publications, 1 (Dublin: The Celtic Society, 1847), p. 183.

11. Cormac, *Sanas Chormaic. Cormac's Glossary*, tr. and annotated by John O'Donovan. Publications (Calcutta and Dublin: The Celtic Society, 1868), p. 160.

12. Ibid., p. 127.

13. Joseph C. Walker, *A Historical Essay on the Dress of the Ancient and Modern Irish*, 1st ed. (Dublin: 1788), p. 20.

14. Ibid., 2nd ed. (Dublin: J. Christie, 1818), p. 8.

15. A. W. Wade-Evans, *Welsh Medieval Law: Being a Text of the Laws of Howel the Good* (Oxford Univ. Pr., 1909), pp. 146, 167.

16. Ibid., pp. 179–180.

17. Gwyn Williams, *An Introduction to Welsh Poetry: From the Beginnings to the 16th Century* (Philadelphia: Dufour, 1952), pp. 7–8.

18. *Encyclopaedia Britannica. Macropedia* (Chicago: Encyclopaedia Britannica, Inc., 1974), vol. 10, pp. 1114–1115.

19. John Toland, *A Critical History of the Celtic Religion and Learning . . .* (London: Lackington, Hughes, Harding and Co., 1815), p. 224.

20. D. W. Nash, *Taliesin; or the Bards and Druids of Britain* (London: John Russell Smith, 1858), p. 33.

21. Williams, *An Introduction to Welsh Poetry*, pp. 12–15.

22. Chadwick and Chadwick, *Growth of Literature*, vol. 1, pp. 613–614.

23. *Beowulf*, tr. by John R. Clark Hall (London: Allen & Unwin, 1911), p. 74.

24. *Runic and Heroic Poems of the Old Teutonic Peoples* (Cambridge: Cambridge Univ. Pr., 1915), p. 77.

25. *Beowulf together with Widsith*, tr. by Benjamin Thorpe (Great Neck, N.Y.: Barron's Educational Series, 1962), p. 226.

26. L. F. Anderson, *The Anglo-Saxon Scop*, Philological Series, no. 1 (Toronto: Univ. of Toronto Studies, 1903), pp. 25–26.

27. Chadwick and Chadwick, *Growth of Literature*, vol. 1, pp. 618–621.

28. William A. Craigie, *Icelandic Sagas*, Cambridge Manuals of Science and Literature (Cambridge: Cambridge Univ. Pr., 1913), p. 11.

29. Ibid.

30. Ibid., p. 18.

31. Abbé De La Rue, *Essais historiques sur les bardes, les jongleurs et les trouvères normands et anglo-normands*, 3 vols. (Caen: 1854), vol. 1, pp. 110ff.

32. Ibid., vol. 1, pp. 103ff.

33. Edmond Faral, *Les jongleurs en France au Moyen Age* (Paris: 1910; New York: Burt Franklin, 1970), pp. 2–18.

34. Ibid., pp. 25–43.

35. Ibid., pp. 61ff.

36. Anthony Bonner, ed. and tr., *Songs of the Troubadours* (New York: Schocken, 1972), pp. 27–29, 223–224; Alois Brandl, "Spielmannsverhältnisse in frühmittelenglischer Zeit," in Preussische Akademie der Wissenschaften, *Sitzungsberichte* (Berlin: The Academy, 1910), pp. 873–892.

37. Same as Notes 31 and 33.

38. Chadwick and Chadwick, *Growth of Literature*, vol. 2, pp. 260–269.

39. Nora Kershaw Chadwick, *Russian Heroic Poetry* (Cambridge: Cambridge Univ. Pr., 1932), pp. 1–32.

40. Chadwick and Chadwick, *Growth of Literature*, vol. 2, p. 261.

41. Ibid., p. 266.

42. Ibid., pp. 300–303.

43. Stavro Skendi, *Albanian and South Slavic Oral Epic Poetry* (Philadelphia: American Folklore Society, 1954), p. 85.

44. Eberhard, *Minstrel Tales from Southeastern Turkey*.

45. Thomas G. Winner, *The Oral Art and Literature of the Kazakhs of Russian Central Asia* (Durham, N.C.: Duke Univ. Pr., 1958), p. 27.

46. Alexander Chodzko, *Specimens of the Popular Poetry of Persia as Found in the Adventures and Improvisations of Kurroglu* . . . (London: 1842), pp. 12–13.

47. Susie Hoogasian-Villa, *100 Armenian Tales and Their Folkloristic Relevance* (Detroit: Wayne State Univ. Pr., 1966), p. 21.

48. Eberhard, *Minstrel Tales from Southeastern Turkey*, pp. 2–4.

49. Winner, *The Oral Art and Literature of the Kazakhs*, p. 29.

50. Chadwick and Chadwick, *Growth of Literature*, vol. 3, p. 178.

51. I. W. Shklovsky, *In Far North-east Siberia* (London: Macmillan, 1916), p. 209.

52. [Henry Ferguson and Joan Ferguson], "Textiles That Tell a Story" (Thompson, Conn.: InterCulture Associates, n.d.).

53. Ibid.

54. Věna Hrdličková, "The Chinese Storytellers and Singers of Ballads: Their Performances and Storytelling Techniques," in *Transactions*, 3rd ser., vol. 10 (Tokyo: Asiatic Society of Japan, 1968), p. 103.

55. Věna Hrdličková, "The Professional Training of Chinese Storytellers and the Storytellers' Guilds," *Archiv Orientální* 33 (1965): 242.

56. Arthur Waley, "Kutune Shirka: The Ainu Epic," in *Botteghe Oscure*, no. 7 (1951), pp. 235–236.

57. Christian Snouck Hurgronje, *The Achehnese*, tr. by A. W. S. O'Sullivan (London: 1906), p. 101.

58. Ibid., p. 88.

59. Katherine Luomala, "Polynesian Literature," in *Encyclopedia of Literature*, ed. by J. T. Shipley, vol. 2 (New York: Philosophical Library, 1946), p. 773.

60. Ibid., p. 777.

61. Ibid., p. 774.

62. Elli K. Maranda and Pierre Maranda, *Structural Models in Folklore and Transformational Essays* (The Hague: Mouton, 1971), p. 11.

63. Roger E. Mitchell, *Micronesian Folktales*, Asian Folklore Studies, 32 (Nagoya: Asian Folklore Institute, 1973), p. 16.

64. Roger Edward Mitchell, "A Study of the Cultural, Historical and Acculturative Factors Influencing the Repertoires of Two Trukese Informants" (Ph.D. diss., University of Indiana, 1967), pp. 170–176.

65. Diego Durán, *Book of the Gods and Rites* and *The Ancient Calendar* (Norman: Univ. of Oklahoma Pr., 1971), p. 299.

66. John Howland Rowe, "Inca Culture at the Time of the Spanish Conquest," in *Handbook of South American Indians*, ed. by Julian H. Steward, Smith-

sonian Institution, Bureau of Ethnology, Bulletin 143 (Washington, D.C.: U.S. Government Printing Office, 1946), pp. 201–202.

67. Ruth Finnegan, *Oral Literature in Africa*, Oxford Library of African Literature (Oxford Univ. Pr., 1970), pp. 108–110.

68. Quoted in Archie Mafeje, "The Role of the Bard in a Contemporary African Community," *Journal of African Languages* 6 (1967): 193.

69. Ibid., pp. 193–223.

70. Daniel P. Biebuyck, "The Epic as a Genre of Congo Oral Literature," in *African Folklore*, ed. by Richard Dorson (Bloomington: Indiana Univ. Pr., 1972), pp. 257–273.

71. See, among others, S. A. Babalola, *The Content and Form of Yoruba Ijala* (Oxford Univ. Pr., 1966); Henry F. Morris, *The Heroic Recitations of the Bahima of Ankole*, Oxford Library of African Literature (Oxford Univ. Pr., 1964); H. T. Norris, *Shinqiti Folk Literature and Song*, Oxford Library of African Literature (Oxford Univ. Pr., 1968).

72. Daniel P. Biebuyck and Kahombo C. Mateene, *The Mwindo Epic from the Banyanga (Congo Republic)* (Berkeley and Los Angeles: Univ. of California Pr., 1969), pp. 12–15.

73. Ibid., pp. 261–262.

74. Same as note 69.

75. Jan Vansina, *Oral Tradition*, tr. from the French by H. M. Wright (Chicago: Aldine Publishing Co., 1965), p. 189.

76. Ibid., p. 119.

77. Ibid., p. 32.

78. Lyndon Harries, *Swahili Poetry* (Oxford Univ. Pr., 1962), p. 24.

79. Finnegan, *Oral Literature in Africa*, p. 174.

80. J. H. Speke, *Journal of the Discovery of the Source of the Nile* (Edinburgh: 1863), p. 344.

81. John Roscoe, *The Baganda*, 2nd ed. (New York: Barnes and Noble, 1966), p. 35 (first pub. in 1911).

82. Morris, *The Heroic Recitations of the Bahima of Ankole*, p. 21.

83. Babalola, *The Content and Form of Yoruba Ijala*, p. 18.

84. Ibid., p. 3.

85. Charles Bird, "Heroic Songs of the Mande Hunters," in *African Folklore*, ed. by Richard Dorson (Bloomington: Indiana Univ. Pr., 1972), p. 278.

86. Ibid., p. 289.

87. Mafeje, "The Role of the Bard," p. 195.

88. Norris, *Shinqiti Folk Literature*, p. 54.

89. *Kitāb al-Wasīt*, quoted in Norris, *Shinqiti Folk Literature*, p. 65.

90. Chadwick and Chadwick, *Growth of Literature*, vol. 3, pp. 524–526.

91. Ibid., p. 526.

92. M. Mondon-Vidailhet, "La Musique Éthiopienne," in *Encyclopédie de la Musique*, ed. by Albert Lavignac (Paris: Delagrave, 1922), pt. 1, vol. 5, p. 3183.

93. Chadwick and Chadwick, *Growth of Literature*, vol. 3, pp. 525–526.

Chapter 3

1. Julian, *Works*, Loeb Classical Library (L. C. L.), p. 79.

2. Ruth Benedict, *Zuni Mythology*, 2 vols., Contributions to Anthropology, 21 (New York: Columbia Univ. Pr., 1935), vol. 1, p. xii.

3. James H. Delargy, *The Gaelic Storyteller*, Rhys Memorial Lecture for 1945. *Proceedings of the British Academy*, 31 (London: The Academy, 1945), p. 19.

4. T. S. Eliot, "Religion and Literature," in his *Essays, Ancient and Modern* (London: Faber and Faber, 1936), p. 105.

5. Linda Dégh, *Folktales and Society: Storytelling in a Hungarian Peasant Community*, tr. from the German by Emily M. Schossburger (Bloomington: Indiana Univ. Pr., 1969), p. 104.

6. Charles Béart, *Jeux et Jouets de l'Ouest Africain*, 2 vols. (Dakar: IFAN, 1955), vol. 2, p. 767.

7. E. Y. Egblewogbe, *Games and Songs as Education Media: A Case Study among the Ewes of Ghana* (Accra: Ghana Publishing Corp., 1975), p. 47.

8. John Mbiti, *Akamba Stories*, Oxford Library of African Literature (Oxford Univ. Pr., 1966), pp. 23–24.

9. H. T. Norris, *Shinqiti Folk Literature and Song*, Oxford Library of African Literature (Oxford Univ. Pr., 1968), p. 118.

10. Dan Ben-Amos, *Sweet Words: Storytelling Events in Benin* (Philadelphia: Institute for the Study of Human Issues, 1975), pp. 23–24.

11. Harold Scheub, *The Xhosa Ntsomi*, Oxford Library of African Literature (Oxford Univ. Pr., 1975), pp. 12–13.

12. Duk-soon Chang, *Folk Treasury of Korea: Sources in Myth, Legend and Folktale* (Seoul: Society of Korean Oral Literature, 1970), pp. 10–11.

13. Alfred Cammann, *Westpreussische Märchen, Fabula*, Supplement Ser., Reihe A, Band 3 (Berlin: W. de Gruyter, 1961), pp. 17–18.

14. Ibid., p. 19.

15. Leza Uffer, *Rätoromanische Märchen und ihre Erzähler*, Schriften, Band 29 (Basel: Schweizerische Gesellschaft für Volkskunde, 1945), p. 63.

16. Ibid., p. 73.

17. Mary Frere, *Hindoo Fairy Legends (Old Deccan Days)* (New York: Dover, 1967), p. xxvii (first pub. 1881).

18. Roger Edward Mitchell, "A Study of the Cultural, Historical and Acculturative Factors Influencing the Repertoires of Two Trukese Informants" (Ph.D. diss., University of Indiana, 1967), pp. 169–170.

19. Louis A. Allen, *Time before Morning: Art and Myth of the Australian Aborigines* (New York: Thomas Y. Crowell, 1975), p. 23.

20. Harriet Ronken Lynton and Mohini Rajan, *The Days of the Beloved* (Berkeley and Los Angeles: Univ. of California Pr., 1974), p. 140.

21. Barre Toelken, "The 'Pretty Languages' of Yellowman: Genre, Mode and Texture in Navajo Coyote Narratives," in *Folklore Genres*, ed. by Dan Ben-Amos (Austin: Univ. of Texas Pr., 1976), p. 155.

22. Ibid., and also Melville Jacobs, *The Content and Style of an Oral Literature: Clackamas Chinook Myths and Tales* (Chicago: Univ. of Chicago Pr., 1959), p. 269; Thelma Adamson, *Folktales of the Coast Salish*, Memoirs, 27 (New York: American Folklore Society, 1934), pp. xii–xlii; Ella E. Clark, *Indian Legends from the Northern Rockies* (Norman: Univ. of Oklahoma Pr., 1966), p. 24; Morris Edward Opler, *Myths and Tales of the Jicarilla Apache Indians*, Memoirs, 31 (New York: American Folklore Society, 1938), p. viii.

23. Daniel J. Crowley, *I Could Talk Old-Story Good: Creativity in Bahamian Folklore*, Publications in Folklore Studies, 17 (Berkeley and Los Angeles: Univ. of California Pr., 1966), p. 12.

24. Rex Gorham, *The Folkways of Brazil* (New York: New York Public Library, 1944), p. 53.

25. Dégh, *Folktales and Society*, p. 118.

26. Hamed Ammar, *Growing Up in an Egyptian Village: Silwa, Province of Aswan* (New York: Octagon, 1966), p. 161.

27. O. F. Raum, *Chaga Childhood: A Description of Indigenous Education in an East African Tribe* (Oxford Univ. Pr., 1940), pp. 217–218.

28. G. Gorer, *Himalayan Village: An Account of the Lepchas of Sikkim*, 2nd ed. (New York: Basic Books, 1967), p. 266 (first pub. in 1938).

29. Nathan Miller, *The Child in Primitive Society* (New York: Brentano's, 1928), pp. 167–172.

30. Carla Bianco, "The Two Rosetos: The Folklore of an Italian-American Community in Northeastern Pennsylvania" (Ph.D. diss., Indiana University, 1972), pp. 127–137.

31. Delargy, *The Gaelic Storyteller*, pp. 9ff.

32. Alexander Carmichael, *Carmina Gadelica*, 2nd ed., vol. 1 (Edinburgh and London: Oliver and Boyd, 1928), p. xxiii.

33. Jiří Cejpek, "Iranian Folk Literature," in *History of Iranian Literature*, ed. by Jan Rypka (Dordrecht: D. Reidel Pub. Co., 1956), p. 653.

34. Dégh, *Folktales and Society*, pp. 95–96.

35. Ibid., pp. 102–103.

36. Otto Brinkmann, *Das Erzählen in einer Dorfgemeinschaft*, Veröffentlichungen der Volkskundlichen Komission des Provinzialinstituts für Westfälische Landes- und Volkskunde, Erste Reihe, Heft 4 (Münster: Aschendorffschen Verlagsbuchhandlung, 1931), p. 9.

37. Gorer, *Himalayan Village*, p. 266.

38. Rupert East, *Akiga's Story: The Tiv Tribe As Seen by One of Its Members* (Oxford Univ. Pr., 1965), pp. 308–309 (first pub. in 1939).

39. Susie Hoogasian-Villa, *100 Armenian Tales and Their Folkloristic Relevance* (Detroit: Wayne State Univ. Pr., 1966), pp. 26–40.

40. Delargy, *The Gaelic Storyteller*, p. 18.

41. Bela Gunda, "Die Funktion des Märchens in der Gemeinschaft der Zigeuner," *Fabula* [Berlin] 6 (1964): 101.

42. Dégh, *Folktales and Society*, pp. 97–98.

43. Yolando Pino-Saavedra, *Folktales of Chile*, tr. by Rockwell Gray (Chicago: Univ. of Chicago Pr., 1967), p. xliii.

44. S. A. Babalola, *The Content and Form of Yoruba Ijala* (Oxford Univ. Pr., 1966), p. 18.

45. Cejpek, "Iranian Folk Literature," p. 653.

46. Gorer, *Himalayan Village*, p. 265.

47. Mervyn W. H. Beech, *The Suk* (New York: Negro Universities Press, 1966), p. 38 (first pub. in 1911).

48. Dégh, *Folktales and Society*, pp. 105–110.

49. *The Sacred Books of the East* (S. B. E.), vol. 29, pp. 355–357.

50. Luc Lacourcière, "Canada," in *Folktales Told around the World*, ed. by Richard Dorson (Chicago: Univ. of Chicago Pr., 1975), p. 450.

51. Delargy, *The Gaelic Storyteller*, p. 20.

52. Elliott Oring, "Ha-Chizbat: The Content and Structure of an Israeli Oral Tradition" (Ph.D. diss., Indiana University, 1974), pp. 35ff.

53. Lacourcière, "Canada," p. 448.

54. Ananda Coomaraswamy, "Picture Showmen," *Indian Historical Quarterly* 5, no. 2 (June 1929): 182ff.

55. Mia I. Gerhardt, *The Art of Story-telling* (Leiden: E. J. Brill, 1963), p. 382ff.

56. A. H. Sayce, "Storytelling in the East," *Living Age*, 5th ser. 64 (October 20, 1888): 176–180.

57. R. Heath, "Storytelling in All Ages," *Leisure Hour* 34 (1885): 199ff.

58. V. C. Scott O'Connor, "Beyond the Grand Atlas," *National Geographic* 61 (March 1932): 261–320.

59. Věna Hrdličková, "The Chinese Storytellers and Singers of Ballads: Their Performances and Storytelling Techniques," in *Transactions*, 3rd ser., vol. 10 (Tokyo: Asiatic Society of Japan, 1968), p. 99.

60. Ibid., p. 100.

61. Robert J. Adams, "Social Identity of a Japanese Storyteller" (Ph.D. diss., Indiana University, 1972), pp. 6ff.

62. Satoshi Kako, "Kamishibai—the Unique Cultural Property of Japan," Tokyo Book Development Centre *Newsletter* 8, no. 2 (September 1976): 6–7; Koji Kata, *Machi no jijyoden (Autobiography of a Street-Person)* (Tokyo: Banseisha, 1977).

63. Kako, "Kamishibai—the Unique Cultural Property of Japan," p. 7.

64. Ibid.

65. Morio Kita, *Nireke no Hitobito (The Nine Families)* (Tokyo: Shinchoshi), p. 231.

66. William A. Coupe, *The German Illustrated Broadsheet in the Seventeenth Century*, Bibliotheca Bibliographica Aureliana, 17 (Baden Baden: Heitz, 1966–1967), vol. 1, pp. 13–17.

67. Hans Fehr, *Massenkunst im 16. Jahrhundert*, Denkmale der Volkskunst, 1 (Berlin: Herbert Stubenrauch, 1924), p. 3.

68. Coupe, *The German Illustrated Broadsheet*, p. 17.

69. Ibid., p. 13; see also *Reallexikon der deutschen Literaturgeschichte*, vol. 1 (Berlin: Walter de Gruyter, 1958), pp. 128–129.

70. Elsbeth Janda and Fritz Nötzoldt, *Die Moritat vom Bänkelsang: oder das Lied der Strasse* (München: Ehrenwirth Verlag, 1959), p. 9.

Chapter 4

1. *The Sacred Books of the East* (S. B. E.)., vol. 44, p. xxiv.

2. Ananda Coomaraswamy, "Picture Showmen," *Indian Historical Quarterly* 5, no. 2 (June 1929), pp. 182–187.

3. Joan Erikson, *Mata ni pachedi: A Book on the Temple Cloth of the Mother Goddess* (Ahmedabad: National Institute of Design, 1968), p. 48.

4. Prabhaker B. Mande, "Dakkalwars and Their Myths," *Folklore* (Calcutta) 14 (January 1973): 69–76.

5. [Henry Ferguson and Joan Ferguson], "Textiles That Tell a Story: Kalamkari" (Thompson, Conn.: InterCulture Associates, n.d.).

6. Heinrich Lüders, "Die Śaubhikas: ein Beitrag zur Geschichte des indischen Dramas," Preussische Akademie der Wissenschaften, *Sitzungsberichte*, June 1916, pp. 698–737.

7. S. B. E., vol. 21, pp. 120–129.

8. S. B. E., vol. 36, pp. 92–96.

9. Jaroslav Průšek, "The Narrators of Buddhist Scriptures and Religious Tales in the Sung Period," *Archiv Orientální* 10 (1938): 376.

10. Ibid., p. 377.

11. Ibid., p. 388.

12. Věna Hrdličková, "The First Translations of Buddhist *Sūtras* in Chinese Literature and Their Place in the Development of Storytelling," *Archiv Orientální* 26 (1958): 114–144.

13. Arthur Waley, *Ballads and Stories from Tun-huang* (New York: Macmillan, 1960), pp. 242–243.

14. Conversation and correspondence with the author, May–September 1977.

15. P. Demiéville, "Translations of Buddhist Literature" and "Tun-huang Texts," in Jaroslav Průšek and Zbigniew Slupski, eds., *Dictionary of Oriental Literatures*, vol. 1 (New York: Basic Books, 1974), p. 186.

16. Ibid., p. 175.

17. Birger Gerhardsson, *Memory and Manuscript: Oral Tradition and Written Transmission in Rabbinic Judaism and Early Christianity*, tr. by Eric J. Sharpe (Lund: C. W. K. Gleerup; Copenhagen: Ejnar Munksgaard, 1961), pp. 62–64.

18. Ibid., pp. 71–78.

19. Ibid., p. 89.

20. Jerome Richard Mintz, *The Legends of the Hasidim: An Introduction to Hasidic Culture and Oral Tradition in the New World* (Chicago: Univ. of Chicago Pr., 1968), pp. 4–8.

21. Toby Shafter, *Storytelling for Jewish Groups* (New York: National Jewish Welfare Board, 1946).

22. Gerhardsson, *Memory and Manuscript*, p. 335.

23. Laurits Bødker, Christina Hole, and G. D'Aronco, *European Folk Tales* (Copenhagen: Rosenkilde and Bagger, 1963), p. xix.

24. Myrtilla Avery, *The Exultet Rolls of South Italy*, vol. 2 (The Hague: Martinus Nijhoff, 1929); J. P. Gilson, "Introduction," in *An Exultet Roll Illuminated in the XIth Century at the Abbey of Monte Cassino* (London: British Museum, 1929).

25. Leopold Schmidt, "Geistlicher Bänkelgesang," Österreichisches Volksliedwerk, *Jahrbuch* 12 (1963): 7.

26. Rolf Wilhelm Brednich, "Zur Vorgeschichte des Bänkelsangs," Österreichisches Volksliedwerk, *Jahrbuch* 21 (1972): 85.

27. H. Munro Chadwick and Nora Kershaw Chadwick, *The Growth of Literature*, vol. 2 (Cambridge: Cambridge Univ. Pr., 1932–1940), pp. 270–283.

28. Ibid., p. 271.

29. Harriet G. Long, *Rich the Treasure: Public Library Service to Children* (Chicago: American Library Association, 1953), pp. 48–49.

30. Edward Porter St. John, *Stories and Storytelling in Moral and Religious Education* (Boston: The Pilgrim Press, 1910).

31. Richard Gerald Alvey, "The Historical Development of Organized Storytelling to Children in the United States" (Ph.D. diss., University of Pennsylvania, 1974), p. 57.

32. *The Story Hour Leader* (Nashville, Tenn: Southern Baptist Convention, 1937–   ).

33. Personal experience of the author.

34. Ibn al-Jawzī, Abū al-Faraj 'Abd al-Rahmān ibn 'Alī, *Kitab al quṣṣāṣ wa-al-mudhakkirīn*, tr. and annotated by Merlin L. Swartz, Recherches de l'Institut de Lettres Orientales, Sér. 1, Pensée Arabe et Musulmane, Tome 47 (Beyrouth: Dar el-Machreq [1971]), p. 103.

35. Ibid., pp. 109–114.

36. Ignaz Goldziher, *Muslim Studies*, 2 vols. (London: Allen & Unwin, 1971), p. 152.

37. Based on personal observations of several Koranic schools in Morocco and Algeria.

38. Martha Warren Beckwith, *Mandan-Hidatsa Myths and Ceremonies*, Memoirs, 32 (New York: American Folklore Society, 1937), p. xvi.

39. Paul Radin, *The Trickster: A Study in American Indian Mythology* (New York: Greenwood Press, 1969), pp. 118–122.

40. Morris Edward Opler, *Myths and Tales of the Jicarilla Apache Indians*, Memoirs, 31 (New York: American Folklore Society, 1938), p. ix.

41. Johannes C. Andersen, *Myths and Legends of the Polynesians* (Rutland, Vt.: Tuttle, 1969), p. 445.

42. Elsdon Best, *The Maori*, 2 vols. Memoirs, 5 (Wellington: Polynesian Society, 1924), p. 65.

43. Daniel P. Biebuyck and Kahombo C. Mateene, *The Mwindo Epic from the Banyanga (Congo Republic)* (Berkeley and Los Angeles: Univ. of California Pr., 1969), p. 14.

Chapter 5

1. Věna Hrdličková, "The Chinese Storytellers and Singers of Ballads: Their Performances and Storytelling Techniques," in *Transactions*, 3rd ser., vol. 10 (Tokyo: Asiatic Society of Japan, 1968), pp. 99–102.

2. Wolfram Eberhard, "Notes on Chinese Storytellers," *Fabula* [Berlin] 11 (1970): 1–31.

3. Věna Hrdličková, "The Professional Training of Chinese Storytellers and the Storytellers' Guilds," *Archiv Orientální* 33 (1965): 225–248.

4. Ibid., p. 234; and "Some Questions Connected with *Tun-huang pien-wen*," *Archiv Orientální* 30 (1962): 211–230. See also note 5 below.

5. Jaroslav Průšek, *The Origins and the Authors of the hua-pen*, Dissertationes Orientales, 14 (Prague: Academia, 1967), pp. 22ff.

6. Hrdličková, "The Professional Training of Chinese Storytellers," p. 234.

7. Ibid., p. 240.

8. Jaroslav Průšek, "The Creative Methods of Chinese Mediaeval Storytellers," in *Charisteria Orientalia*, by Felix Tauer and others (Prague: Nakladatelstvi Československe Akademie Věd, 1956), p. 265.

9. György Kara, *Chants d'un Barde Mongol* (Budapest: Akadémiai Kiadó, 1970), p. 8.

10. Ibid., p. 50.

11. F. Brinkley, ed., *Japan Described and Illustrated by the Japanese*, 10 vols. (Boston: J. B. Millet Co., 1897), vol. 8, p. 286.

12. Jules Adam, *Japanese Storytellers*, tr. from the French by Osman Edwards (Tokyo: T. Hasegawa, 1912), unp.

13. Kurt Meissner, "Die Yose," Deutsche Gesellschaft für Natur- und Völkerkunde Ostasiens, *Mitteilungen* 14 (1913): 230–240.

14. Adam, *Japanese Storytellers*, pp. 1–30.

15. Meissner, "Die Yose," p. 233.

16. Ibid., pp. 236–241.

17. Ibid., p. 234; Adam, *Japanese Storytellers*.

18. J. Barth, "Kodan und Rakugo," Deutsche Gesellschaft für Natur- und Völkerkunde Ostasiens, *Mitteilungen* 22 (1928): Teil D.

19. Ibid., pp. 2–4.

20. Ibid., p. 4.

21. Ibid., p. 11.

22. Věna Hrdličková, "Japanese Professional Storytellers," in *Folklore Genres*, ed. by Dan Ben-Amos (Austin: Univ. of Texas Pr., 1976), pp. 171–190; and "The Zenza, the Storyteller's Apprentice," International Conference of Orientalists in Japan, *Transactions* 13 (1968): 31–41.

23. Hrdličková, "Japanese Professional Storytellers," pp. 185–187.

24. Ibid., p. 187 and plate 23.

25. Charlotte Rougemont, ... *dann leben sie noch heute: Erlebnisse und Erfahrungen beim Märchenerzählen* (Münster: Verlag Aschendorff, 1962), pp. 17–19.

26. Elsa Sophia von Kamphoevener, *An Nachtfeuern der Karawan-Serail: Märchen und Geschichten Alttürkischer Nomaden*, vol. 1 (Hamburg: Christian Wegner, 1956), p. 7.

27. Conversation with the author, September 1976.

28. Observed by the author in a performance at the College of Saint Teresa, Winona, Minnesota.

29. Frances Clarke Sayers, *Anne Carroll Moore: A Biography* (New York: Atheneum, 1972), pp. 81ff.

30. Yuri M. Sokolov, *Russian Folklore*, tr. by Catherine Ruth Smith (New York: Macmillan, 1950), pp. 416–417.

31. Polly Bowditch McVicker, "Storytelling in Java," *Horn Book* 40 (December 1964): 596–601.

32. Moebirman, *Wanang Purwa: The Shadow Play of Indonesia*, tr. from the French, rev. ed. (The Hague: Van Deventer-Maasstichting, 1960), p. 14.

33. Ananda Coomaraswamy, "Picture Showmen," *Indian Historical Quarterly* 5, no 2 (June 1929): 187.

Chapter 6

1. Elizabeth Porter Clarke, "Storytelling, Reading Aloud and Other Special Features of Work in Children's Rooms," *Library Journal* 27 (April 1902): 189.

2. Jeanne B. Hardendorff, "Storytelling and the Story Hour," *Library Trends* 12 (July 1963): 52–63.

3. Mary Ella Dousman, "Children's Departments," *Library Journal* 21 (September 1896): 407.

4. Ibid., p. 408.

5. Anne Carroll Moore, "The Story Hour at Pratt Institute Free Library," *Library Journal* 30 (April 1905): 210.

6. Ibid., p. 206.

7. Audrey Kennedy, "History of the Boys and Girls Department of the Carnegie Library of Pittsburgh" (Master's thesis, Carnegie Institute of Technology, 1949), p. 23.

8. Ibid.

9. Frances J. Olcutt, "Storytelling, Lectures and Other Adjuncts of the Children's Room," *Public Libraries* 5 (July 1900): 283.

10. Ibid., p. 284.

11. *Stories to Tell to Children*, 4th ed. (Pittsburgh: Carnegie Library, 1926), p. 11.

12. Kennedy, "History of the Boys and Girls Department," pp. 23–24.

13. Richard Gerald Alvey, "The Historical Development of Organized Storytelling to Children in the United States" (Ph.D. diss., University of Pennsylvania, 1974), pp. 400–401.

14. Olcutt, "Storytelling, Lectures and Other Adjuncts," p. 284, mentions the fact that Omaha and Cedar Rapids, Iowa, had story hours of a similar nature; in addition to these were the story hours in Pratt Institute, Carnegie (Pittsburgh), and Buffalo.

15. Frances Clarke Sayers, *Anne Carroll Moore: A Biography* (New York: Atheneum, 1972), pp. 81ff. This entire section on Marie Shedlock and her influence on library storytelling is summarized from the segment in Mrs. Sayers' book.

16. Almost every other issue of *Library Journal* and of *Public Libraries* from 1902–1907 has a mention of a visit by Miss Shedlock to one or another of the library schools as a lecturer on storytelling.

17. Sayers, *Anne Carroll Moore*, p. 83.

18. May Hill Arbuthnot, *Children and Books*, 1st ed. (Chicago: Scott, Foresman, 1947), p. 249.

19. Alvey, "The Historical Development of Organized Storytelling," p. 244.

20. Ibid., p. 90.

21. Kennedy, "History of the Boys and Girls Department," p. 24.

22. Sayers, *Anne Carroll Moore*, pp. 81ff.

23. John Cotton Dana, "Storytelling in Libraries," *Public Libraries* 13 (November 1908): 349–350.

24. Rose Gymer, "Storytelling in the Cleveland Public Library, *ALA Bulletin*, 3 (1909): 417–418.

25. American Library Association, *A Survey of Libraries in the United States*, vol. 3 (Chicago: American Library Association, 1927), p. 44.

26. Alvey, "The Historical Development of Organized Storytelling," pp. 22–23.

27. Elizabeth Henry Gross, *Public Library Service to Children* (Dobbs Ferry: Oceana Publications, 1967), p. 96.

28. Ardis Huls, "Pre-school Story Hour," *Wilson Library Bulletin* 16 (May 1942): 726–727, 730.

29. Candace McDowell Chamberlin, "The Pre-School Story Hour," *Library Journal* 69 (November 1, 1944): 927–928.

30. F. Marie Foster, *A Round of Picture Book Programs* (Albany: N.Y. State Education Department, Division of Adult Education and Library Extension, c. 1944).

31. Alice Kane, "The Changing Face of the Story Hour," *Ontario Library Review* 14 (August 1965): 141–142.

32. Alvey, "The Historical Development of Organized Storytelling," p. 638.

33. Ethna Sheehan and Martha C. Bentley, "A Public Library Reassesses Storytelling," *Illinois Libraries* 44 (December 1962): 653–657.

34. Alvey, "The Historical Development of Organized Storytelling," p. 313.

Chapter 7

1. Richard Gerald Alvey, "The Historical Development of Oorganized Storytelling to Children in the United States" (Ph.D. diss., University of Pennsylvania, 1974), pp. 1–6.

2. Harriet G. Long, *Rich the Treasure: Public Library Service to Children* (Chicago: American Library Association, 1953), p. 8.

3. Jacob A. Riis, *The Making of an American* (New York: Macmillan, 1901), p. 16.

4. Jane Addams, *Twenty Years at Hull-House* (New York: Macmillan, 1910), p. 101.

5. Ibid., p. 103.

6. Maud Summers, "Storytelling in Playgrounds," *The Story Hour* 1, no. 1 (1908): 26.

7. Ibid., p. 27.

8. Anne Carroll Moore, "Report of the Committee on Storytelling," *Playground* 4 (August 1910): 162ff; reprinted in Alice I. Hazeltine, *Library Work with Children* (New York: H. W. Wilson, 1917), pp. 297–315.

9. Gudrun Thorne-Thomsen, "The Practical Results of Storytelling in Chicago's Park Reading Rooms," *ALA Bulletin* 3 (1909): 408–410.

10. Alvey, "Historical Development of Organized Storytelling," pp. 18–19.

11. Anne Carroll Moore, "Report of the Committee on Storytelling," p. 169.

12. Ibid., p. 171.

13. Alvey, "Historical Development of Organized Storytelling," p. 103.

14. Ibid., p. 556; see also *Playground* 16 (January 1923): 479.

15. Boy Scouts of America, *Handbook for Scoutmasters*, 1st ed., 9th reprint (New York: Boy Scouts of America, 1919), pp. 78ff.

16. Franklin K. Mathiews, ed., *The Boy Scouts Book of Campfire Stories* (New York: Appleton, 1921), p. v.

Chapter 8

1. James H. Delargy, *The Gaelic Storyteller*, Rhys Memorial Lecture for 1945, *Proceedings of the British Academy*, 31 (London: The Academy, 1945), pp. 10, 19.

2. Martha Warren Beckwith, *Mandan-Hidatsa Myths and Ceremonies*, Memoirs, 32 (New York: American Folklore Society, 1937), p. xvi.

3. Otto Brinkmann, *Das Erzählen in einer Dorfgemeinschaft*, Veröffentlichungen der Volkskundlichen Komission des Provinzialinstituts für Westfälische Landes- und Volkskunde, Erste Reihe, Heft 4 (Münster i. W.: Aschendorffschen Verlagsbuchhandlung, 1931), pp. 28–52.

4. Mary Kingsley, *West African Studies*, 3rd ed. (New York: Barnes and Noble, 1964), pp. 126–127 (first pub. in 1899).

5. Robert S. Rattray, *The Ashanti* (Oxford Univ. Pr., 1923), p. 162.

6. Verna Aardema, *Tales from the Story Hat* (New York: Coward McCann, 1960).

7. Henri A. Junod, *The Life of a South African Tribe*, 2 vols. (New York: University Books, 1962), vol. 1, p. 351.

8. Amin Sweeney, "Professional Malay Storytelling: Some Questions of Style and Presentation," in *Studies in Malaysian Oral and Musical Traditions* (Ann Arbor: Center for South and Southeast Asian Studies, University of Michigan, 1974), p. 59.

9. Věna Hrdličková, "The Zenza, the Storyteller's Apprentice," International Conference of Orientalists in Japan, *Transactions* 13 (1968): 39.

10. Elsie Clews Parsons, *Taos Tales*, Memoirs, 34 (New York: American Folklore Society, 1940), p. 1.

11. Ella E. Clark, *Indian Legends from the Northern Rockies* (Norman: Univ. of Oklahoma Pr., 1966), p. 24.

12. Thelma Adamson, *Folktales of the Coast Salish*, Memoirs, 27 (New York: American Folklore Society, 1934), pp. xii–xiii.

13. Henri A. Junod, *The Life of a South African Tribe*, vol. 2, p. 209.

14. Harold Scheub, *The Xhosa Ntsomi*, Oxford Library of African Literature (Oxford Univ. Pr., 1975), pp. 9–11.

15. G. S. Kirk, *The Songs of Homer* (Cambridge: Cambridge Univ. Pr., 1962), pp. 90ff.

16. C. M. Bowra, *Heroic Poetry* (London: Macmillan, 1952), pp. 280–281.

17. Ibid., p. 281; and Albert B. Lord, *The Singer of Tales*, Harvard Studies in Comparative Literature, 24 (Cambridge: Harvard Univ. Pr., 1960), pp. 68–98.

18. William Butler Yeats, *Fairy and Folktales of Ireland*. Foreword by Kathleen Raine (New York: Macmillan, 1973), p. viii (first pub. in 1888).

19. Aleksandr Afanas'ev, *Russian Fairy Tales* (New York: Pantheon, 1945), p. 521.

20. Bokar N'Diaye, *Veillées au Mali* (Bamako: Editions Populaires, 1970), p. 8.

21. Arthur Perera, *Sinhalese Folklore Notes* (Bombay: 1917).

22. Keigo Seki, *Folktales of Japan* (Chicago: Univ. of Chicago Pr., 1963), p. xv.

23. Warren S. Walker and Ahmet E. Uysal, *Tales Alive in Turkey* (Cambridge: Harvard Univ. Pr., 1966), p. 10.

24. Melville Jacobs, *The Content and Style of an Oral Literature: Clackamas Chinook Myths and Tales* (Chicago: Univ. of Chicago Pr., 1959), pp. 220–221.

25. Grenville Goodwin, *Myths and Tales of the White Mountain Apache*, Memoirs, 33 (New York: American Folklore Society, 1939), p. 2.

26. Franc J. Newcomb, *Navajo Folk Tales* (Santa Fe: Museum of Navajo Ceremonial Art, 1967), p. xvi.

27. Harold Scheub, "South Africa," in *Folktales Told around the World*, ed. by Richard Dorson (Chicago: Univ. of Chicago Pr., 1975), pp. 388–426.

28. Rupert East, *Akiga's Story; the Tiv Tribe As Seen by One of Its Members* (Oxford Univ. Pr., 1965), pp. 308–309 (first pub. in 1939).

29. Patricia Ann O'Connell, "Bandi Oral Narratives" (Master's thesis, Indiana University, 1976), p. 1.

30. Thomas G. Winner, *The Oral Art and Literature of the Kazakhs of Russian Central Asia* (Durham, N.C.: Duke Univ. Pr., 1958), p. 46.

31. Roman Jacobson, "Commentary," in Alexander Afanas'ev, *Russian Fairy Tales*, p. 645.

32. Philip A. Noss, "Description in Gbaya Literary Art," in *African Folklore*, ed. by Richard Dorson (Bloomington: Indiana Univ. Pr., 1972), pp. 73–101.

33. A. J. N. Tremearne, *Hausa Superstitions and Customs: An Introduction to the Folklore and the Folk* (London: Frank Cass and Co., 1970), pp. 10–11 (first pub. in 1913); Frank Edgar, *Hausa Tales and Traditions*, ed. and tr. from the Hausa by Neil Skinner, vol. 1 (New York: Africana Pub. Corp., 1969), p. xxiv (first pub. in 1911).

34. Dan Ben-Amos, *Sweet Words: Storytelling Events in Benin* (Philadelphia: Institute for the Study of Human Issues, 1975), pp. 50–51.

35. Linda Dégh, *Folktales and Society: Storytelling in a Hungarian Peasant Community*, tr. from the German by Emily M. Schossburger (Bloomington: Indiana Univ. Pr., 1969), pp. 75, 360.

36. Daniel J. Crowley, *I Could Talk Old-Story Good: Creativity in Bahamian Folklore*, Publications in Folklore Studies, 17 (Berkeley and Los Angeles: Univ. of Chicago Pr., 1966), pp. 19–22.

37. Geneviève Massignon, *Folktales of France*, tr. by Jacqueline Hyland (Chicago: Univ. of Chicago Pr., 1968), p. xli.

38. Elsie Clews Parsons, *Folktales of Andros Island, Bahamas*, Memoirs, 13 (New York: American Folklore Society, 1918), pp. xi–xii.

39. Yolando Pino-Saavedra, *Folktales of Chile*, tr. by Rockwell Gray (Chicago: Univ. of Chicago Pr., 1967), p. 159.

40. *Fairy Tales and Legends from Romania*, tr. by Ioana Sturdza and others (New York: Twayne Publishers, 1972), pp. 64, 75.

41. John S. Mbiti, *Akamba Stories*, Oxford Library of African Literature (Oxford Univ. Pr., 1966), p. v.

42. Stanley L. Robe, *Amapa Storytellers*, Folklore Studies, 24 (Berkeley and Los Angeles: Univ. of California Pr., 1972), pp. 1–10.

Chapter 9

1. John Ball, "Style in the Folktale," *Folk-lore* 65 (1954): 170–172.

2. Robert A. Georges, "Toward an Understanding of Storytelling Events," *Journal of American Folklore* 82 (1969): 313–328.

3. Melville Jacobs, *The Content and Style of an Oral Literature: Clackamas Chinook Myths and Tales* (Chicago: Univ. of Chicago Pr., 1959).

4. Ibid., pp. 266–267.

5. Ibid., p. 5.

6. Gladys A. Reichard, *An Analysis of Coeur d'Alene Indian Myths* (Philadelphia: American Folklore Society, 1947; New York: Kraus Reprint Co., 1969), p. 26.

7. Elsie Clews Parsons, *Kiowa Tales*, Memoirs, 22 (New York: American Folklore Society, 1929), p. x.

8. Barre Toelken, "The 'Pretty Languages' of Yellowman: Genre, Mode and Texture in Navajo Coyote Narratives," in *Folklore Genres*, ed. by Dan Ben-Amos (Austin: Univ. of Texas Pr., 1976), p. 155.

9. Ella E. Clark, *Indian Legends from the Northern Rockies* (Norman: Univ. of Oklahoma Pr., 1966), p. 317; Robert H. Lowie, *Myths and Traditions of the Crow Indians*, Anthropological Papers, vol. 25, part 1 (New York: American Museum of Natural History, 1918), p. 13.

10. Morris Edward Opler, *Myths and Legends of the Jicarilla Apache Indians*, Memoirs, 31 (New York: American Folklore Society, 1938), pp. viii–ix.

11. Martha Warren Beckwith, *Mandan-Hidatsa Myths and Ceremonies*, Memoirs, 32 (New York: American Folklore Society, 1937), pp. xviff.

12. Thelma Adamson, *Folktales of the Coast Salish*, Memoirs, 27 (New York: American Folklore Society, 1934), pp. xii–xiii.

13. Edwin S. Hall, *The Eskimo Storyteller* (Knoxville: Univ. of Tennessee Pr., 1975), p. 412.

14. Henry M. Stanley, *My Dark Companions and Their Strange Stories* (New York: Charles Scribner's Sons, 1893), pp. 232ff.

15. Heli Chatelain, *Folktales of Angola*, Memoirs of the American Folklore Society, 1 (Boston: Houghton Mifflin, 1894; New York: Negro Universities Press, 1969), pp. 21ff.

16. A. B. Ellis, *The Yoruba-Speaking Peoples of the Slave Coast of West Africa* (London: 1894; New York: Anthropological Publications, 1970), pp. 243ff.

17. Edward W. Lane, *An Account of the Manners and Customs of the Modern Egyptians* . . ., 5th ed. (London: John Murray, 1871). Chapters 21, 22, and 23 deal with "Public Recitations of Romances."

18. Chatelain, *Folktales of Angola*, pp. viiff.

19. A. B. Ellis, *The Yoruba-Speaking Peoples*, pp. 243ff.

20. E. W. Lane, *Modern Egyptians*, p. 360.

21. J. Torrend, *Specimens of Bantu Folklore from Northern Rhodesia* (New York: Negro Universities Press, 1969), p. 5 (first pub. in 1921).

22. A. C. Jordan, "Tale, Teller and Audience," in *Proceedings of a Conference on African Languages and Literatures, Northwestern University, April 28–30, 1966* (Evanston, Ill.: Northwestern University, n.d.), pp. 33–44.

23. Harold Scheub, *The Xhosa Ntsomi*, Oxford Library of African Literature (Oxford Univ. Pr., 1975).

24. Ibid., p. 6.

25. Ibid.

26. Ibid., pp. 7–8.

27. E. E. Evans-Pritchard, *The Zande Trickster*, Oxford Library of African Literature (Oxford: Oxford Univ. Pr./Clarendon, 1967), p. 34.

28. Charles Béart, *Jeux et Jouets de l'Ouest Africain*, 2 vols. (Dakar, IFAN, 1955), vol. 2, p. 778.

29. John S. Mbiti, *Akamba Stories*, Oxford Library of African Literature (Oxford Univ. Pr., 1966), p. 24.

30. Dan Ben-Amos, *Sweet Words: Storytelling Events in Benin* (Philadelphia: Institute for the Study of Human Issues, 1975), pp. 23–24.

31. Ibid., pp. 49, 51.

32. Ibid., pp. 52–53.

33. Ibid., pp. 42–43.

34. Ellis, *The Yoruba-Speaking Peoples*, p. 243.

35. Samuel Johnson, *The History of the Yorubas* (London: Routledge and Kegan Paul, 1921), pp. 125–126.

36. Ellis, *The Yoruba-Speaking Peoples*, p. 243.

37. Johnson, *The History of the Yorubas*, p. 58.

38. Ebiegberi Joe Alagoa, "Oral Tradition among the Ijo of the Niger Delta," *Journal of African History* 7 (1966): 410.

39. S. A. Babalola, *The Content and Form of Yoruba Ijala* (Oxford Univ. Pr., 1966), p. vi.

40. Robert S. Rattray, *Religion and Art in Ashanti* (Oxford Univ. Pr., 1927), p. 219.

41. Daniel P. Biebuyck and Kahombo C. Mateene, *The Mwindo Epic from the Banyanga (Congo Republic)* (Berkeley and Los Angeles: Univ. of California Pr., 1969), pp. 6–14.

42. Melville J. Herskovits and Frances S. Herskovits, *Dahomean Narrative* (Evanston: Northwestern Univ. Pr., 1958), p. 17.

43. Biebuyck and Mateene, *The Mwindo Epic*, p. 8.

44. Henry F. Morris, *The Heroic Recitations of the Bahima of Ankole*, Oxford Library of African Literature (Oxford Univ. Pr., 1964), pp. 19–39.

45. A. C. Jordan, *Tales from Southern Africa* (Berkeley and Los Angeles: Univ. of California Pr., 1973), pp. 2ff.

46. Same as Note 44.

47. S. A. Babalola, *The Content and Form*, p. 18.

48. Charles Bird, "Heroic Songs of the Mande Hunters," in *African Folklore*, ed. by Richard Dorson (Bloomington: Indiana Univ. Pr., 1972), p. 278.

49. Trevor Cope, *Izibongo: Zulu Praise Poems*, Oxford Library of African Literature (Oxford Univ. Pr., 1968), p. 29.

50. O. F. Raum, *Chaga Childhood: A Description of Indigenous Education in an East African Tribe* (Oxford Univ. Pr., 1940), p. 222.

51. Yuri M. Sokolov, *Russian Folklore*, tr. by Catherine Ruth Smith (New York: Macmillan, 1950), p. 311.

52. Mark Azadovsky, *Eine Sibirische Märchenerzählerin*, Folklore Fellows Communications, no. 68 (Helsinki, 1926), pp. 36ff.

53. Sokolov, *Russian Folklore*, pp. 405–406.

54. Carl-Herman Tillhagen, *Taikon Berättar* (Stockholm: P. A. Norstedt & Söners, 1946), pp. 11–12.

55. Knut Liestøl, *The Origin of the Icelandic Family Sagas*, Instituttet for Sammenlignende Kulturforskning, Ser. A, Forelesninger, no. 10 (Oslo: W. Aschehoug & Co., 1930), p. 103.

56. Karl Haiding, *Von der Gebärdensprache der Märchenerzähler*, Folklore Fellows Communications, no. 155 (Helsinki: 1955), pp. 9–10.

57. Otto Brinkmann, *Das Erzählen in einer Dorfgemeinschaft*, Veröffentlichungen der Volkskundlichen Komission des Provinzialinstituts für Westfälische Landes- und Volkskunde, Erste Reihe, Heft 4 (Münster i. W.: Aschendorffschen Verlagsbuchhandlung, 1931), p. 11.

58. Leza Uffer, *Rätoromanische Märchen und ihre Erzähler*, Schriften, Band 29 (Basel: Schweizerische Gesellschaft für Volkskunde, 1945), p. 81.

59. Linda Kégh, *Folktales and Society: Story-telling in a Hungarian Peasant Community*, tr. from the German by Emily M. Schosssurger (Bloomington: Indiana Univ. Pr., 1969), p. 227.

60. Ibid., p. 253.

61. Ibid., p. 183.

62. Ibid., p. 184.

63. James H. Delargy, *The Gaelic Storyteller*, Rhys Memorial Lecture for 1945, *Proceedings of the British Academy*, 31 (London: The Academy, 1945), p. 16.

64. Alexander Carmichael, *Carmina Gadelica*, 2nd ed. (Edinburgh and London: Oliver and Boyd, 1928), p. xxii.

65. Kenneth Hurlstone Jackson, *The International Popular Tale and Early Welsh Tradition* (Cardiff: Univ. of Wales Pr., 1961), p. 55.

66. Geneviève Massignon, *Folktales of France*, tr. by Jacqueline Hyland (Chicago: Univ. of Chicago Pr., 1968), pp. xli–xliii.

67. Věna Hrdličková, "Japanese Professional Storytellers," in *Folklore Genres*, ed. by Dan Ben-Amos (Austin: Univ. of Texas Pr., 1976), pp. 171–190.

68. "Japan: Dirty Stories," *Newsweek* 81 (June 4, 1973): 51.

69. Wolfram Eberhard, *Minstrel Tales from Southeastern Turkey*, Folklore Studies, 5 (Berkeley and Los Angeles: Univ. of California Pr., 1955), pp. 1ff.

70. Barbara K. Walker, "The Folks Who Tell Folktales: Field Collecting in Turkey," *Horn Book* 47, no. 6 (December 1971): 636–642.

71. Harriet Ronken Lynton and Mohini Rajan, *The Days of the Beloved* (Berkeley and Los Angeles: Univ. of California Pr., 1974), p. 140; Kunjabehari Das, *A Study of Orissan Folklore* (Santinketan, India: Visvabharati, 1953), p. 8; Arthur Perera, *Sinhalese Folklore Notes* (Bombay: 1917), n.p.

72. Suzan Lapai, "Burma," in *Folktales Told around the World*, ed. by Richard Dorson (Chicago: Univ. of Chicago Pr., 1975), p. 277.

73. Roy Franklin Barton, *The Mythology of the Ifugaos*, Memoirs, 46 (Philadelphia: American Folklore Society, 1955), p. 11.

74. Roger Edward Mitchell, "A Study of the Cultural, Historical and Acculturative Factors Influencing the Repertoires of Two Trukese Informants" (Ph.D. diss., University of Indiana, 1967), p. 176.

75. Tupou Posesi Fanua, *Po Fananga: Folktales of Tonga* (San Diego, Calif.: Tofua Press, 1975), p. 7.

76. Elli Köngäs Maranda and Pierre Maranda, *Structural Models in Folklore and Transformational Essays* (The Hague: Mouton, 1971), pp. 11–13.

77. Geoffrey Gorer, *Himalayan Village: An Account of the Lepchas of Sikkim*, 2nd ed. (New York: Basic Books, 1967), pp. 266–267.

78. Susie Hoogasian-Villa, *100 Armenian Tales and Their Folkloristic Relevance* (Detroit: Wayne State Univ. Pr., 1966), pp. 535–537; Leon Surmelian, *Apples of Immortality: Folktales of Armenia*, UNESCO Collection of Representative Works (Berkeley and Los Angeles: Univ. of California Pr., 1968), pp. 11ff.

79. Carla Bianco, "The Two Rosetos: The Folklore of an Italian-American Community in Northeastern Pennsylvania" (Ph.D. diss., Indiana University, 1972), p. 137.

80. Barbro Sklute, "Legends and Folk Beliefs in a Swedish-American Community: A Study in Folklore and Acculturation" (Ph.D. diss., Indiana University, 1970), p. 174.

81. Richard Dorson, "Oral Styles of American Folk Narrators," in his *Folklore: Selected Essays* (Bloomington: Indiana Univ. Pr., 1972), pp. 99–146.

82. Benjamin Botkin, *A Treasury of Southern Folklore* (New York: Crown, 1949), p. ix.

83. Marie Campbell, *Tales from the Cloud-Walking Country* (Bloomington: Indiana Univ. Pr., 1958).

84. J. Frank Dobie, "Storytellers I Have Known," in *Singers and Storytellers*, by Mody C. Boatright and others (Dallas: Southern Methodist Univ. Pr., 1961), pp. 3–29.

85. Jerome Richard Mintz, *The Legends of the Hasidim: An Introduction to Hasidic Culture and Oral Tradition in the New World* (Chicago: Univ. of Chicago Pr., 1968), pp. 3–8.

249

86. Audrey Kennedy, "History of the Boys and Girls Department of the Carnegie Library of Pittsburgh" (Master's thesis, Carnegie Institute of Technology, 1949), p. 23.

Chapter 10

1. H. T. Norris, *Shinqiti Folk Literature and Song*, Oxford Library of African Literature (Oxford Univ. Pr., 1968), p. 61.

2. *Berimbau*. 16mm film. 12 min. Color. Directed by Toby Talbot. Narrated by Emile de Antonio. New York: New Yorker Films, 1971.

3. Dan Ben-Amos, *Sweet Words: Storytelling Events in Benin* (Philadelphia: Institute for the Study of Human Issues, 1975), pp. 25–29, 42–49.

4. Henri Frankfort, *The Art and Architecture of the Ancient Orient* (Baltimore: Penguin Books, 1969), pp. 35–36.

5. G. S. Kirk, *The Songs of Homer* (Cambridge: Cambridge Univ. Pr., 1962), pp. 90–91.

6. Ibid., pp. 313–314.

7. H. Munro Chadwick and Nora Kershaw Chadwick, *The Growth of Literature*, vol. 2 (Cambridge: Cambridge Univ. Pr., 1932–1940), p. 271.

8. L. F. Anderson, *The Anglo-Saxon Scop*, Philological Ser., no. 1 (Toronto: Univ. of Toronto Studies, 1903), p. 13.

9. Norris, *Shinqiti Folk Literature and Song*, pp. 64–65.

10. Charles Bird, "Heroic Songs of the Mande Hunters," in *African Folklore*, ed. by Richard Dorson (Bloomington: Indiana Univ. Pr., 1972), p. 279.

11. Norris, *Shinqiti Folk Literature and Song*, pp. 62–63.

12. Kurt Meissner, "Die Yose," Deutsche Gesellschaft für Natur- und Völkerkunde Ostasiens, *Mitteilungen* 14 (1913): 240–241.

13. J. Barth, "Kodan und Rakugo," Deutsche Gesellschaft für Natur- und Völkerkunde Ostasiens, *Mitteilungen* 22 (1928): Teil D, p. 3.

14. Christine Oppong, *Growing Up in Dagbon* (Accra: Ghana Publishing Corp., 1973), p. 57.

15. Chadwick and Chadwick, *Growth of Literature*, vol. 2, p. 271; Peter Alexseevich Bessonov, *Kalêki Perekhozhie*, 6 parts (Moscow: 1861–1864), plates.

16. Thomas G. Winner, *The Oral Art and Literature of the Kazakhs of Russian Central Asia* (Durham, N.C.: Duke Univ. Pr., 1958), p. 29.

17. Chadwick and Chadwick, *The Growth of Literature*, vol. 2, p. 242.

18. Same as Note 16.

19. Wolfram Eberhard, *Minstrel Tales from Southeastern Turkey*, Folklore Studies, 5 (Berkeley and Los Angeles: Univ. of California Pr., 1955), pp. 1, 8.

20. Kirk, *The Songs of Homer*, p. 90; Albert B. Lord, *The Singer of Tales*, Harvard Studies in Comparative Literature, 24 (Cambridge: Harvard Univ. Pr., 1960), p. 21.

21. Chadwick and Chadwick, *Growth of Literature*, vol. 2, p. 22.

22. György Kara, *Chants d'un Barde Mongol* (Budapest: Akadémiai Kiadó, 1970), pp. 46–47.

23. Amin Sweeney, "Professional Malay Storytelling: Some Questions of Style and Presentation," in *Studies in Malaysian Oral and Musical Traditions* (Ann Arbor, Mich.: Center for South and Southeast Asian Studies, University of Michigan, 1974), pp. 47–55.

24. Chadwick and Chadwick, *Growth of Literature*, vol. 3, pp. 668–669.

25. M. Mondon-Vidailhet, "La Musique Éthiopienne," in *Encyclopédie de la Musique*, ed. by Albert Lavignac (Paris: Delagrave, 1922), pt. 1, vol. 5, p. 3181.

26. Prabhaker B. Mande, "Dakkalwars and Their Myths," *Folklore* (Calcutta) 14 (January 1973): 70.

27. Same as Note 3.

28. A. M. Jones, *African Music in Northern Rhodesia and Some Other Places*, Rhodes-Livingston Museum, Occasional Papers, new series, no. 4, 1958, p. 29 (originally issued as no. 2 in 1943).

29. Daniel P. Biebuyck and Kahombo C. Mateene, *The Mwindo Epic from the Banyanga (Congo Republic)* (Berkeley and Los Angeles: Univ. of California Pr., 1969), p. 13.

30. Same as Note 23.

31. Same as Note 10.

32. Oppong, *Growing Up in Dagbon*, p. 54.

33. S. A. Babalola, *The Content and Form of Yoruba Ijala* (Oxford Univ. Pr., 1966), pp. 54–55.

34. Same as Note 23.

35. Chadwick and Chadwick, *Growth of Literature*, vol. 3, p. 423.

36. Ibid.

37. Same as Note 16.

38. Biebuyck and Mateene, *The Mwindo Epic*, p. 7.

Chapter 11

1. "Children Like Pictures: The Wagko Story Hour Stimulates the Child's Interest," *Publishers' Weekly* 126 (August 25, 1934): 589.

2. See also Myrtilla Avery, *The Exultet Rolls of South Italy*, vol. 2 (The Hague: Martinus Nijhoff; Princeton: Princeton Univ. Pr., 1936).

3. J. P. Gilson, "Introduction," in *An Exultet Roll Illuminated in the XIth Century at the Abbey of Monte Cassino* (London: British Museum, 1929), pp. 5–7.

4. Rolf Wilhelm Brednich, "Zur Vorgeschichte des Bänkelsangs," Österreichisches Volksliedwerk, *Jahrbuch* (Wien) 21 (1972): 78–92.

5. Leopold Schmidt, "Geistlicher Bänkelgesang," Österreichisches Volksliedwerk, *Jahrbuch* 12 (1963): 1–16.

6. William A. Coupe, *The German Illustrated Broadsheet in the Seventeenth Century*, Bibliotheca Bibliographica Aureliana, 17 (Baden-Baden: Heitz, 1966–1967), pp. 13–17.

7. Elsbeth Janda and Fritz Nötzoldt, *Die Moritat vom Bänkelsang: oder das Lied der Strasse* (München: Ehrenwirth Verlag, 1959), p. 9.

8. Correspondence of the author and Fritz Nötzoldt.

9. Brednich, "Zur Vorgeschichte des Bänkelsangs," p. 84.

10. Johann Wolfgang von Goethe, *Wilhelm Meister's Theatralische Sendung*, vol. 51 of his *Werke* (Weimar, 1911), p. 150.

11. Janda and Nötzoldt, *Die Moritat vom Bänkelsang*, pp. 9ff.

12. Ananda Coomaraswamy, "Picture Showmen," *Indian Historical Quarterly* 5, no. 2 (June 1929): 182.

13. Quoted in Coomaraswamy, "Picture Showmen," p. 186.

14. [Henry Ferguson and Joan Ferguson], "Textiles That Tell a Story" (Thompson, Conn.: InterCulture Associates, n.d.), unp.

15. Ibid.

16. Joan Erikson, *Mata ni Pachedi: A Book on the Temple Cloth of the Mother Goddess* (Ahmedabad: National Institute of Design, 1968), pp. 9ff.

17. Prabhaker B. Mande, "Dakkalwars and their Myths," *Folklore* (Calcutta) 14 (January 1973): 69–76.

18. See the description from Morio Kita's novel, quoted in Chapter Three.

19. Koji Kata, *Machi no jijyoden* (*Autobiography of a Street-Person*) (Tokyo: Bansei-sha, 1977).

20. Ibid.

21. Ardis Huls, "Pre-school Story Hour," *Wilson Library Bulletin* 16 (May 1942): 730.

22. Marie L. Shedlock, *The Art of the Storyteller* (New York: Dover, 1951), pp. 13–14 (first pub. in 1915).

23. Gwendolyn Marie Fannin, "A Resumé of the History, Growth and Development of the Story Hour in the New York Public Library" (Master's thesis, Atlanta University, 1958), p. 10.

24. Ibid., p. 14.

25. Florence Sanborn, "How to Use Picture-Story Books," *Library Journal* 74 (February 15, 1949): 272–274.

26. F. Marie Foster, *A Round of Picture Book Programs* (Albany: New York State Education Dept., Division of Adult Education and Library Extension, c. 1944), unp.

27. Adeline Corrigan, "The Next Step—the Picture Book Hour," *Library Journal* 81 (September 15, 1956): 2014–2016.

28. Alice Kane, "The Changing Face of the Story Hour," *Ontario Library Review* 49 (August 1965): 141–142.

29. Based on personal observation.

30. Lyle A. Dickey, *String Figures from Hawaii*, Bulletin 54 (Honolulu: Bernice P. Bishop Museum, 1928), p. 11.

31. Charles P. Mountford, "Exploring Stone Age Arnhem Land," *National Geographic* 96 (December 1949): 745–782.

32. K. G. Lindblom, *String Figures in Africa*, Populära Etnologiska Skrifter, Smärre meddelanden, 9 (Stockholm: Statens Etnografiska Museum, 1930), p. 11.

33. M. D. Leakey and L. S. B. Leakey, *Some String Figures from North East Angola* (Lisboa: Companhia de Diamantes de Angola, Serviços Culturais, 1949), p. 7.

34. Věna Hrdličková, "Japanese Professional Storytellers," in *Folklore Genres*, ed. by Dan Ben-Amos (Austin: Univ. of Texas Pr., 1976), p. 175.

35. Věna Hrdličková, "The Chinese Storytellers and Singers of Ballads: Their Performances and Storytelling Techniques," in *Transactions*, 3rd ser., vol. 10 (Tokyo: Asiatic Society of Japan, 1968), p. 103.

36. Geoffrey Gorer, *Himalayan Village: An Account of the Lepchas of Sikkim*, 2nd ed. (New York: Basic Books, 1967), p. 267 (first pub. in 1938).

37. Daniel J. Crowley, *I Could Talk Old-Story Good: Creativity in Bahamian Folklore*, Publications in Folklore Studies, 17 (Berkeley and Los Angeles: Univ. of California Pr., 1966), p. 28.

38. H. Munro Chadwick and Nora Kershaw Chadwick, *The Growth of Literature*, vol. 2 (Cambridge: Cambridge Univ. Pr., 1932–1940), p. 265.

39. Amin Sweeney, "Professional Malay Storytelling: Some Questions of Style and Presentation," in *Studies in Malaysian Oral and Musical Traditions* (Ann Arbor, Mich.: Center for South and Southeast Asian Studies, University of Michigan, 1974), p. 54.

40. Chadwick and Chadwick, *Growth of Literature*, vol. 2, pp. 263ff.

41. Daniel P. Biebuyck, "The Epic as a Genre in Congo Oral Literature," in *African Folklore*, ed. by Richard Dorson (Bloomington: Indiana Univ. Pr., 1972), p. 262.

42. Gilbert Rouget, "Court Songs and Traditional History in the Ancient Kingdoms of Porto-Novo and Abomey," in *Essays on Music and History in Africa*, ed. by Klaus P. Wachsmann (Evanston, Ill.: Northwestern Univ. Pr., 1971), pp. 39–41.

43. Henry F. Morris, *The Heroic Recitations of the Bahima of Ankole*, Oxford Library of African Literature (Oxford Univ. Pr., 1964), p. 21.

44. G. S. Kirk, *The Songs of Homer* (Cambridge: Cambridge Univ. Pr., 1962), pp. 314–315.

Chapter 12

1. Barbara Walker, "Folk Tales in Turkey," *Horn Book* 40 (February 1964): 42–46.

2. Elsie Clews Parsons, *Folktales of Andros Island, Bahamas*, Memoirs, 13 (New York: American Folklore Society, 1918), p. xi.

3. Elsie Clews Parsons, *Folklore of the Sea Islands, South Carolina* (Cambridge, Mass., and New York: American Folklore Society, 1923), p. xviii.

4. Geneviève Massignon, *Folktales of France*, tr. by Jacqueline Hyland (Chicago: Univ. of Chicago Pr., 1968), p. 142.

5. Melville Jacobs, *The Content and Style of an Oral Literature: Clackamas Chinook Myths and Tales* (Chicago: Univ. of Chicago Pr., 1959), p. 220.

6. James H. Delargy, *The Gaelic Storyteller*, Rhys Memorial Lecture for 1945, *Proceedings of the British Academy*, 31 (London: The Academy, 1945), p. 20.

7. Georgios Megas, *Folktales of Greece*, tr. by Helen Colaclides (Chicago: Univ. of Chicago Pr., 1970), p. xlviii.

8. Daniel J. Crowley, *I Could Talk Old-Story Good: Creativity in Bahamian Folklore*, Publications in Folklore Studies, 17 (Berkeley and Los Angeles: Univ. of California Pr., 1966), p. 32.

9. Anthony Alpers, *Legends of the South Seas* (New York: Thomas Y. Crowell, 1970), p. 41.

10. Keigo Seki, *Folktales of Japan* (Chicago: Univ. of Chicago Pr., 1963), p. 125.

11. Elsie Clews Parsons, *Taos Tales*, Memoirs, 34 (New York: American Folklore Society, 1940), p. 1.

12. Melville J. Herskovits and Frances S. Herskovits, *Dahomean Narrative* (Evanston, Ill.: Northwestern Univ. Pr., 1958), pp. 53–54.

13. Ella E. Clark, *Indian Legends from the Northern Rockies* (Norman: Univ. of Oklahoma Pr., 1966), p. 317; Harriet Ronken Lynton and Mohini Rajan, *The Days of the Beloved* (Berkeley and Los Angeles: Univ. of California Pr., 1974), p. 140; Mrs. Meer Hasan Ali, *Observations on the Mussulmauns of India* . . ., 2nd ed. (Oxford Univ. Pr., 1917), pp. 251–252; Roger Edward Mitchell, "A Study of the Cultural, Historical and Acculturative Factors Influencing the Repertoires of Two Trukese Informants" (Ph.D. diss., University of Indiana, 1967), p. 176; Arthur Perera, *Sinhalese Folklore Notes* (Bombay: 1917), unp.

14. Thelma Adamson, *Folktales of the Coast Salish*, Memoirs, 27 (New York: American Folklore Society, 1934), p. xiii.

15. Morris Edward Opler, *Myths and Tales of the Jicarilla Apache Indians*, Memoirs, 31 (New York: American Folklore Society, 1938), p. ix.

Chapter 13

1. Věna Hrdličková, "The Professional Training of Chinese Storytellers and the Storytellers' Guilds," *Archiv Orientální* 33 (1965): 228.

2. H. Munro Chadwick and Nora Kershaw Chadwick, *The Growth of Literature*, vol. 1 (Cambridge: Cambridge Univ. Pr., 1932–1940), p. 605.

3. Daniel Corkery, "The Bardic Schools of Munster," *The Blarney Annual* 1 (1948): 19–24.

4. Chadwick and Chadwick, *Growth of Literature*, vol. 1, p. 603.

5. Same as Note 3.

6. Christine Oppong, *Growing Up in Dagbon* (Accra: Ghana Publishing Corp., 1973), p. 54.

7. Ibid., pp. 55–56.

8. Ibid., p. 55.

9. Ibid., pp. 57–58.

10. Ibid., p. 58.

11. H. T. Norris, *Shinqiti Folk Literature and Song*, Oxford Library of African Literature (Oxford Univ. Pr., 1968), p. 65.

12. Ibid.

13. Ibid., p. 54.

14. E. S. Craighill Handy, *Marquesan Legends*, Bulletin 69 (Honolulu: Bernice P. Bishop Museum, 1930), p. 20.

15. Elsdon Best, *The Maori*, Memoirs, 5 (Wellington: Polynesian Society, 1924), vol. 1, pp. 57–84.

16. Paul Radin, *The Trickster: A Study in American Indian Mythology* (New York: Greenwood Press, 1969), p. 122.

17. Chadwick and Chadwick, *Growth of Literature*, vol. 2, pp. 251–253.

18. Bronislaw Malinowski, *Argonauts of the Western Pacific* (London: Routledge and Kegan Paul, 1922), pp. 185–186, 291.

19. L. F. Anderson, *The Anglo-Saxon Scop*, Philological Ser. no. 1 (Toronto: Univ. of Toronto Studies, 1903).

20. John Howland Rowe, "Inca Culture at the Time of the Spanish Conquest," in *Handbook of South American Indians*, ed. by Julian H. Steward, Smithsonian Institution, Bureau of Ethnology, Bulletin, 143 (Washington, D.C.: U.S. Government Printing Office, 1946), pp. 201–202.

21. Věna Hrdličková, "Japanese Professional Storytellers," in *Folklore Genres*, ed. by Dan Ben-Amos (Austin: Univ. of Texas Pr., 1976); and "The Zenza, the Storyteller's Apprentice," International Conference of Orientalists in Japan, *Transactions* 13 (1968): 31–41.

22. Hrdličková, "The Professional Training of Chinese Storytellers," pp. 227ff.

23. Jiří Cejpek, "Iranian Folk Literature," in *History of Iranian Literature*, ed. by Jan Rypka (Dordrecht, Holland: D. Reidel Pub. Co., 1956), p. 654.

24. Charles Bird, "Heroic Songs of the Mande Hunters," in *African Folklore*, ed. by Richard Dorson (Bloomington: Indiana Univ. Pr., 1972), p. 279.

25. S. A. Babalola, *The Content and Form of Yoruba Ijala* (Oxford Univ. Pr., 1966), p. 41.

26. Daniel P. Biebuyck and Kahombo C. Mateene, *The Mwindo Epic from the Banyanga (Congo Republic)* (Berkeley and Los Angeles: Univ. of California Pr., 1969), pp. 11–12.

27. Ibid., p. 12.

28. Dan Ben-Amos, *Sweet Words: Storytelling Events in Benin* (Philadelphia: Institute for the Study of Human Issues, 1975), pp. 37ff.

29. Harold Scheub, *The Xhosa Ntsomi*, Oxford Library of African Literature (Oxford Univ. Pr., 1975), p. 21.

30. Ibid., p. 19.

31. Albert B. Lord, *The Singer of Tales*, Harvard Studies in Comparative Literature, 24 (Cambridge: Harvard Univ. Pr., 1960), pp. 13–29.

32. Ibid.

33. Thomas G. Winner, *The Oral Art and Literature of the Kazakhs of Russian Central Asia* (Durham, N.C.: Duke Univ. Pr., 1958), pp. 33–34.

34. Carnegie Library of Pittsburgh, *Annual Report*, 1900.

35. Announcement of Pratt Institute, *Library Journal* 24 (February 1899): 72.

36. Announcement of program of study, *Library Journal* 26 (September 1901): 697.

37. *Pratt Institute Monthly* 10 (December 1901): 46.

38. Library School of Western Reserve University, *Catalog 1904–1905*.

39. Announced in *Wilson Library Bulletin* 4 (June 1908): 56.

40. New York Public Library, Library School, [*Catalog*] 1912.

41. St. Louis Public Library, Library School, *Circular of Information 1917–18*.

42. Columbia University, Library School, *Catalog*, 1928.

43. Ibid.

44. Rose L. Abernethy, " A Study of Existing Practices and Principles of Storytelling for Children in the United States" (Ph.D. diss., Northwestern University, 1964).

45. Gwendolyn Marie Fannin, "A Resumé of the History, Growth and Development of the Story Hour in the New York Public Library" (Master's thesis, Atlanta University, School of Library Service, 1958), p. 13.

46. Hrdličková, "The Professional Training of Chinese Storytellers," p. 238.

47. Chautauqua Library School, *Handbook and Register 1901–1910* (Chautauqua: 1911).

48. *The Story Hour* 1 (1908): 38.

49. This short summary of the work of Richard T. Wyche and the National Storyteller's League is taken from Richard Gerald Alvey, "The Historical Development of Organized Storytelling to Children in the United States" (Ph.D. diss., University of Pennsylvania, 1974), pp. 182–220.

50. Compiled from the bibliography of ibid., and from Anne Pellowski, *The World of Children's Literature* (New York: R. R. Bowker, 1968).

51. Alvey, "The Historical Development of Organized Storytelling."

52. Reported in a personal conversation with the author, Tokyo, October 1975.

53. Reported in a personal conversation with the author, Detroit, June 1977.

54. Anne Izard, "I Study Very Hard. I Thank You Very Much," *Top of the News* 29 (January 1973): 130–132.

55. James H. Delargy, *The Gaelic Storyteller*, Rhys Memorial Lecture for 1945, *Proceedings of the British Academy*, 31 (London: The Academy, 1945), pp. 22ff.

56. Edwin S. Hall, *The Eskimo Storyteller* (Knoxville: Univ. of Tennessee Pr., 1975), p. 38.

57. Prajuab Tirabutana, "A Simple One: The Story of a Siamese Girlhood," Data Paper, no. 30 (Ithaca: Cornell University, Department of Far Eastern Studies, Southeast Asia Program, 1958), pp. 10–11.

58. Robin Flower, *The Western Island or the Great Blasket* (Oxford Univ. Pr., 1945), p. 53.

59. Gottfried Henssen, *Überlieferung und Persönlichkeit: Die Erzählung und Lieder des Egbert Gerrits* (Münster i. W.: Aschendorffsche Verlagsbuchhandlung, 1951), pp. 1–3.

60. Linda Dégh, *Folktales and Society: Storytelling in a Hungarian Peasant Community*, tr. from the German by Emily M. Schossburger (Bloomington: Indiana Univ. Pr., 1969), Chapters 6, 7, and 8.

61. Ibid., p. 186.

62. Ibid., p. 195.

63. Seán O'Sullivan, *A Handbook of Irish Folklore* (Detroit: Singing Tree Press, 1970), p. 555.

64. Dégh, *Folktales and Society*, pp. 192–194.

65. Hall, *The Eskimo Storyteller*, p. 41.

66. Harriet Ronken Lynton and Mohini Rajan, *The Days of the Beloved* (Berkeley and Los Angeles: Univ. of California Pr., 1974), p. 140.

67. Mary Frere, *Hindoo Fairy Legends (Old Deccan Days)* (New York: Dover, 1967), p. xxvii (first pub. in 1881).

68. Ella E. Clark, *Indian Legends from the Northern Rockies* (Norman: Univ. of Oklahoma Pr., 1966), p. xiii.

69. Cited in Reidar Thorwald Christiansen, *Folktales of Norway* (Chicago: Univ. of Chicago Pr., 1964), p. xli.

70. Jaroslav Průšek, "The Creative Methods of Chinese Mediaeval Storytellers," in *Charisteria Orientalia*, by Felix Tauer and others (Prague: Nakladatelstvi Československe Akademie Věd, 1956), p. 253.

Chapter 14

1. Richard Dorson, *Buying the Wind* (Chicago: Univ. of Chicago Pr., 1964), pp. 1–20.

2. See especially Laura Ingalls Wilder, *Little House in the Big Woods* and *Little Town on the Prairie* (New York: Harper and Row, 1953).

3. Joseph Jacobs, "Master of All Masters," in his *English Folk and Fairy Tales* (New York: Dover, n.d.); "There Was an Old Woman All Skin and Bone," learned from an oral version sung by Jean Ritchie.

4. Robert Lowie, *Social Organization* (New York: Holt, Rinehart and Winston, 1948), pp. 131–134.

5. Linda Dégh, *Folktales and Society: Storytelling in a Hungarian Peasant Community*, tr. from the German by Emily M. Schossburger (Bloomington: Indiana Univ. Pr., 1969), pp. 89, 185.

6. Noted on jacket copy of Elphinstone Dayrell, *Why the Sun and the Moon Live in the Sky*. Illus. by Blair Lent. (Boston: Houghton Mifflin, 1968).

Bibliography

Books and Periodicals

Abernethy, Rose L. "A Study of Existing Practices and Principles of Story-telling for Children in the United States." Ph.D. dissertation, Northwestern University, 1964.

Adam, Jules. *Japanese Storytellers*. Tr. from the French by Osman Edwards. Tokyo: T. Hasegawa, 1912.

Adams, Robert J. "Social Identity of a Japanese Storyteller." Ph.D. dissertation, Indiana University, 1972.

Adamson, Thelma. *Folktales of the Coast Salish*. Memoirs, 27. New York: American Folklore Society, 1934.

Addams, Jane. *Twenty Years at Hull-House*. New York: Macmillan, 1910.

Adler, Felix. *The Moral Instruction of Children*. New York: D. Appleton and Co., 1892.

Afanas'ev, Aleksandr. *Russian Fairy Tales*. New York: Pantheon, 1945.

Alagoa, Ebiegberi Joe. "Oral Tradition among the Ijo of the Niger Delta." *Journal of African History* 7 (1966): 405–419.

Allen, Arthur T. "The Ethos of the Teller of Tales." *Wilson Library Bulletin*, December 1965, pp. 356–358.

Allen, Louis A. *Time before Morning: Art and Myth of the Australian Aborigines*. New York: Thomas Y. Crowell, 1975.

Alpers, Anthony. *Legends of the South Seas.* New York: Thomas Y. Crowell, 1970.

Alvey, Richard Gerald. "The Historical Development of Organized Story-telling to Children in the United States." Ph.D. dissertation, University of Pennsylvania, 1974.

American Library Association. *A Survey of Libraries in the United States.* Chicago: ALA, 1927.

Ammar, Hamed. *Growing Up in an Egyptian Village: Silwa, Province of Aswan.* New York: Octagon, 1966.

Andersen, Johannes C. *Myths and Legends of the Polynesians.* Rutland, Vt.: Tuttle, 1969.

Anderson, L. F. *The Anglo-Saxon Scop.* Studies, Philological Series, no. 1. Toronto: University of Toronto, 1903.

Andersson, Theodore M. *The Icelandic Family Saga.* Cambridge: Harvard Univ. Pr., 1967.

Anyumba, H. O. "The *Nyatiti* Lament Songs." In *East Africa Past and Present.* Paris: Presence Africaine, 1964.

Arbuthnot, May Hill. *Children and Books*, 1st ed. Chicago: Scott, Foresman, 1947.

Attagara, Kingkeo. "The Folk Religion of Ban Nai, a Hamlet in Central Thailand." Ph.D. dissertation, Indiana University, 1967.

Avery, Myrtilla. *The Exultet Rolls of South Italy.* 2 vols. The Hague: Martinus Nijhoff, 1936; Princeton: Princeton Univ. Pr., 1936.

Azadovsky, Mark. *Eine Sibirische Märchenerzählerin.* Folklore Fellows Communications, no. 68. Helsinki, 1926.

Azevedo, Warren L. d'. "Uses of the Past in Gola Discourse." *Journal of African History* 3 (1962): 11–34.

Babalola, Adeboye. "One Type of Yoruba Folk Narrative Called Àrò." *Fabula* 14 (1973): 179–193.

Babalola, S. A. *The Content and Form of Yoruba Ijala.* Oxford Univ. Pr., 1966.

Bain, R. Nisbet, ed. and tr. *Cossack Fairy Tales and Folk Tales.* New York: Fred A. Stokes, n.d.

Baker, Augusta, and Greene, Ellin. *Storytelling: Art and Technique.* New York: R. R. Bowker, 1977.

Ball, John. "Style in the Folktale." *Folk-lore* 65 (1954): 170–172.

Barth, J. "Kodan und Rakugo." In *Mitteilungen*, vol. 22, pt. D. Tokyo: Deutsche Gesellschaft für Natur- und Völkerkunde Ostasiens, 1928.

Barton, Roy Franklin. *The Mythology of the Ifugaos.* Memoirs, 44. Philadelphia: American Folklore Society, 1955.

Bascom, William R. "The Forms of Folklore: Prose Narratives." *Journal of American Folklore* 78 (1965): 3–20.

Béart, Charles. *Jeux et Jouets de l'Ouest Africain.* 2 vols. Dakar: IFAN, 1955.

Bechtum, Martin. *Beweggründe und Bedeutung des Vagantentums in der lateinischen Kirche des Mittelalters.* Beiträge zur mittelalterlichen, neueren und allgemeinen Geschichte, 14. Jena: Gustav Fischer, 1941.

Beckwith, Martha Warren. *Mandan-Hidatsa Myths and Ceremonies*. Memoirs, 32. New York: American Folklore Society, 1937.

Beech, Mervyn W. H. *The Suk*. New York: Negro Universities Press, 1966. (Originally pub. 1911 by Clarendon Press.)

Ben-Amos, Dan. *Sweet Words: Storytelling Events in Benin*. Philadelphia: Institute for the Study of Human Issues, 1975.

Benedict, Ruth. *Zuni Mythology*. 2 vols. Contributions to Anthropology, 21. New York: Columbia Univ., 1935.

Beowulf. Tr. by John R. Clark Hall. London: Allen and Unwin, 1911.

Beowulf together with Widsith. Tr. by Benjamin Thorpe. Great Neck, N.Y.: Barron's Educational Series, 1962.

Bessonov, Peter Alexseevich. *Kalêki Perekhozhie*. 6 parts. Moscow, 1861–1864.

Best, Elsdon. *The Maori*. 2 vols. Memoirs, 5. Wellington: Polynesian Society, 1924.

Bianco, Carla. "The Two Rosetos: The Folklore of an Italian-American Community in Northeastern Pennsylvania." Ph.D. dissertation, Indiana University, 1972.

Biebuyck, Daniel P. "The Epic as a Genre in Congo Oral Literature." In *African Folklore*, ed. by Richard Dorson. Bloomington: Indiana Univ. Pr., 1972.

_____ . *Lega Culture: Art, Initiation, and Moral Philosophy among a Central African People*. Berkeley and Los Angeles: Univ. of California Pr., 1973.

_____ , and Mateene, Kahombo C. *The Mwindo Epic from the Banyanga (Congo Republic)*. Berkeley and Los Angeles: Univ. of California Pr., 1969.

Bird, Charles. "Heroic Songs of the Mande Hunters." In *African Folklore*, ed. by Richard Dorson. Bloomington: Indiana Univ. Pr., 1972.

Blacking, John. *Venda Children's Songs*. Johannesburg: Witwatersrand Univ. Pr., 1967.

Boas, Franz. *Tsimshian Mythology*. Smithsonian Institution, U.S. Bureau of Ethnology, 31st Annual Report. Washington, D.C.: U.S. Government Printing Office, 1916.

Bødker, Laurits, Hole, Christina, and D'Aronco, G. *European Folk Tales*. Copenhagen: Rosenkilde and Bagger, 1963.

Bolte, Johannes, and Polivka, Georg. *Anmerkungen zu den Kinder- und Hausmärchen der Brüder Grimm*. 5 vols. Leipzig: Dieterich, 1913–1932.

Bonner, Anthony, ed. and tr. *Songs of the Troubadours*. New York: Schocken, 1972.

Bowra, C. M. *Heroic Poetry*. London: Macmillan, 1952.

Boy Scouts of America. *Handbook for Scoutmasters*, 1st ed., 9th reprint. New York: Boy Scouts of America, 1919.

Brandl, Alois. "Spielmannsverhältnisse in frühmittelenglischer Zeit." In Preussische Akademie der Wissenschaften, *Sitzungsberichte*, pp. 873–892. Berlin: The Academy, 1910.

261

Brednick, Rolf Wilhelm. "Zur Vorgeschichte des Bänkelsangs." Österreichisches Volksliedwerk, *Jahrbuch* 21 (1972): 78–92.

Brinkley, F., ed. *Japan Described and Illustrated by the Japanese.* Written by eminent Japanese authorities and scholars. 10 vols. Boston: J. B. Millet Co., 1897.

Brinkmann, Otto. *Das Erzählen in einer Dorfgemeinschaft.* Veröffentlichungen der Volkskundlichen Komission des Provinzialinstituts für Westfälische Landes- und Volkskunde. Erste Reihe, Heft 4. Münster i. W.: Aschendorffschen Verlagsbuchhandlung, 1931.

Bruford, Alan. *Gaelic Folktales and Medieval Romances.* Dublin: Folklore of Ireland Society, 1969.

Bryant, Sara Cone. *How to Tell Stories to Children.* Detroit: Gale Research Co., 1973; Boston: Houghton Mifflin, 1905.

Bynum, David E. "The Generic Nature of Oral Epic Poetry." In *Folklore Genres*, ed. by Dan Ben-Amos, pp. 35–58. Austin: Univ. of Texas Pr., 1976.

Cammann, Alfred. *Westpreussische Märchen. Fabula*, Supplement Series, Reihe A, Band 3. Berlin: W. de Gruyter, 1961.

Campbell, J. F. *Popular Tales of the West Highlands*, vol. 1. London: Alexander Gardner, 1890.

Campbell, Marie. *Tales from the Cloud-Walking Country.* Bloomington: Indiana Univ. Pr., 1958.

Cardinall, Allan Wolsey. *Tales Told in Togoland.* Oxford Univ. Pr., 1931; Westport, Conn.: Negro Universities Press, 1970.

Carlson, Ruth Kearney. *Folklore and Folktales around the World.* Perspectives in Reading, 15. Newark, Del.: International Reading Assn., 1972.

Carmichael, Alexander. *Carmina Gadelica*, 2nd ed. Edinburgh and London: Oliver and Boyd, 1928.

Carnegie Library. *Story Hour, 1915–16.* Atlanta, Georgia: Carnegie Library, 1915.

Carnegie Library of Pittsburgh. *Story Hour Courses for Children from Greek Myths, The Iliad and The Odyssey.* Pittsburgh: Carnegie Library of Pittsburgh, 1906.

Carvalho-Neto, Paulo de. *The Concept of Folklore.* Tr. by Jacques M. P. Wilson. Miami: Univ. of Miami Pr., 1965.

Cejpek, Jiří. "Iranian Folk Literature." In *History of Iranian Literature*, ed. by Jan Rypka. Dordrecht, Holland: D. Reidel Pub. Co., 1956.

Centner, Th. H. *L'enfant africain et ses jeux dans le cadre de la vie traditionelle au Katanga.* Elizabethville: CEPSI, 1963.

Cerulli, Enrico. *The Folk-Literature of the Galla of Southern Abyssinia.* Harvard African Studies, 3. Varia Africana 3. Cambridge: Harvard Univ. Pr., 1922.

Chadwick, H. Munro and Chadwick, Nora Kershaw. *The Growth of Literature.* 3 vols. Cambridge: Cambridge Univ. Pr., 1932–1940.

Chadwick, Nora Kershaw. *Russian Heroic Poetry*. Cambridge: Cambridge Univ. Pr., 1932.

Chamberlin, Candace McDowell. "The Pre-School Story Hour." *Library Journal* 69 (November 1, 1944): 927–928.

Chang, Duk-soon. *The Folk Treasury of Korea: Sources in Myth, Legend and Folktale*. Seoul: Society of Korean Oral Literature, 1970.

Chatelain, Heli. *Folktales of Angola*. American Folklore Society, Memoirs, 1. Boston: Houghton Mifflin, 1894.

Chaudhury, P. C. Roy. *Folk Tales of Bihar*. New Delhi: Sahitya Akademi, 1968.

Chautauqua Library School. *Handbook and Register 1901–1910*. Chautauqua: 1911.

"Children Like Pictures: The Wagko Story Hour Stimulates the Child's Interest." *Publishers Weekly*, August 25, 1934, p. 589.

Chodzko, Alexander. *Specimens of the Popular Poetry of Persia as Found in the Adventures and Improvisations of Kurroglu. . . .* London: 1842.

Christiansen, Reidar Thorwald. *Folktales of Norway*. Chicago: Univ. of Chicago Pr., 1964.

Clark, Ella E. *Indian Legends from the Northern Rockies*. Norman: Univ. of Oklahoma Pr., 1966.

Clarke, Elizabeth Porter. "Storytelling, Reading Aloud and Other Special Features of Work in Children's Rooms." *Library Journal* 27 (April 1902): 189–190.

Clarke, Kenneth, and Clarke, Mary. *A Concise Dictionary of Folklore*. Bowling Green: Kentucky Folklore Society, 1965.

————. *Introducing Folklore*. New York: Holt, Rinehart and Winston, 1965.

Colum, Padraic. *A Treasury of Irish Folklore*. New York: Crown, 1967.

Coomaraswamy, Ananda. "Picture Showmen." *Indian Historical Quarterly* 5, no. 2 (June 1929): 182–187.

Cope, Trevor. *Izibongo: Zulu Praise Poems*. Oxford Library of African Literature. Oxford Univ. Pr., 1968.

Corkery, Daniel. "The Bardic Schools of Munster." *The Blarney Annual* 1 (1948): 19–24.

Cormac. *Sanas Chormaic. Cormac's Glossary*. Tr. and annotated by John O'Donovan. Calcutta and Dublin: The Celtic Society, 1868.

Corrigan, Adeline. "The Next Step—the Picture Book Hour." *Library Journal* 81 (September 15, 1956): 2014–2016.

Coupe, William A. *The German Illustrated Broadsheet in the Seventeenth Century*. Bibliotheca Bibliographica Aureliana, 17. Baden-Baden: Heitz, 1966–1967.

Courlander, Harold. *The Drum and the Hoe: Life and Lore of the Haitian People*. Berkeley and Los Angeles: Univ. of California Pr., 1960.

———. *A Treasury of African Folklore.* New York: Crown, 1975.

Craigie, William A. *Icelandic Sagas.* Cambridge Manuals of Science and Literature. Cambridge Univ. Pr., 1913.

Cronise, Florence M., and Ward, Henry W. *Cunnie Rabbit, Mr. Spider and the Other Beef: West African Folk Tales.* New York: E. P. Dutton, 1903; Chicago: Afro-Am Press, 1969.

Crowley, Daniel J. *I Could Talk Old-Story Good: Creativity in Bahamian Folklore.* Publications in Folklore Studies, 17. Berkeley and Los Angeles: Univ. of California Pr., 1966.

Damane, M. and Sanders, P. B. *Lithoko: Sotho Praise-Poems.* Oxford Library of African Literature. Oxford Univ. Pr., 1974.

Dana, John Cotton. "Storytelling in Libraries." *Public Libraries* 13 (November 1908): 349–350.

Das, Kunjabehari. *A Study of Orissan Folklore.* Santinketan, India: Visvabharati, 1953.

Day, Lal Behari. *Bengal Peasant Life; Folk-Tales of Bengal; Recollections of My School Days.* Calcutta: Editions Indian, 1969.

Dayrell, Elphinstone. *Folk Stories from Southern Nigeria West Africa.* London: Longmans, Green, 1910.

Dégh, Linda. "Folk Narrative." In *Folklore and Folklife,* ed. by Richard Dorson, pp. 53–83. Chicago: Univ. of Chicago Pr., 1972.

———. *Folktales and Society: Storytelling in a Hungarian Peasant Community.* Tr. from the German by Emily M. Schossburger. Bloomington: Indiana Univ. Pr., 1969.

———, and Vázsonyi, Andrew. "Legend and Belief." In *Folklore Genres,* ed. by Dan Ben-Amos, pp. 93–123. Austin: Univ. of Texas Pr., 1976.

Delargy, James H. *The Gaelic Storyteller.* Rhys Memorial Lecture for 1945. *Proceedings of the British Academy,* 31. London: The Academy, 1945.

Demiéville, Paul. "Translations of Buddhist Literature" and "Tun-huang Texts." In *Dictionary of Oriental Literatures,* ed. by Jaroslav Průšek and Zbigniew Słupski, vol. 1, pp. 174–175, 185–187. New York: Basic Books, 1974.

Desroches-Noblecourt, Christiane. *Ancient Egypt.* Greenwich, Conn.: New York Graphic Society, 1960.

Dickey, Lyle A. *String Figures from Hawaii.* Bernice P. Bishop Museum, Bulletin 54. Honolulu: The Museum, 1927.

A Dictionary of the Yoruba Language. London: Oxford Univ. Pr. and Geoffrey Cumberlege, 1950.

Diop, Birago. *Tales of Amadou Koumba.* Tr. by Dorothy S. Blair. Oxford Library of African Literature. Oxford Univ. Pr., 1966.

Dobie, J. Frank. "Storytellers I Have Known." In *Singers and Storytellers,* by Mody C. Boatright and others, pp. 3–29. Dallas: Southern Methodist Univ. Pr., 1961.

Doke, Clement M. *Lamba Folk-lore.* Memoirs, 20. New York: American Folklore Society, 1927.

Dorson, Richard, ed. *African Folklore*. Bloomington: Indiana Univ. Pr., 1972.

_____ . *Bloodstoppers and Bearwalkers: Folk Traditions of the Upper Peninsula*. Cambridge: Harvard Univ. Pr., 1952.

_____ . *Buying the Wind*. Chicago: Univ. of Chicago Pr., 1964.

_____ , ed. *Folktales Told around the World*. Chicago: Univ. of Chicago Pr., 1975.

_____ . "Oral Styles of American Folk Narrators." In his *Folklore: Selected Essays*, pp. 99–146. Bloomington: Indiana Univ. Pr., 1972.

Dousman, Mary Ella. "Children's Departments." *Library Journal* 21 (September 1896): 406–408.

Durán, Fray Diego. *Book of the Gods and Rites* and *The Ancient Calendar*. Tr. and ed. by Fernando Horcasitas and Doris Heyden. Norman: Univ. of Oklahoma Pr., 1971.

East, Rupert. *Akiga's Story; the Tiv Tribe As Seen by One of Its Members*. Oxford Univ. Pr., 1965. (First pub. 1939.)

Eberhard, Wolfram. *Folktales of China*. Chicago: Univ. of Chicago Pr., 1965.

_____ . *Minstrel Tales from Southeastern Turkey*. Folklore Studies, 5. Berkeley and Los Angeles: Univ. of California Pr., 1955.

_____ . "Notes on Chinese Storytellers," *Fabula* [Berlin] 11 (1970): 1–31.

_____ . *Studies in Taiwanese Folktales*. Asian Folklore and Social Life Monographs, 1. Taiwan: Orient Cultural Service, 1970.

Edgar, Frank. *Hausa Tales and Traditions*. Tr. and ed. from the Hausa by Neil Skinner, vol. 1. New York: Africana Pub. Corp., 1969. (First pub. 1911.)

Egblewogbe, E. Y. *Games and Songs As Education Media: A Case Study among the Ewes of Ghana*. Accra: Ghana Pub. Corp., 1975.

Egyptian Literature. Tr. and ed. by Epiphanius Wilson. London and New York: The Colonial Press, 1901.

Elbert, Samuel H., and Monberg, Torben. *From the Two Canoes: Oral Traditions of Rennell and Bellona Islands*. Honolulu: Univ. of Hawaii; and Copenhagen: Danish National Museum, 1965.

Eliot, T. S. "Religion and Literature." In his *Essays, Ancient and Modern*. London: Faber and Faber, 1936.

Ellis, A. B. *The Yoruba-Speaking Peoples of the Slave Coast of West Africa*. London: 1894.

Ennis, Merlin. *Umbundu: Folk Tales from Angola*. Boston: Beacon Press, 1962.

Erikson, Joan. *Mata ni Pachedi: A Book on the Temple Cloth of the Mother Goddess*. Ahmedabad: National Institute of Design, 1968.

Evans-Pritchard, E. E. *The Zande Trickster*. Oxford Library of African Literature. Oxford Univ. Pr./Clarendon, 1967.

Fairy Tales and Legends from Romania. Tr. by Ioana Sturdza and others. New York: Twayne Publishers, 1972.

Fannin, Gwendolyn Marie. "A Resumé of the History, Growth and Development of the Story Hour in the New York Public Library." Master's thesis, Atlanta University, School of Library Service, 1958.

Fanua, Tupou Posesi. *Po Fananga. Folktales of Tonga.* San Diego: Tofua Press, 1975.

Faragó, József. "Storytellers with Rich Repertoires." *Acta Ethnographica* 20 (1971): 439–443.

Faral, Edmond. *Les jongleurs en France au Moyen Age.* Paris, 1910; New York: Burt Franklin, 1970.

Fehr, Hans. *Massenkunst im 16. Jahrhundert.* Denkmale der Volkskunst, vol. 1. Berlin: Herbert Stubenrauch, 1924.

Felkin, Robert W. "Notes on the Waganda Tribe of Central Africa." In Royal Society of Edinburgh, *Proceedings, 1885–1886,* pp. 699–770.

[Ferguson, Henry, and Ferguson, Joan]. "Textiles That Tell a Story." Series of three sheets accompanying cloths. Thompson, Conn.: InterCulture Associates, n.d.

Filstrup, Jane Merrill. "The Enchanted Cradle: Early Storytelling in Boston." *Horn Book* 52 (December 1976): 601–610.

Finnegan, Ruth. *Oral Literature in Africa.* Oxford Library of African Literature. Oxford Univ. Pr., 1970.

Flerina, E. A., and Shabad, E. *Rasskazyvanie dliâ doshkol'nogo vozrasta.* Moscow: 1937.

Flower, Robin. *The Western Island or the Great Blasket.* Oxford Univ. Pr., 1945.

Foster, F. Marie. *A Round of Picture Book Programs.* Albany: Division of Adult Education and Library Extension, N.Y. State Education Dept., c. 1944.

Frankfort, Henri. *The Art and Architecture of the Ancient Orient.* Baltimore: Penguin Books, 1969.

Freeman, Douglas Southall. "Foreword" to *A Treasury of Southern Folklore,* ed. by B. A. Botkin. New York: Crown, 1949.

Frere, Mary. *Hindoo Fairy Legends (Old Deccan Days).* New York: Dover, 1967. (First pub. 1881.)

Georges, Robert A. "Toward an Understanding of Storytelling Events." *Journal of American Folklore* 82 (1969): 313–328.

Gerhardsson, Birger. *Memory and Manuscript: Oral Tradition and Written Transmission in Rabbinic Judaism and Early Christianity.* Tr. by Eric J. Sharpe. Lund: C. W. K. Gleerup, and Copenhagen: Ejnar Munksgaard, 1961.

Gerhardt, Mia I. *The Art of Storytelling.* Leiden: E. J. Brill, 1963.

Gilson, J. P. "Introduction," in *An Exultet Roll Illuminated in the XIth Century at the Abbey of Monte Cassino.* Reproduced from Add. Ms. 30337. London: British Museum, 1929.

Gimblett, Barbara Kirshenblatt. "Traditional Storytelling in the Toronto Jewish Community: A Study in Performance and Creativity in an Immigrant Culture." Ph.D. dissertation, Indiana University, 1972.

Giteau, Madeleine. *Khmer Sculpture and the Angkor Civilization.* New York: Harry Abrams, 1965.

Goethe, Johann Wolfgang von. *Wilhelm Meister's Theatralische Sendung,* vol. 51 of his *Werke.* Weimar: 1911.

Goldziher, Ignaz. *Muslim Studies.* 2 vols. London: Allen & Unwin, 1971.

Goodwin, Grenville. *Myths and Tales of the White Mountain Apache.* Memoirs, 33. New York: American Folklore Society, 1939.

Gorer, Geoffrey. *Himalayan Village: An Account of the Lepchas of Sikkim,* 2nd ed. New York: Basic Books, 1967. (First pub. 1938.)

Gorham, Rex. *The Folkways of Brazil.* New York: New York Public Library, 1944.

Grant, James Augustus. *A Walk across Africa.* Edinborough and London: William Blackwood, 1864.

Gross, Elizabeth Henry. *Public Library Service to Children.* Dobbs Ferry: Oceana Publications, 1967.

Guirma, Frederic. *Tales of Mogho.* Foreword by Elliott P. Skinner. New York: Macmillan, 1971.

Guma, S. M. *The Form, Content and Technique of Traditional Literature in Southern Sotho.* Hiddingh-Currie Publications, University of South Africa, no. 8. Pretoria: J. L. Van Schaik, 1967.

Gunda, Bela. "Die Funktion des Märchens in der Gemeinschaft der Zigeuner." *Fabula* [Berlin] 6 (1964): 95–107.

Gunkel, Hermann. *Das Märchen im Alten Testament.* Die Religion des Alten Testaments, 2nd Series, 23/6. Tübingen: J. S. B. Mohr, 1921.

Gymer, Rose. "Storytelling in the Cleveland Public Library." *ALA Bulletin* 3 (1909): 417–420.

Hadel, Richard E. "Five Versions of the Riding Horse Tale: A Comparative Study." *Folklore Annual* (Austin, Texas) 2 (1970): 1–22.

Haiding, Karl. *Von der Gebärdensprache der Märchenerzähler.* Folklore Fellows Communications, no. 155. Helsinki, 1955.

Hall, Edwin S. *The Eskimo Storyteller.* Illustrated by Claire Fejes. Knoxville: Univ. of Tennessee Pr., 1975.

Handy, E. S. Craighill. *History and Culture in the Society Islands.* Bernice P. Bishop Museum, Bulletin 79. Honolulu: The Museum, 1930.

———. *Marquesan Legends.* Bernice P. Bishop Museum, Bulletin 69. Honolulu: The Museum, 1930.

Hardendorff, Jeanne B. "Storytelling and the Story Hour." *Library Trends* 12 (July 1963): 52–63.

Hardiman, James. *Irish Minstrelsy or Bardic Remains of Ireland.* 2 vols. London: J. Robins, 1831.

Harries, Lyndon. *Swahili Poetry.* Oxford Univ. Pr., 1962.

Harrison, Harry P., and Detzer, Karl. *Culture Under Canvas: The Story of the Tent Chautauqua.* New York: Hastings House, 1958.

Hartland, Edwin Sidney. *The Science of Fairy Tales.* New York: Frederick A. Stokes, [c1891].

267

Hazeltine, Alice I. "Storytelling in the Carnegie Library of Pittsburgh." *ALA Bulletin* 3 (1909): 413–415.

Heath, R. "Storytelling in All Ages." *Leisure Hour* 34 (1885): 199ff; 273ff; 351ff.

Henssen, Gottfried. *Überlieferung und Persönlichkeit: Die Erzählung und Lieder des Egbert Gerrits.* Münster i. W.: Aschendorffsche Verlagsbuchhandlung, 1951.

Herskovits, Melville J., and Herskovits, Frances S. *Dahomean Narrative.* Evanston, Ill.: Northwestern Univ. Pr., 1958.

Hill, Janet. *Children Are People: The Librarian in the Community.* London: Hamish Hamilton, 1973.

Hollis, A. C. *The Nandi: Their Language and Folklore.* Oxford Univ. Pr., 1909.

Holmes, Urban Tigner. *A History of Old French Literature from the Origins to 1300.* New York: F. S. Crofts, 1938.

Hoogasian-Villa, Susie, ed. *100 Armenian Tales and Their Folkloristic Relevance.* Detroit: Wayne State Univ. Pr., 1966.

Hopkins, E. Washburn. *India Old and New.* New York: Scribner's, 1901.

Horio, S., and Inaba, K., eds. *Kamishibai.* Tokyo: Doshinsha, 1972.

Hornell, James. *String Figures from Fiji and Western Polynesia.* Bernice P. Bishop Museum, Bulletin 39. Honolulu: The Museum, 1927.

Hrdličková, Věna. "The Chinese Storytellers and Singers of Ballads: Their Performances and Storytelling Techniques." Asiatic Society of Japan, *Transactions*, 3rd ser., vol. 10. (Tokyo: Asiatic Society of Japan, 1968), pp. 97–115.

——— . "The First Translations of Buddhist Sūtras in Chinese Literature and Their Place in the Development of Storytelling." *Archiv Orientální* 26 (1958): 114–144.

——— . "Japanese Professional Storytellers." In *Folklore Genres*, ed. by Dan Ben-Amos, pp. 171–190. Austin: Univ. of Texas Pr., 1976.

——— . "The Professional Training of Chinese Storytellers and the Storytellers' Guilds." *Archiv Orientální* 33 (1965): 225–248.

——— . "Some Questions Connected with *Tun-huang pien-wen.*" *Archiv Orientální* 30 (1962): 211–230.

——— . "The Zenza, the Storyteller's Apprentice." International Conference of Orientalists in Japan, *Transactions* 13 (1968): 31–41.

Htin Aung, Maung. *Burmese Monk's Tales.* New York: Columbia Univ. Pr., 1966.

Huizinga, Johan. *Homo Ludens.* Boston: Beacon Press, 1955.

Huls, Ardis. "Pre-school Story Hour." *Wilson Library Bulletin*, May 1942, pp. 726–727, 730.

Hultkrantz, Åke. "Religious Aspects of the Wind River Shoshoni Folk Literature." In *Culture in History*, ed. by Stanley Diamond, pp. 552–569. Pub. for Brandeis Univ. by Columbia Univ. Pr., 1960.

Hürlimann, Bettina. *Three Centuries of Children's Books in Europe.* Oxford Univ. Pr., 1967.

Hurreiz, Sayyid. "Afro-Arab Relations in the Sudanese Folktale." In *African Folklore*, ed. by Richard Dorson, pp. 157–163. Bloomington: Indiana Univ. Pr., 1972.

Hymes, Dell. "Models of the Interaction of Language and Social Life." In *Directions in Sociolinguistics*, ed. by J. J. Gumperz and Dell Hymes. pp. 35–71. New York: Holt, Rinehart and Winston, 1972.

Ibn al-Jawzī, Abū al-Faraj 'Abd al-Rahmān ibn 'Alī. *Kitāb al qussās wa-al-mudhakkirīn*. Tr. and annotated by Merlin L. Swartz. Recherches de l'Institut de Lettres Orientales Série 1, Pensée Arabe et Musulmane, Tome 47. Beyrouth: Dar el-Machreq, [1971].

Izard, Anne. "I Study Very Hard. I Thank You Very Much." *Top of the News* 29 (January 1973): 130–132.

Jablow, Alta. *Gassire's Lute*. Illustrated by Leo and Diane Dillon. New York: E. P. Dutton, 1971.

———. *Yes and No: The Intimate Folklore of Africa*. New York: Horizon, 1961.

Jackson, Kenneth Hurlstone. *The International Popular Tale and Early Welsh Tradition*. Cardiff: Univ. of Wales Pr., 1961.

———. *The Oldest Irish Tradition: A Window on the Iron Age*. The Rede Lecture. Cambridge: Cambridge Univ. Pr., 1964.

Jacobs, Melville. *The Content and Style of an Oral Literature: Clackamas Chinook Myths and Tales*. Chicago: Univ. of Chicago Pr., 1959.

Jan, Isabelle. *On Children's Literature*. New York: Schocken, 1974.

Janda, Elsbeth, and Nötzoldt, Fritz. *Die Moritat vom Bänkelsang: oder das Lied der Strasse*. München: Ehrenwirth Verlag, 1959.

Jansen, William Hugh. "Classifying Performance in the Study of Verbal Folklore." In *Studies in Folklore*, ed. by W. Edson Richmond, pp. 110–118. Bloomington: Indiana Univ. Pr., 1957.

"Japan: Dirty Stories." *Newsweek*, June 4, 1973, p. 51.

Johnson, Samuel. *The History of the Yorubas*. London: Routledge and Kegan Paul, 1921.

Johnston, H. A.S. *A Selection of Hausa Stories*. Oxford Univ. Pr., 1966.

Jolles, André. *Einfache Formen*, 2nd ed. Tübingen: Max Niemeyer, 1958.

Jones, A. M. *African Music in Northern Rhodesia and Some Other Places*. Rhodes-Livingston Museum, Occasional Papers, new series, no. 4, 1958. (Originally issued as no. 2 in 1943.)

Jordan, A. C. "Tale, Teller and Audience." In *Proceedings of a Conference on African Languages and Literatures, Northwestern University, April 28–30, 1966*, pp. 33–44. Evanston, Ill.: Northwestern University, n.d.

———. *Tales from Southern Africa*. Illustrated by Feni Dumile; foreword by Z. Pallo Jordan; introduction and commentaries by Harold Scheub. Berkeley and Los Angeles: Univ. of California Pr., 1973.

Junod, Henri A. *The Life of a South African Tribe*. 2 vols. New York: University Books, 1962.

Kako, Satoshi. "Kamishibai—the Unique Cultural Property of Japan." Tokyo Book Development Centre, *Newsletter* 8, no. 2 (September 1976): 6–7.

Kamphoevener, Elsa Sophia von. *An Nachtfeuern der Karawan-Serail: Märchen und Geschichten Alttürkischer Nomaden.* 2 vols. Hamburg: Christian Wegner, 1956.

Kane, Alice. "The Changing Face of the Story Hour." *Ontario Library Review* 49 (August 1965): 141–142.

Kara, György. *Chants d'un Barde Mongol.* Budapest: Akadémiai Kiadó, 1970.

Kata, Koji. *Machi no jijyoden (Autobiography of a Street-Person).* Tokyo: Bansei-sha, 1977.

Kennedy, Audrey. "History of the Boys and Girls Department of the Carnegie Library of Pittsburgh." Master's thesis, Carnegie Institute of Technology, 1949.

Ker, Annie. *Papuan Fairy Tales.* New York: Macmillan, 1910.

Keyes, Angela M. *Stories and Storytelling.* New York: D. Appleton & Co., 1911.

Killip, Margaret. *The Folklore of the Isle of Man.* Totowa, N.J.: Rowman and Littlefield, 1976.

Kingsley, Mary. *West African Studies,* 3rd ed. New York: Barnes and Noble, 1964. (First pub. 1899.)

Kirk, G. S. *Myth: Its Meaning and Functions in the Ancient and Other Cultures.* Cambridge Univ. Pr.; Berkeley and Los Angeles: Univ. of California Pr., 1971.

––––––. *The Songs of Homer.* Cambridge Univ. Pr., 1962.

Kita, Morio. *Nireke no Hitobito (The Nine Families).* Tokyo: Shinchoshi, 1964.

Knowles, James Hinton. *Folk-Tales of Kashmir.* London: Trübner & Co., 1888.

Kramer, S. N. *Sumerian Mythology.* Philadelphia: American Philosophical Society, 1944.

Lacourcière, Luc. "Canada." In *Folktales Told around the World,* ed. by Richard Dorson, pp. 429–467. Chicago: Univ. of Chicago Pr., 1975.

Lane, Edward William. *An Account of the Manners and Customs of the Modern Egyptians . . . ,* 5th ed. London: John Murray, 1871.

Lapai, Suzan. "Burma." In *Folktales Told around the World,* ed. by Richard Dorson, pp. 277–286. Chicago: Univ. of Chicago Pr., 1975.

La Rue, Abbé de. *Essais historiques sur les bardes, les jongleurs et les trouvères normands et anglo-normands.* 3 vols. Caen: 1854.

Law, Bimala Churn. *The Magadhas in Ancient India.* Royal Asiatic Society. Monographs, no. 24. Calcutta: The Society, 1946.

Laya, Dioulde. "Tradition orale et recherche historique en Afrique: méthodes, réalisations, perspectives." *Journal of World History* 12, no. 4 (1970): 560–587.

Leabhar na g-ceart or The Book of Rights. Tr. by John O'Donovan. Dublin: The Celtic Society, 1847.

Leach, MacEdward. "Problems of Collecting Oral Literature." *Publications of the Modern Language Association* 77 (1972): 335–340.

Leach, Maria, and Fried, Jerome. *Standard Dictionary of Folklore Mythology and Legend.* New York: Funk and Wagnalls, 1972.

Leakey, M. D., and Leakey, L. S. B. *Some String Figures from North East Angola.* Lisboa: Companhia de Diamantes de Angola, Serviços Culturais, 1949.

Lenz, Rodolfo. "Un grupo de consejas chilenas." *Revista de Folklore Chileno* 3 (1912): 1.

Lestrange, Monique de. "Contes et legendes des Fulakunda du Badyar." *Études Guinéennes*, no. 7 (1951): 6–7.

Liestøl, Knut. *The Origin of the Icelandic Family Sagas.* Instituttet for Sammenlignende Kulturforskning. Serie A. Forelesninger, no. 10. Oslo: W. Aschehoug & Co., 1930.

Lindblom, K. G. *String Figures in Africa.* Populära Etnologiska Skrifter, Smärre meddelanden, 9. Stockholm: Riksmuseets Etnografiska Avdelning, 1930.

Loeb Classical Library. Founded by James Loeb. Vol. 1– . Cambridge: Harvard Univ. Pr.; London: William Heinemann, 1912– .

Long, Harriet G. *Public Library Service to Children: Foundation and Development.* Metuchen, N.J.: Scarecrow Press, 1969.

———. *Rich the Treasure: Public Library Service to Children.* Chicago: American Library Association, 1953.

Lord, Albert B. *The Singer of Tales.* Harvard Studies in Comparative Literature, 24. Cambridge: Harvard Univ. Pr., 1960.

Lowie, Robert H. *Myths and Traditions of the Crow Indians.* Anthropological Papers, vol. 25, pt. 1. New York: American Museum of Natural History, 1918.

Lüders, Heinrich. "Die Śaubhikas: ein Beitrag zur Geschichte des indischen Dramas." Preussische Akademie der Wissenschaften, *Sitzungsberichte*, June 1916, pp. 698–737.

Luomala, Katherine. "Polynesian Literature." In *Encyclopedia of Literature*, ed. by Joseph T. Shipley, vol. 2, pp. 772–789. New York: Philosophical Library, 1946.

Lynton, Harriet Ronken, and Rojan, Mohini. *The Days of the Beloved.* Berkeley and Los Angeles: Univ. of California Pr., 1974.

MacDonald, Donald A. "Fieldwork: Collecting Oral Literature." In *Folklore and Folklife*, ed. by Richard Dorson, pp. 407–428. Chicago: Univ. of Chicago Pr., 1972.

MacDonnell, Anne. *The Italian Fairy Book.* New York: Frederick Stokes, n.d.

McGinniss, Dorothy A., ed. *Oral Presentations and the Librarian.* Syracuse: Syracuse Univ. Pr., 1971.

MacManus, Seumas. *Donegal Fairy Book.* New York: Doubleday, 1932.

———. *A Renaissance in Story Telling.* Publications, 110. New York: National Recreation Association, 1912.

McVicker, Polly Bowditch. "Storytelling in Java." *Horn Book* 40 (December 1964): 596–601.

Mafeje, Archie. "The Role of the Bard in a Contemporary African Community." *Journal of African Languages* 6 (1967): 193–223.

Malinowski, Bronislaw. *Argonauts of the Western Pacific*. London: Routledge and Kegan Paul, 1922.

_____ . "Myth in Primitive Psychology." In his *Magic, Science and Religion and Other Essays*, pp. 93–148. New York: Doubleday/Anchor Books, 1954. (First pub. 1926.)

Mande, Prabhaker B. "Dakkalwars and Their Myths." *Folklore* (Calcutta) 14 (January 1973): 69–76.

Maranda, Elli Köngäs, and Maranda, Pierre. *Structural Models in Folklore and Transformational Essays*. The Hague: Mouton, 1971.

Massignon, Geneviève. *Folktales of France*. Tr. by Jacqueline Hyland. Chicago: Univ. of Chicago Pr., 1968.

Mathiews, Franklin K., ed. *The Boy Scouts Book of Campfire Stories*. New York: Appleton, 1921.

Maus, Cynthia Pearl. *Youth and Storytelling*. Chicago: The International Council of Religious Education, 1928.

Mbiti, John S. *Akamba Stories*. Oxford Library of African Literature. Oxford Univ. Pr., 1966.

Meer Hasan Ali, Mrs. *Observations on the Mussulmauns of India* . . ., 2nd ed. Oxford Univ. Pr., 1917. (First pub. 1832.)

Megas, Georgios. *Folktales of Greece*. Tr. by Helen Colaclides. Chicago: Univ. of Chicago Pr., 1970.

Meissner, Kurt. "Die Yose." Deutsche Gesellschaft für Natur- und Völkerkunde Ostasiens, *Mitteilungen* 14 (1913): 230–241.

Miller, Nathan. *The Child in Primitive Society*. New York: Brentano's, 1928.

The Minnesingers: Portraits from the Weingartner Manuscript. Basle: Amerbach Publishing Comp., 1947.

Mintz, Jerome Richard. *The Legends of the Hasidim: An Introduction to Hasidic Culture and Oral Tradition in the New World*. Chicago: Univ. of Chicago Pr., 1968.

Mitchell, Roger E. *Micronesian Folktales*. Asian Folklore Studies, 32. Nagoya: Asian Folklore Institute, 1973.

_____ . "A Study of the Cultural, Historical and Acculturative Factors Influencing the Repertoires of Two Trukese Informants." Ph.D. dissertation, University of Indiana, 1967.

Moebirman. *Wanang Purwa: The Shadow Play of Indonesia*. Tr. from the French. Rev. ed. The Hague: Van Deventer-Maasstichting, 1960.

Mondon-Vidailhet, M. "La Musique Éthiopienne." In *Encyclopédie de la Musique*, ed. by Albert Lavignac, pt. 1, vol. 5, pp. 3179–3196. Paris: Delagrave, 1922.

Moore, Anne Carroll. "Report of the Committee on Storytelling." *Playground* 4 (August 1910): 162ff; reprint in Alice I. Hazeltine, *Library Work with Children*, pp. 297–315. New York: H. W. Wilson, 1917.

————. "Ruth Sawyer, Storyteller." *Horn Book* 12 (January 1936): 34–38.

————. "The Story Hour at Pratt Institute Free Library." *Library Journal* 30 (April 1905): 204–211.

Moore, Vardine. *The Pre-School Story Hour*. Metuchen, N.J.: Scarecrow Press, 1972.

Morris, Henry F. *The Heroic Recitations of the Bahima of Ankole*. Oxford Library of African Literature. Oxford Univ. Pr., 1964.

Motherwell, William. *Minstrelsy: Ancient and Modern*. Boston: W. D. Ticknor, 1846.

Mountford, Charles P. "Exploring Stone Age Arnhem Land." *National Geographic* 96 (December 1949): 745–782.

Müller, F. Max, ed. *The Sacred Books of the East*. Tr. by various Oriental scholars. 50 vols. Oxford: Oxford Univ. Pr./Clarendon, 1879; Delhi: Motilal Banarsidass, 1965.

Nahmad, H. M. *A Portion in Paradise and Other Jewish Folktales*. New York: W. W. Norton, 1970.

Nance, R. Morton. *An English-Cornish Dictionary*. London: Haycock Printers, 1965.

Nash, D. W. *Taliesin; or the Bards and Druids of Britain*. London: John Russell Smith, 1858.

N'Diaye, Bokar. *Veillées au Mali*. Bamako: Editions Populaires, 1970.

Nesbitt, Elizabeth. "The Art of Storytelling." *Horn Book* 21 (November-December 1945): 439–444.

————. "Hold to That Which Is Good." *Horn Book* 16 (January-February 1940): 7–15.

Newcomb, Franc J. *Navajo Folk Tales*. Santa Fe: Museum of Navajo Ceremonial Art, 1967.

Norris, H. T. *Shinqiti Folk Literature and Song*. Oxford Library of African Literature. Oxford Univ. Pr., 1968.

Noss, Philip A. "Cameroun (Gbaya People)." In *Folktales Told around the World*, ed. by Richard Dorson, pp. 360–379. Chicago: Univ. of Chicago Pr., 1975.

————. "Description in Gbaya Literary Art." In *African Folklore*, ed. by Richard Dorson, pp. 73–101. Bloomington: Indiana Univ. Pr., 1972.

O'Connell, Patricia Ann. "Bandi Oral Narratives." Master's thesis, Indiana University, 1976.

O'Connor, V. C. Scott. "Beyond the Grand Atlas." *National Geographic* 61 (March 1932): 261–320.

Okeke, Uche. *Tales of the Land of Death: Igbo Folk Tales*. New York: Doubleday, 1971.

Olcutt, Frances J. "Story-telling, Lectures and Other Adjuncts of the Children's Room," *Public Libraries* 5 (July 1900): 282–284.

O'Lochlainn. *Irish Street Ballads*. New York: Citadel, 1960.

Olrik, Axel. "Epic Laws of Folk Narrative." In *The Study of Folklore*, ed. by Alan Dundes, pp. 129–141. New York: Prentice-Hall, 1965.

Opler, Morris Edward. *Myths and Tales of the Jicarilla Apache Indians*. Memoirs, 31. New York: American Folklore Society, 1938.

Oppong, Christine. *Growing Up in Dagbon*. Accra: Ghana Publishing Corp., 1973.

Orbell, Margaret. *Maori Folktales in Maori and English*. Auckland: Blackwood and Janet Paul Ltd., 1968.

Oring, Elliott. "Ha-Chizbat: The Content and Structure of an Israeli Oral Tradition." Ph.D. dissertation, Indiana University, 1974.

O'Sullivan, Seán. *The Folklore of Ireland*. New York: Hastings House, 1974.

_____ . *A Handbook of Irish Folklore*. Detroit: Singing Tree Press, 1970.

Pakrasi, Mira. *Folk Tales of Assam*. Folk Tales of India, no. 3. Delhi and Jullundur: Sterling Pub. Co., 1969.

The Panchatantra. Tr. from the Sanskrit by Arthur W. Ryder. Chicago: Univ. of Chicago Pr., 1956.

Parsons, Elsie Clews. *Folklore of the Sea Islands, South Carolina*. Cambridge, Mass., and New York: American Folklore Society, 1923.

_____ . *Folktales of Andros Island, Bahamas*. Memoirs, 13. New York: American Folklore Society, 1918.

_____ . *Kiowa Tales*. Memoirs, 22. New York: American Folklore Society, 1929.

_____ . *Taos Tales*. Memoirs, 34. New York: American Folklore Society, 1940.

Patai, Raphael, Utley, Francis Lee, and Noy, Dov. *Studies in Biblical and Jewish Folklore*. Bloomington: Indiana Univ. Pr., 1960.

Perera, Arthur. *Sinhalese Folklore Notes*. Bombay: 1917.

Phillips, Herbert P. *Thai Peasant Personality*. Berkeley and Los Angeles: Univ. of California Pr., 1966.

Phillott, D. C. "Some Current Persian Tales." Asiatic Society of Bengal (Calcutta), *Memoirs* 1, no. 18 (1906): 375–412.

Pickard, P. M. *I Could A Tale Unfold: Violence, Horror and Sensationalism in Stories for Children*. New York: Humanities Press, 1961.

Pino-Saavedra, Yolando. *Folktales of Chile*. Tr. by Rockwell Gray. Chicago: Univ. of Chicago Pr., 1967.

Polish Folklore. Vol. 3 (1958)–Vol. 5 (1960). Cambridge Springs, Pa.: Alliance College.

Postma, Minnie. *Tales from the Basotho*. Austin: Univ. of Texas Pr., 1974.

Power, Effie Lee. *Syllabus for the Study of Storytelling for Use in Connection with Library Service S178*. New York: Columbia University, School of Library Service, 1936.

Powlison, Paul Stewart. "Yagua Mythology and Its Epic Tendencies." Ph.D. dissertation, Indiana University, 1969.

Pratt Institute. *Report of the Free Library for the Year Ending June 30, 1900.* Brooklyn, N.Y.

Průšek, Jaroslav. "The Creative Methods of Chinese Mediaeval Story-tellers." In *Charisteria Orientalia*, by Felix Tauer and others, pp. 253–273. Prague: Nakladatelstvi Československe Akademie Věd, 1956.

――――. "The Narrators of Buddhist Scriptures and Religious Tales in the Sung Period." *Archiv Orientální*, 10 (1938): 375–388; 23 (1955): 620ff.

――――. *The Origins and the Authors of the hua-pen.* Dissertationes Orientales, 14. Prague: Academia, 1967.

――――. "Shuo-ch'ang wen-hsüeh." In *Dictionary of Oriental Literatures*, vol. 1, pp. 161–162. New York: Basic Books, 1974.

Radin, Paul. *The Trickster: A Study in American Indian Mythology.* New York: Greenwood Press, 1969.

Raine, Kathleen. "Foreword," in *Fairy and Folk Tales of Ireland*, by William Butler Yeats. New York: Macmillan, 1973.

Ransome, Arthur. *A History of Storytelling: Studies in the Development of Narrative.* London: T. C. & E. C. Jack, 1909.

Rattray, Robert S. *The Ashanti.* Oxford Univ. Pr., 1923.

――――. *Religion and Art in Ashanti.* Oxford Univ. Pr., 1927.

Raum, O. F. *Chaga Childhood: A Description of Indigenous Education in an East African Tribe.* Oxford Univ. Pr., 1940.

Read, Margaret. *Children of Their Fathers: The Ngoni of Nyasaland.* New Haven: Yale Univ. Pr., 1960.

Reallexikon der deutschen Literaturgeschichte. Berlin: Walter de Gruyter, 1958.

Reichard, Gladys A. *An Analysis of Coeur d'Alene Indian Myths.* Philadelphia: American Folklore Society, 1947.

Die Religion in Geschichte und Gegenwart, 3rd ed. Tübingen: J. C. B. Mohr, 1965.

Reventberg, E. "Böcker på lekplatsen." *Biblioteksbladet* 40, no. 3 (1955): 170–171.

Riis, Jacob A. *The Making of an American.* New York: Macmillan, 1901.

Robe, Stanley L. *Amapa Storytellers.* Folklore Studies, 24. Berkeley and Los Angeles: Univ. of Calif. Pr., 1972.

Röhrich, Lutz. *Märchen und Wirklichkeit; eine volkskundliche Untersuchung*, 2nd ed. Wiesbaden: F. Steiner, 1964.

Roscoe, John. *The Baganda*, 2nd ed. New York: Barnes and Noble, 1966. (First pub. 1911.)

Rossell, Mary E. "History of Storytelling in England, Germany, and France." Thesis, New York Public Library, Library School, 1915.

Rougemont, Charlotte. . . . . *dann leben sie noch heute; Erlebnisse und Erfahrungen beim Märchenerzählen.* Münster: Verlag Aschendorff, 1962.

Rouget, Gilbert. "Court Songs and Traditional History in the Ancient Kingdoms of Porto-Novo and Abomey." In *Essays on Music and History in*

Africa, ed. by Klaus P. Wachsmann, pp. 27–64. Evanston: Northwestern Univ. Pr., 1971.

Rowe, John Howland. "Inca Culture at the Time of the Spanish Conquest." In *Handbook of South American Indians*, ed. by Julian H. Steward, pp. 183–330. Smithsonian Institution, Washington, D.C.: U.S. Government Printing Office, 1946. Bureau of Ethnology, Bulletin 143.

Runic and Heroic Poems of the Old Teutonic Peoples. Cambridge: Cambridge Univ. Pr., 1915.

Sahagun, *Historia de las cosas de Nueva España*. In *Antiquities of Mexico* by Lord Kingsborough. London: Robert Havell, 1831. Vol. 4 and vol. 7.

St. John, Edward Porter. *Stories and Storytelling in Moral and Religious Education*. Boston: The Pilgrim Press, 1910.

Sanborn, Florence. "How to Use Picture-Story Books." *Library Journal* 74 (February 15, 1949): 272–274.

Saul, George Brandon. *Traditional Irish Literature and Its Backgrounds: A Brief Introduction*. Lewisburg: Bucknell Univ. Pr., 1970.

Sawyer, Ruth. *The Way of the Storyteller*. New York: Viking, 1965. (First pub. 1942.)

Sayce, A. H. "Storytelling in the East." *Living Age*, 5th series. 64 (October 20, 1888): 176–180.

Sayers, Frances Clarke. *Anne Carroll Moore: A Biography*. New York: Atheneum, 1972.

———. "Notes on Storytelling." *Top of the News* 14 (March 1958): 10–11.

Schapera, I. *Praise-Poems of Tswana Chiefs*. Oxford Library of African Literature. Oxford Univ. Pr., 1965.

Scheub, Harold. "The Art of Nongenile Mazithathu Zenani, a Gcaleka Ntsomi Performer." In *African Folklore*, ed. by Richard Dorson, pp. 115–142. Bloomington: Indiana Univ. Pr., 1972.

———. "South Africa." in *Folktales Told around the World*, ed. by Richard Dorson, pp. 388–426. Chicago: Univ. of Chicago Pr., 1975.

———. *The Xhosa Ntsomi*. Oxford Library of African Literature. Oxford Univ. Pr., 1975.

Schmidt, Leopold. "Geistlicher Bänkelgesang." Österreichisches Volksliedwerk, *Jahrbuch* 12 (1963): 1–16.

Schwarzbaum, Haim. *Studies in Jewish and World Folklore*. Berlin: Walter de Gruyter and Co., 1968.

Scott, Edna Lyman. *Story Telling: What to Tell and How to Tell It*, rev. ed. Chicago: A. C. McClurg, 1923.

Seki, Keigo. *Folktales of Japan*. Chicago: Univ. of Chicago Pr., 1963.

Shafter, Toby. *Story-telling for Jewish Groups*. New York: National Jewish Welfare Board, 1946.

Shah, Idries. *Tales of the Dervishes*. New York: E. P. Dutton, 1970.

Shedlock, Marie L. *The Art of the Storyteller*. New York: Dover, 1951. (First pub. 1915.)

Sheehan, Ethna, and Bentley, Martha C. "A Public Library Reassesses Storytelling." *Illinois Libraries* 44 (December 1962): 653–657.

Shepard, Leslie. *The Broadside Ballad: A Study in Origins and Meaning.* London: H. Jenkins, 1962.

Shklovsky, I. W. *In Far North-east Siberia.* London: Macmillan, 1916.

Sidahome, Joseph E. *Stories of the Benin Empire.* London and Ibadan: Oxford Univ. Pr., 1964.

Sidhanta, N. K. *The Heroic Age of India.* London: Kegan, Paul, Trench, Trubner, 1929.

Simmons, D. C. "Specimens of Efik Literature." *Folklore* 66 (1955): 417–418.

Simpson, Jacqueline. *Icelandic Folktales and Legends.* Berkeley and Los Angeles: Univ. of California Pr., 1972.

Skendi, Stavro. *Albanian and South Slavic Oral Epic Poetry.* Philadelphia: American Folklore Society, 1954.

Sklute, Barbro. "Legends and Folk Beliefs in a Swedish-American Community: A Study in Folklore and Acculturation." Ph.D. dissertation, Indiana University, 1970.

Smith, Mary F., ed. *Baba of Karo: A Woman of the Muslim Hausa.* London: Faber and Faber, 1954.

Smith, M. G. "The Social Functions and Meaning of Hausa Praise-Singing." *Africa* 27 (1957): 27.

Snouck Hurgronje, Christian. *The Achehnese.* Tr. by A. W. S. O'Sullivan. London: 1906.

Sokolov, Yuri M. *Russian Folklore.* Tr. by Catherine Ruth Smith. New York: Macmillan, 1950.

Speke, J. H. *Journal of the Discovery of the Source of the Nile.* Edinburgh: 1863.

Srivastava, Sahab Lal. *Folk Culture and Oral Tradition.* New Delhi: Abhinav Publications, 1974.

Stanley, Henry M. *My Dark Companions and Their Strange Stories.* New York: Charles Scribner's Sons, 1893.

Stefaniszyn, B. "The Hunting Songs of the Ambo." *African Studies* 10 (1951): 1–12.

Stevenson, Tilly E. "The Religious Life of the Zuni Child." American Bureau of Ethnology. *Annual Report*, vol. 5, pp. 533–555. New York: 1897.

The Story Hour Leader. Quarterly. Nashville, Tenn., Southern Baptist Convention, 1937–

"Storytelling around the World: A Symposium." *Library Journal* 65 (April 1, 1940): 285–289.

Summers, Maud. "Storytelling in Playgrounds." *The Story Hour* 1, no. 1 (1908): 24–27.

Surmelian, Leon. *Apples of Immortality; Folktales of Armenia.* UNESCO Collection of Representative Works. Berkeley and Los Angeles: Univ. of California Pr., 1968.

Sweeney, Amin. "Professional Malay Storytelling: Some Questions of Style and Presentation." In *Studies in Malaysian Oral and Musical Traditions*, pp. 47–99. Ann Arbor: Center for South and Southeast Asian Studies, University of Michigan, 1974.

Sydow, C. W. von. "Folktale Studies and Philology: Some Points of View." In *The Study of Folklore*, Alan Dundes, pp. 219–242. New York: Prentice-Hall, 1965.

Tetzner, Lisa. *Vom Märchenerzählen im Volke*. Jena: Verlag Eugene Diederichs, 1925.

Thompson, Stith. *The Folktale*. New York: Dryden Press, 1946.

————. "Story-Telling to Story-Writing." In *Proceedings of the 5th Congress of the International Comparative Literature Association*, pp. 433–442. Amsterdam: Swets and Zeitlinger, 1969.

Thomson, James Alexander Ker. *The Art of the Logos*. London: George Allen and Unwin, Ltd., 1935.

Thorne-Thomsen, Gudrun. "The Practical Results of Storytelling in Chicago's Park Reading Rooms." *ALA Bulletin* 3 (1909): 408–410.

Tillhagen, Carl-Herman. *Taikon Berättar*. Stockholm: P. A. Norstedt Söners, 1946.

Tirabutana, Prajuab. "A Simple One: The Story of a Siamese Girlhood." Data Paper no. 30. Ithaca: Southeast Asia Program, Dept. of Far Eastern Studies, Cornell University, 1958.

Toelken, Barre. "The 'Pretty Languages' of Yellowman: Genre, Mode and Texture in Navajo Coyote Narratives." In *Folklore Genres*, ed. by Dan Ben-Amos, pp. 93–123. Austin: Univ. of Texas Pr., 1976.

Toland, John. *A Critical History of the Celtic Religion and Learning* . . . London: Lackington, Hughes, Harding and Co., 1815. (First pub. 1719.)

Torrend, J. *Specimens of Bantu Folklore from Northern Rhodesia*. New York: Negro Universities Press, 1969. (First pub. 1921.)

Towo-Atangana, Gaspard. "Le *mvet*, genre majeur de la littérature orale des populations pahouines (Bulu, Béti, Fang-Ntumu)." *Abbia* 9/10 (1965): 163–179.

Tremearne, A. J. N. *Hausa Superstitions and Customs: An Introduction to the Folklore and the Folk*. London: Frank Cass and Co., 1970. (First pub. 1913.)

Uffer, Leza. *Rätoromanische Märchen und ihre Erzähler*. Schriften, Band 29. Basel: Schweizerische Gesellschaft für Volkskunde, 1945.

Upadhyaya, K. D. "The Classification and Chief Characteristics of Indian (Hindi) Folk Tales." *Fabula* 7 (1965): 225–229.

Vaillant, G. C. *The Aztecs of Mexico*. New York: Doubleday, 1962.

Vansina, Jan. *Oral Tradition*. Tr. from the French by H. M. Wright. Chicago: Aldine Pub. Co., 1965.

Wade-Evans, A. W. *Welsh Medieval Law: Being a Text of the Laws of Howel the Good*. Oxford Univ. Pr., 1909.

Waley, Arthur. *Ballads and Stories from Tun-huang*. New York: Macmillan, 1960.

278

_____ . "Kutune Shirka: The Ainu Epic." In *Botteghe Oscure*, no. 7, 1951, pp. 214–236.

Walker, Barbara K. "The Folks Who Tell Folktales: Field Collecting in Turkey." *Horn Book* 47 (December 1971): 636–642.

Walker, Joseph C. *A Historical Essay on the Dress of the Ancient and Modern Irish*, 2nd ed. 2 vols. Dublin: J. Christie, 1818. 1st ed. Dublin: 1788.

Walker, Warren S., and Uysal, Ahmet E. *Tales Alive in Turkey*. Cambridge: Harvard Univ. Pr., 1966.

Wandira, Asavia. *Indigenous Education in Uganda*. Kampala: Makerere University Dept. of Education, 1971.

Westermann, Diedrich. *The Shilluk People: Their Language and Folklore*. Westport, Conn.: Negro Universities Press, 1970. (First pub. 1912.)

Wheeler, Howard T. *Tales from Jalisco Mexico*. Memoirs, 35. Philadelphia: American Folklore Society, 1943.

Wheeler, Post. *Tales from the Japanese Storytellers*. Selected and ed. by Harold G. Henderson. Rutland, Vt.: Charles E. Tuttle, 1964.

Wiggin, Kate Douglas. *Children's Rights*. Boston: Houghton Mifflin, 1892.

Williams, Gwyn. *An Introduction to Welsh Poetry: From the Beginnings to the 16th Century*. Philadelphia: Dufour, 1952.

Winner, Thomas G. *The Oral Art and Literature of the Kazakhs of Russian Central Asia*. Durham, N.C.: Duke Univ. Pr., 1958.

Wintgens, Hans-Herbert. *Das Erzählen im Religionsunterricht*. Gütersloh: Gerd. Mohn, 1971.

Wisser, Wilhelm. *Auf der Märchensuche; die Entstehung meiner Märchensammlung*. Hamburg and Berlin: Hanseatische Verlagsanwalt, c. 1920.

The Work of the Cleveland Public Library with the Children and the Means Used to Reach Them. Cleveland: Cleveland Public Library, 1908.

Young, Frances. "Primitive Story-telling in Greece." Thesis, New York Public Library, Library School, 1915.

Nonprint Materials

Berimbau. 16mm film. 12 minutes. Color. Directed by Toby Talbot. Narrated by Emile de Antonio. New York: New Yorker Films, 1971.

The Fine Art of Storytelling. Videocassette Series. Ed. by Philip A. Cecchettini. Davis: University of California, 1975.

Index of Films and Videotapes on American Folklore. Memphis: Center for Southern Folklore, 1976.

The Pleasure Is Mutual: How to Conduct Effective Picture Book Presentations. 16mm film. 26 minutes. Color. Produced and directed by Joanna Foster and William D. Stoneback. Stamford: Connecticut Films, 1966.

"Recordings. Phonodisc. Cassette." In Marilyn Berg Iarusso, comp., *Stories: A List of Stories to Tell and to Read Aloud*, 7th ed., pp. 64–67. New York: The New York Public Library, 1977.

There's Something about a Story. 16mm film. 27 minutes. Color. Dayton: Public Library of Dayton and Montgomery County, 1969.

Index